Your Past Can Set You Free

How Insights from Past Lives Can Heal Current Issues

Karin Stettler with Maitra

ISBN: 9798322639916

Library of Congress Information (pending)

Opening the Lotus Publishers rev. date: 4/8/23

Acknowledgements

We deeply appreciate all the people who have "gone the extra mile" in support of the *Opening the Lotus* work and this book. These include, but are not limited to:

Barbara Stone, not only for her sensitive translation of the German original, but for "hanging in there" with us through the many revisions, and giving us the benefit of her professional experience without which we would have been lost. She's our hero.

Tenzin Lhamo for the title, *Your Past Can Set You Free*, which came so spontaneously that I thought it must be a channeled blessing;

Kevin Young, who found Barbara Stone, our translator and editor, and connected her with Karin and Maitra;

The continued support of those friends who were in the Lotus classes or had Readings—you know who you are—whose openness and love were so valuable during the creative process of this book;

Karin's long-standing meditation group, Stefan Birrer, Brigitta Gunziger, Regula Bacas, Yolanda Bosch, and Giuseppe Santamaria, who always encouraged Karin to keep at it throughout the writing of this book.

All our manuscript readers, who did such a professional job: Sharyn Adams, Gayla Bastas, Alena Byrnes, Carol Grossmann, Rev. Dr. Bobbie Groth, Aisha Hudson, Rachael Sharp, Tomi Speed, Sufen Yen. And especially to Razelle Drescher, our master proofreader!

Melanie Redman for her invaluable advice as we neared the end;

Bayley Logan for her graphic talents and unstinting support;

Sam Brown's painting for the cover; we both fell in love with it;

Ladina Kindschi, who opened the door to Europe in the first place, and her partner Bea Ender, who together have supported the Lotus work all these years;

And to our families, whose love continues to give meaning and purpose to our lives.

Karin & Maitra, whose loving appreciation for each other lights up the world and has created this book!

Karin Stettler　　　　**Maitra**

Your own Self-Realization is the greatest service you can render the world.
—Ramana Maharshi (1879-1950)

The moment you change your perception is the moment you rewrite the chemistry of your body.
—Bruce Lipton

*To all the courageous people who open their lives to be read—
those who are included in this book and those who are not—
who have shown such a deep level of trust
that we are often in awe of what is revealed.*

CONTENTS

FOREWORD BY BARBARA S. STONE, TRANSLATOR

When I began this translation, the topic of past lives was totally new to me. I grew up in an academic family of Viennese refugees who had emigrated to the United States in the late 1930s. Freud and the unconscious were always lurking in the background, affecting how I viewed and understood the world around me. I have always brought a level of Freud's 'healthy skepticism' to my own psychoanalytic work and explorations, all of which were grounded very deeply in the Western tradition.

But life takes its own paths, and my laissez-faire response to a posting on *Craigslist* a few years back by Kevin Young, a dear friend of Karin's, resulted in my translation of Karin's first book, *On the Path to Freedom* (2018). This was a wonderful experience. It introduced me to Karin's way of understanding the world, her creativity, and her way with words. I found many passages in that work to be moving and memorable.

I was very excited when Karin invited me to collaborate on a translation of this book of Maitra's Readings. These Readings were done over several years, and the interviews took place more recently. Clients were given a CD of their Readings so that they could review and work with them over the subsequent period. The Readings and interviews were done in English or German, with a bit of Swiss German thrown into the mix.

I had heard Karin speak highly of Maitra from the get-go, but at the time, I had no idea that her invitation to translate this book, which had originally been published in German, would lead to more than two years of work with Maitra, twice a week over Skype or Zoom. We edited and discussed the texts to ensure that the English version captured her voice, her gifts, and her work as a teacher. We began with the original texts, editing them for readability, and removing some of the repetition and phrasing that worked well in speech but not in a reader-friendly text. Being new to these kinds of Readings and the Akashic tradition* (Note: An asterisk denotes a word that is defined in the Glossary), I would frequently ask her to clarify terms and ideas. This "pushed" Maitra to come up with further clarifications in the Readings and interviews. The more we worked together, the more it became clear to us that, although Karin had composed her book in large part to honor Maitra, it could also serve as a 'teaching tool,' and a way to reassure others that one could learn from her, even if one came to the work with a 'healthy skepticism' about past lives and reincarnation. As she writes, "I don't care if you don't believe in past lives, I tell stories that illumine the Way."

I have found this translation work an inspiration. It has introduced me to new ways of thinking, a new vocabulary, and new ways of learning. It has been a very freeing experience and has helped me look at aspects of my own life and the world around me in a new way.

Our work together over these past two years has been especially beneficial, in that it offered me a way to be engaged in a meaningful project during a worldwide pandemic. Alas, the pandemic prevented the three of us from meeting in person, but this will surely happen.

A big thanks to Karin for her friendship, and for trusting me with this project. And, a big thanks also to Maitra for her warmth, her patience, her partnership, and her wisdom. For me, our work together has been a model of collaboration.

With the publication of this book, I look forward to Maitra's work being shared with a larger audience. And readers, I hope that your explorations of these life stories will be a healing and freeing experience.

April, 2023

My work with Maitra, a psychic from California, inspired me to give her powerful work a form, a face. When asked if she would ever write a book about her life as a spiritual teacher, as a seer, she answered, "Probably not ... my living work with people, in Readings and workshops is the book." Today this has changed. As time went on and Maitra continued her work, she found her voice as a writer, and this book became a collaboration that revealed the powerful nature of her work.

At the time, Maitra was in her eighty-first year; she was still traveling and teaching, coming to Europe, and every time she was here, the calendar filled with individual sessions. Her work touched and liberated people through her clear presence, intuitive insights, and her teachings.

My First Encounter with Maitra

In 2011, friends sent me an invitation to a talk by Maitra, a psychic, spiritual teacher who was new to me. They already knew her from previous gatherings and were looking forward to returning to Lucerne to hear her speak. So I went, open and curious, to the evening talk. It was in a relatively small space. Soon the room was full, and the organizer had to provide more chairs so that everyone had a seat. As I recall, Maitra talked about sensitivity and the third eye*, and that there are ways to train and develop one's intuition and inner vision. The most important thing for me was the feeling that someone with a natural sense of intuition and an open third eye was expressing what had been burning inside of me for so long. It felt like I had come home to myself.

At the same time, I was touched by her soft, luminous presence, and her naturalness and clarity as she stood before us and spoke to us.

As with all her presentations, Maitra also offered mini-Readings that evening. Those present could ask questions and receive her insights and explanations. I got excited because I had so many questions, but foremost I thought, *Should I ask her, here in the middle of this large group of people who know me? What will they think of me, if one of my secrets is revealed by the answer?*

I found my courage and asked my questions, because here was a great opportunity to learn something about myself. In this phase of my life, I was very busy with family and work. I felt a lot of inner pressure, and I had health problems. As I remember it, I was stuck, and I sought answers about my inner physical and mental states. Simply put, I wanted to become more aware. Something in me was seeking solutions, better health, progress, and liberation.

When Maitra turned to me, I was deeply touched because I felt seen by her. A powerful, loving, and bright spark sprang from her to me. That's what I remember now when I write about it. The most touching moment was when she started to sing a song for me. I asked myself: 'How is it that she sings a song for me here in this group of people?' It was so incredible and extraordinary for me to receive so much attention and that sweet song; I felt richly gifted. After the talk, I let myself fall into her arms, which felt just as intense for me, as I was usually rather restrained. She confirmed in the mini-Reading that my true way of being was open and loving. She noted that as I walk through my life, I could and would like to embrace everyone, but I hold back because of my restricted conditioning. At that moment, she lifted me directly into my heart, and a part of my Being was allowed again.

I went to another talk six months later, when Maitra came back to Lucerne and I booked my first individual session with her. Through this Reading, I gained further vital inspiration when she asked me a few questions. In retrospect, my answers were groundbreaking for my life. Among others, there was this question: "You are standing on a platform and the train is leaving shortly and your intuition tells you that you should go. You do not know where, but you know that it's important. Are you ready to get on board?" After a few moments, I answered, "Yes." At the time, I did not know what that meant exactly, but inside I had a feeling it was right. It was time for a change.

Then I told her about my dreams, which I did not fully understand. During this phase of my life, I often had dreams in which the brightness was so strong that I could not see anything; I was momentarily blinded. In the recurring dream, I had to find my way through this bright, dazzling light. I tried to interpret it as meaning that I simply could not see certain things, or that my perception was obstructed. I often felt lost, and sometimes I wondered if I would go blind.

But what Maitra then simply answered was so amazing to me: "That's your light. You are that."

Never before could I have seen it that way. It was such a simple answer; but, to see myself as part of this light, to understand that we are all this light, surrounded by it, and coming from this light, was such an overwhelming idea. I believe today that these moments gave me a first glimpse of what it means to heal, and I began to understand with what extraordinary, deep perception, she sees the people who come to her. It opens us up to who we are. She sees the brightness of the soul and our inner beauty and helps us to recognize and accept it. This connects us again with the True Self and brings body, mind, and soul back into harmony.

After this first one-on-one meeting, Maitra introduced me to her seminar program and said it would be beneficial for me. For many years, she has been leading groups in a two-year seminar cycle on metaphysics, reincarnation and karmic work, tarot, and inner vision: *Opening the Lotus Seminars* (<u>www.m aitra.net</u>). I took her brochure and the CD with my recorded Reading and went home after this intense encounter.

It did not take me long to think about it, and I signed up for this adventure.

Already during the seminars, an intensive inner learning and a slow awakening were activated in me. The organizers soon asked me if I would arrange talks and individual sessions (Readings) for Maitra in the Lucerne area.

I agreed and, beginning in 2011, organized the first talk in a large, pleasant room. Over sixty people attended and it was a very moving evening. A whole week's worth of individual Readings was fully booked. In addition to all the people and friends I was able to reach through my practice, which I had had for many years, many people came who had known Maitra for years and had also been deeply affected by her work. I was a bit overwhelmed myself, and thankful that so many people found their way to us quickly. I was invited to start translating the individual Readings with Maitra, and was deeply touched by every encounter, and the intensity of the discussions that took place during these Readings.

—Karin Stettler

Our Book Project

I have known Maitra for eight years, initially as a student, and more recently as her translator and sponsor during her teaching trips to Europe. I have personally experienced her work with individuals and groups through her Readings, seminars, talks, and workshops. What touches me most about her work as a seer and spiritual teacher, is how she helps people transform their lives through insights into their past lives.

My personal experiences and the assistance that I have received from Maitra led me to visualize a book about her work, in order to honor her by sharing her work with others. Her insights into layers of the human soul and her interpretations of life situations are deep, detailed, and often so surprising that they are difficult to describe. The effects of her guidance and encounters with people of all ages and life situations leave no doubt that her work is of great value.

With this book project, I have reached out to many of those who have sought advice from Maitra through the years. This includes those who were counseled by her, had Readings, or participated in classes, workshops, talks, and seminars. I see my writing as that of an author working with the recorded Readings, which make direct references to previous lives, and give clarifications that are useful for life in the present.

In order to tackle such a book project, I have relied on everyone's openness, trust, and consent to make the recordings of Maitra's Readings available for translation and inclusion in this book. The intent of this book is to make Maitra's work and life-long engagement as a seer and spiritual teacher available to many people.

A further important aspect of this project is the impact, insights, and reflections following each individual session that include a description of changes in the client's life situation. This required personal interviews.

The opportunity to glance into the human soul through Maitra's work has been both a great gift and a very precious learning process for me.

Thank You to everybody who contributed to the understanding of Maitra's work in this book.

—Karin Stettler

Karin Stettler and Maitra

Part I ~ Maitra's Story

I have had psychic visions, visitations, and guidance since my childhood in Montana. In 1973, now in California, I began to meditate with Muktananda, a well-known spiritual teacher from India. With his influence, my psychic abilities began to expand, and I found that the resulting transformation defined my life's work: Psychic Healing, through Readings and other transformative work.

By 1977, after some training at Family of Man, a small metaphysical church founded and led by Marsha Mossman, my natural abilities were further awakened and I began doing Readings professionally and teaching classes and workshops. I also worked internationally in Europe and Asia. I am clairsentient, which means I "sense" in my body what is going on with clients. I also channel and read the energy field around the body, known as the *aura**. This can give information on past lives, current challenges, relationships, and health.

I find my best skills lie in the area of helping people further align with their Higher Selves, identify their life's purpose, and make better life decisions by understanding themselves and their karmic* situations.

The first step in teaching others to develop their psychic abilities is to identify the students' level of openness in their third eye and define whatever might be preventing them from developing further. This frequently is fear, resulting from karmic memories and painful experiences in past lives, which are recorded in the Akashic record, the permanent record of the soul. By bringing these memories into consciousness, we can heal them and clear the way for further development of a student's psychic abilities.

The third eye works differently with each person, so it's paramount to discover the nature of each person's inherent abilities. Here is a listing of some of the ways the third eye works:

- **Clairvoyance:**
  "clear seeing"—what is not perceived with traditional sight.

- **Clairaudience:**
  "clear hearing"—can be physical or the mind's inner hearing.

- **Clairsentience:**
  "clear feeling"—sensing other's emotions in your physical body.

- **Claircognizance:**
  "clear knowing"—a thought previously unknown to us that presents as truth.

- **Clairalience**:
  "clear smelling"—ability to smell odors that do not have a physical source.

- **Note:** Intuition is NOT located in the third eye.
  It is located in each person's center and may incorporate any or all of the above.

As a teacher, my goal is to help each person discover their strengths and weaknesses, develop and nurture their strengths, and devise ways to minimize their weaknesses. Once we've done this, we can use the psychic tools that I teach my students not only to help others but to help them move more confidently into their potential.

Many years ago, I stood in front of the altar at Family of Man and asked the Universe to use me: "I want to travel the world and reveal to everyone their own indescribable beauty." Karin's dedication, generosity, and love in creating this book tell me that my prayer has been answered.

Chapter 1: Setting the Stage

In October 2017, I was asked to give an extemporaneous talk at the Basel Psi-Verein Symposium's 50th Anniversary. When Lucius Werthmüller, the director, asked me what I wanted to talk about, I proposed three or four ideas, but he said, "No, No, No! Tell them about your life path." As it's the only thing I am an expert on, I agreed. And sometimes I can surprise myself so much that I wonder if I'm an expert on my own story. I hope that you are surprising yourself sometimes too, because that is what opens the door to our unlimited nature. Here's my talk:

"Tonight, I want to share some highlights of my journey, with particular emphasis on the karma* with my mother and my family. Maybe it will give you a glimpse into your own personal processes.

"When I was three years old, I had the first experience of realizing that I was different, that what was happening with me wasn't happening with most other people.

"I was in the garden with my mother. It was a beautiful sunshiny day and my mother, happy and singing, was hanging up the clothes she had washed. I was sitting over to one side in the grass, watching ants climbing up the flowers. I noticed several little globes of light, 2 or 2 1/2 inches in diameter, coming toward me and jumping around me. When they began to talk to me, it didn't seem strange at all. We had a conversation for a few minutes.

Later, I understood that those were little fairies. My mother heard me talking, and she asked, 'Who are you talking to?' I said, 'To that little light there.' I had been watching my mother's aura. Her energy field was very big, she was happy, and it was a beautiful day. When I told her what I was seeing, and pointed to that little light, her aura shrank much smaller, and even at three years old, I understood that she was afraid.

"It was my first lesson in understanding with whom I could share what I was experiencing and how I see things. In some ways, my mother was always interested in non-ordinary phenomena. She had books about it. But when it came right down to it, she was too afraid. In all the years of teaching, I have noticed that fear comes up for many people when confronted with such things.

"We all have a third eye. It doesn't work the same for everybody, but it is there for everybody if they want to develop it. When I started studying this in my thirties, many of my spiritual teachers said, 'Don't open the third eye. Don't go in that direction because it takes you off your spiritual path.' But what I observed during the next years was that, for many people, the third eye opens spontaneously. For example, I think that everybody here has some openness. I don't think you would be here if you didn't have some experience with the third eye. But to deliberately pursue that path is another matter, and that's when the fear that comes up has to be addressed. I feel it's important to acknowledge the experiences that many of you in the audience have had.

"I'd like to share with you a few more highlights of my life. I want to start by telling you about an experience with my mother when I was in my early forties.

"I was living in Northern California and my house was a small Light Center, where I was giving Readings and talks and offering courses in Psychic Development.

"Let's back up a little: I always knew that my mother, Joyce, didn't like me. We were not close. Sometimes four or five years went by and we didn't see each other. She lived in Montana, I lived in California. Until the incident that I am about to describe, I never understood why.

"I hadn't seen her for several years when she came to visit me in California. She liked what was going on in my small Light Center. She wanted to have a Past-Life Regression* to learn more about her past life. Regressions were one of the main things we were doing there. We decided that it would be better for her to do it with someone other than me, and so she went into the session with one of my students. Twenty minutes later they came out and said that it didn't work. So I said 'OK, let me try.' We went back into the room and I put her in a state of light hypnosis and she immediately started receiving extremely vivid images and the emotions that went with them. I can't recall if I had ever seen my mother cry before, but she was crying that day.

"The following is my recollection of what happened in my mother's Hypnotic Regression. Her story turned out to be my story, too.

"My mother remembered being the high priest of The Temple of Baal on the shores of the Mediterranean. It was springtime and they were doing a sacrifice for the planting season. The temple was round and it had a big hole in the roof. It also had a pit in the floor, which was full of fire. People were standing all around the fire. As she was speaking about it, I started to see it too. And I could feel it, the heat from it. The high priest (my mother), was waiting for the sacrificial offering to be brought in. The sacrifice was a young girl who I recognized as my youngest daughter in this current lifetime. My older daughter (also from this current lifetime) and I were the priests who brought her in.

"We brought her in and my mother held her up and threw her into the fire. She was about eight years old. It was very emotional for both of us. My mother (then and now) was screaming. We kept looking into the fire and my daughter rose out of the fire in her etheric body*, and pointed her finger at my mother (in the past lifetime) and said, 'You know that this is wrong. You have to stop it.' My mother, as the high priest, was so overcome that she jumped into the fire herself. The other priest and I (my older daughter today), tried to change this practice. We were unsuccessful and were subsequently cast out. We left the area and went on the road. Earlier, we had known that this was wrong, but we hadn't had the courage to do anything to change it.

"So that is the past life. In this life, my mother Joyce, when she was about five years old, was in the kitchen with her mother, who was canning vegetables. She was carrying a big pot of boiling water from the stove to the table and Joyce, playing on the floor, accidentally bumped into her and was burned when the boiling water spilled. She had terrible, big scars down her neck and shoulder, and down her chest and upper arm.

"When I was eleven months old, my mother put me in a crib for a nap and left the house to visit her mother. My grandmother lived a quarter mile away, across a field. It was a cold day, and my mother left a kerosene heater burning in the bedroom. I wonder if any of you remember those heaters. They got red hot. They were quite dangerous, and we don't have them anymore. My mother, when she finally told me about this, when I was in my 30s, said that she didn't know that I could get out of the crib by myself. I was toddling. That means I would hang on to something and go two steps and hang on to something else. So, I got out of the crib, went a few steps and I put my hands on the red-hot kerosene heater. When I pulled them off, all the skin on my palms was gone; the skin had stuck to the heater. My parents said that later, when they came into the room, there were bloody hand-prints on all the walls and all the furniture and that I was going around the room, hanging onto the wall and screaming.

"I saw my father come to the window and look in. What he saw frightened him so much that he left again to look for my mother. Upon hearing this, I finally understood why my mother didn't like to be with me. She felt so sad and guilty when I was burned that she could hardly bear to look at me. My parents had never explained to me what had happened to my hands. Finally, in my thirties, I was able to learn about what had happened. After the regression, I understood about the past life fire and my burns in the present life, and my mother understood about her burns and terrible scars. At last, we were able to heal our relationship. I think this was such a big karmic burden that I only started to live fully after I understood it.

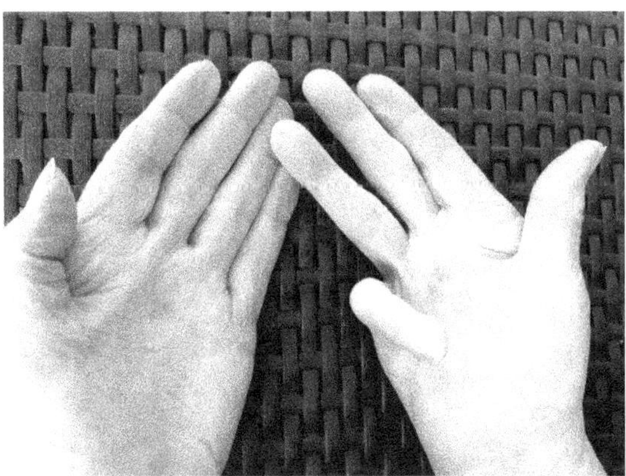

"Karma is real. It affects us in our everyday lives, and it can block us from reaching our potential. After the regression experience with my mother, the pain of being an unloved child lifted away, and doors began opening for me in many ways. It was not only the healing with my mother. I also started to trust myself much more."

"Sometime after that regression with my mother, I was taken by a friend to meet a well-known spiritual teacher, Muktananda, who came from northern India to America in the 1970s. The first time I met him when my friend took me to see him, he was sitting on the floor in a circle with a small group of people, in his Ashram in Oakland, California. When we entered the room, he saw us in the doorway, and he got up and came across the room and greeted me. I thought this was something he did with everybody. But it wasn't. It was very unusual and people suddenly treated me with a lot of respect after that happened, although I didn't understand that it was anything special at the time.

"Some months later, I was in a Meditation Intensive (workshop) with him. There were probably 300 or 400 people there, and he would walk between the people and hit them with his peacock feathers, or he would touch some people with his hand on their shoulder or head. He was giving Shaktipat, which is the energy that an enlightened being can use to assist any person he chooses to touch. When he came to me, he put his thumb in my third eye. Tears of joy flew straight out of my eyes.

"Through this experience of his touch, of Shaktipat, he gave me a big boost and it opened many doors for me in the next years. I think it made it possible for me to do the healing work that I do today. Slowly, I began to understand that I had a type of perception that was different than most people have and that I also had the power to heal.

"One aspect of my work is to help people to open and understand how to use their psychic abilities and how to conquer their fear. Right now I think the increase has to do with a healing crisis. So much of the suffering, of the negativity that's here in the present, is part of this healing crisis. We are preparing ourselves for a great leap in consciousness.

"The opportunity right now is to be able to look straight at the things that are so frightening and hold onto the reality that 'this too shall pass.' This is all part of the preparation for peace on earth. I know there are days when it seems almost hopeless. We have to hold onto the consciousness of Oneness that is part of us, really hold onto it, in the face of everything that is so frightening. We must address the fear within ourselves, knowing that each cell (person) in the body of mankind that is conscious of our Oneness will make a difference.

"Muktananda has been gone since 1982, but his presence remains real for me. For a long time, whenever I had a big question about how to do things, he would come to me in a dream and give me a lesson.

"Money questions come up for many people who do healing work or therapies. Muktananda gave me a teaching about money.

"Some years ago, I was giving a talk and there were several ladies present who were what I call 'old-time psychics.' That means people (mostly women) who have an active third eye and are doing Readings. Usually, they were married or widowed and were financially secure. They were mostly good, well-meaning souls. The main difference I see between them and the people who are doing this work today is that most people today are constantly working on themselves, to stay clear for the healing work. There is much more self-awareness among psychics today.

"As I was speaking, one of them raised her hand and said to me, 'If you keep charging money for your readings, you will lose your gift.' The other ladies were all sagely nodding their heads. I wasn't prepared for such a statement, and it stopped me cold. Finally, I said to her, 'If I don't charge for the service I provide, I can't keep doing it—I would have to get a job and I just don't have enough energy for both.'

"I went home after this exchange, and for a couple of nights I was having difficulty sleeping, asking myself, over and over again, 'Am I doing the right thing, charging for my work?' Finally, I had a dream.

"I was sitting in a large audience listening to my teacher, Muktananda, and he invited me, gesturing, to come sit with him in front of everyone. I went reluctantly up onto the stage, rather self-conscious. He was sitting on a heavy sheet of plywood which was balanced on four glasses of water, one in each corner of the wood. Naturally, I was reluctant to climb up, fearing to upset the balance, but he insisted, pulling me so I was sitting very close to him. I was so overwhelmed that I could hardly breathe.

"We sat there for a few minutes and he went on teaching. Then he startled me by reaching for my hand. He had a velvet pouch in his other hand and he emptied it into my hand—gold coins spilling into and overflowing my hand. The message I got was that money is another form of energy, another form of God, as is all form. And that it is my sacred right to receive it in exchange for my healing help.

"I woke up feeling overwhelmingly grateful for this whole experience; I can feel it again now. Thank you, dear Guru Muktananda."

CHAPTER 2: MY INTRODUCTION TO FREEDOM

I was part of a circle of ten to fifteen people who met irregularly in Santa Cruz and Berkeley, California, which was formed spontaneously in the 1970s. We were people of all descriptions passing through in the Great Awakening of Consciousness that was ebbing and flowing at that time. Change, and the embracing of it, was on the menu. William James was the teacher, a clear visionary who accompanied us all through our challenges. He had no agenda. I never saw him manipulate people. His teaching was my introduction to freedom, to a better way to live.

William was a psychologist who loved women. He "slept" with any women who would like to join him in that exploration. He was ethical about it—to my knowledge, he never lied to anyone, never made promises that he didn't keep, never implied it was something it was not, and most importantly, his heart was wide open. The women knew he loved them but it wasn't possessive, it wasn't personal; rather, it was universal, unconditional.

One night a man, who was new to the group, not understanding, decided to confront him: "Just who do you think you are, screwing around with all these women, William?"

The group was very quiet as the man listed all the things that were wrong with William because of his behavior with women. William listened attentively, palms together, head bowed, and said "Yes, that's me too." And we went on with the group.

The next person who spoke felt she wanted to defend William. She addressed the man, saying, "We come to William because he's teaching us how to love, and the way he is, is the teaching. He doesn't ask us to be like him, he just shows us how to trust ourselves."

She said more, praising William and giving examples of how we had all benefited from his example. Then everyone turned to William, who bowed his head again, his hands in the prayer position, and said to her, and all of us, "Yes, that's me too."

Whatever it is, positive or negative: "Yes, that's me too." No defensiveness, no denial. No taking anything personally. No explanation. This living lesson makes self-acceptance and happiness possible.

Try it.

CHAPTER 3: HEALING FOR PROTECTION AND SUBSEQUENT DREAM

In the early 2000s, while I was living in the Santa Cruz area, I was preparing to return to Europe to teach and do Readings. I was distressed by frequent influenza-type illnesses that were sapping my energy and causing me to feel exhausted all the time. My doctor could find no cause. I was in doubt about continuing my work, wondering if it was time to give up the travel and most importantly, the work that I love.

My friend Tenzin Lhamo urgently suggested that I visit a Brazilian healer/Lhama who could, she said, help me find out why I was unable to heal. Reluctantly, I made an appointment and went to see him. Without looking at me, without any kind of preamble, he said, "You've had a shock—your protection is gone." I denied having had any shock and said that I had been feeling so exhausted that any kind of activity was out of the question. He insisted, saying it might have been some years ago.

Finally, I said, "Well, five years ago my daughter died."

"How did she die?" he asked.

"Suicide," I replied. "OK," I thought, "that was definitely a shock."

He said, "We need to do a *Puja*, a healing ritual, to restore your protection. I can do it just before I leave the country in one week, up in Sebastopol."

I agreed as it was also just before my trip to Europe.

The day before the appointment I drove up to see him, a three-hour drive. I stayed with friends who live nearby in Santa Rosa. The next morning, I prepared to drive the half hour to his place in Sebastopol. I was on the road an hour early because he had the reputation of turning people away for being late.

What a drive! My car would not go the way I wanted it to—it kept turning in another direction and I would get lost trying to get back on track again. I called his Center several times, asking for help to get back on the correct road. When I finally arrived, I was two hours late and I thought for sure they would turn me away.

Instead, they said I had had significant interference and that the Puja would take about three hours. I was taken to the healing room immediately. There were three monks, the healer, and two younger monks, to do the Puja ritual. A pot of cold tea was used; the monks poured it a little at a time over my head, my hands, and my bare feet, while intoning a steady chanting. They constantly referred to a book. I don't remember being aware of much but I was definitely in an altered state at the end and had to walk around and get grounded before the uneventful drive back to my friend's house.

Three days later, I flew to Europe and began my work there. A week after that, I was in Lugano, Switzerland, and I had a dream. In the dream, I was in the healing room again, sitting on the floor at a low table with the healer. He asked me, "What makes you think you deserve my help?" in a demanding voice, not very friendly. I went completely blank; my mind couldn't come up with a single thing. I opened my mouth to say that when abruptly I was sitting up on the ceiling, chatting away with him about some nonsense, while he was still sitting calmly below me at the table. Suddenly I noticed that there was a whirlwind, which was picking up everything in the room except us, and whirling it around in circles—papers, books, furniture, plants, holy objects, and more were flying around the room. I panicked and the next thing I knew, I was waking up at 3 a.m. in Lugano with the covers on the bed all tangled around my neck, something that had never happened to me before.

I was saying, 'I'm not worthy, I'm not worthy,' over and over again. Then a warm, blissful feeling started to flow up through my feet, and as it flowed up my body, what came out of my mouth was 'O-o-o-h, I AM worthy, I AM worthy!'—and then I drifted tearfully, blissfully off to sleep again.

I knew then that the healing was complete. The illness and the exhaustion were behind me. Deep gratitude to all concerned.

CHAPTER 4: A SHORT EXPLANATION OF HOW I READ

Often when I am working with a person, I am doing what I call "following the energy." When I ask seemingly unrelated questions, one after another, I am looking for where I can feel the energy is stuck or blocked. When I find it, I look for an opening where I can enter their energy field and reveal or name, what I see is blocking the person's ability to free themselves.

Sometimes, what is revealed is a past life in which the issues are unresolved in some way. When I see past lives, I am using my third eye to access the "permanent record of the soul," which is called the **Akashic Record**.

What may also be revealed is a childhood event that traumatized or otherwise may be blocking the person. Often, simply naming something precisely and correctly will be enough to release the energy and begin the healing process. Other times, I need to "move some energy," and perhaps ask the person to "own" a feeling such as anger or shame, or ask them to name their "bottom line," i.e., what they want in the situation. This process of inviting someone to come fully into the present moment and accept themselves where they are can open the way to the freedom we all want.

What Is a "Reading"?

Imagine that you run into a friend whom you haven't seen for a while. Without your friend saying a word, you can "see" immediately that they are under extreme stress and if you are a sensitive person, you know whether you should mention it or not. Or perhaps your friend is radiant with happiness and you know something wonderful has taken place. You are "reading their energy." This can also work on the phone—the minute you hear their voice, you are aware of whatever is going on with that person. Now imagine that you expand this awareness through diligent practice and a desire to help. As you practice, you see more and more, until like me, you may become aware of past lives and what I call "in-between" lives and other dimensions that are beyond ordinary consciousness. If you think of it as a deep meditative state (theta*), then you'll begin to get a feeling for the process of "reading."

Also, I am aware that every Reading is a teaching, a response to the client's wish to liberate themselves from suffering. I am blessed to do this work—it has benefits for me as well. Sometimes their questions are questions that I didn't know I had!

**As you start to walk on the Way,
the Way appears.
Your heart knows the Way.
Run in that direction.**

—Rumi

After Karin received Sam Brown's Spiral Painting, she painted one also, inspired by Sam's amazing artwork.
Karin's is a joyful celebration of the changing consciousness on our precious planet.
Use the QR Code to view a video of Temple Villa Maria

Part II ~ Akashic Journeys With Clients

Recorded and Transcribed Readings and Interviews

I don't care if you don't believe in past lives, I tell stories that illumine the Way.

—Maitra

In this section of the book, you will find twenty-eight Readings containing accounts of past lives from the Akashic Records, the permanent record of the soul. You will see how past experiences in other lifetimes, and events in the present incarnation never leave us until we understand and integrate them within ourselves. Only then can we attain the wisdom they were meant to bring us.

All the elements of our unresolved issues remain with us in our present lives. Remembering past lives is one effective way to reach the understanding that we need to resolve them. As William Faulkner wrote, "The past is never dead. It's not even past."

Following each Reading, you will find an interview with the client, in which they recount the effects of the Reading as they continue to move through their lives.

Quotations or poems offering yet more insights relevant to the healing life lessons given in the Reading come after each interview.

Finally, Maitra has provided a "For Your Toolkit" at the end of each chapter. The goal is to give people tools that provide practical application of the metaphysical principles or concepts she teaches. As we come to understand the principles, we can apply the tools to our lives. You'll find that many of the tools apply to several of the Readings. These tools will help you make the changes that you want in your life. They will help you appreciate, love, and accept yourself more. We trust they will make for a happier, more successful *You*. A happier *You* becomes a Blessing for the world!

The names of individuals, and a few other details, as necessary, have been altered in all of the following Readings, to protect their identity. We have also made a few other changes for readability.

These readings shine the light on challenges we all share and offer fresh perspectives and new ways of thinking about issues that are common to all of us. They were chosen to answer concerns we all have about family and partner relationships. We want to explore work, career, and in a deeper sense, what we want to do with our lives. We share concerns about financial issues, including decisions about housing, where to live, and future plans. We want to understand the fears that block us from achieving our goals. Whether you are married, single, have children or not, are a healer, or the CEO of a company, there's something here for everybody.

Let's continue and explore the metaphysical world, the world of the Akashic Records, and their impact on our lives.

M = abbreviation for Maitra

All other abbreviations refer to the client.

Chapter 5: My Child Can't Sleep

For Your Toolkit: Owning the Situation

(Kristin, Nina's mother, born 1975)

Kristin, a highly-trained acupuncturist, is an American; she married a Swiss man and lives in Switzerland. She came to hear Maitra speak and then made an appointment for a Reading. She had a five-year-old daughter, Nina. Nina had always had difficulties sleeping. She was afraid of being alone and sleeping alone. As soon as she was born, Kristin could tell that these feelings ran very deep. Sometimes Nina even got panic attacks. She needed to have somebody with her until she could fall asleep. She always held Kristin's hand or would cling to her body, and was often wide awake, even though she was very tired.

If Nina was sitting alone in the car because Kristin had to get out to open her door, she would begin to scream. Kristin would have to leave her door open, and then open Nina's door to take her out. Only then could she close both doors. Over time, Kristin got used to this, but she wanted to understand what was behind it.

Through the following Reading, Kristin received insight into one of her daughter's past lives:

"In her past life, Nina was a seven-year-old girl. She had a sister who was two years older. They lived with their parents in a small hut in Vietnam. It was night. Soldiers were outside with the parents. There was an incident in which both parents were shot by the soldiers. The door to the hut was locked from the outside and the two girls were locked inside. They could hear the shots. They found out later that their parents were dead. The younger child didn't live much longer in that life. She died early, as a teenager, without having healed from the loss of her parents. She has brought this shock with her into her current life. She has returned with this trauma inside her new body."

Maitra explained that the trauma of past experiences is often reactivated when a person reaches the age of the earlier trauma in a past life. It can also be triggered by a similar, current experience. The unprocessed memories begin to have an effect as they become more conscious, whereas before, they had been below the level of consciousness. This makes it possible for them to be resolved so that things can get easier.

Kristin's and Nina's Transformations

Two years later, during a follow-up conversation, Kristin described how her Reading gave her the tools to help her daughter change her behavior. This dramatically changed the family dynamics.

"Since Nina's seventh birthday, we have experienced a change in her entire being. Soon after the Reading, she became lighter. Her story in the Reading confirmed our experience. It wasn't only that my thoughts and feelings had changed, but now I also had a better understanding of Nina's behavior. There were sometimes still minor conflicts with my husband because he believed that Nina should be able to sleep alone by now and that it was wrong of us to stay in bed with her until she was able to fall asleep.

"Now I was relieved, and I felt that I had handled things well. I remained with Nina instinctively, so that she would feel safe and secure, and I took her fears seriously.

"We also worked with kinesiology (the scientific study of human body movement). This work helped me to feel supported. All of this, in addition to my insights into this traumatic past life, assured me that something was beginning to change. This was all very helpful, and a great relief.

"I got goose bumps while listening to this story about my daughter during the Reading, and I knew there was something true in it. Something was making life very difficult for her, and she was deeply preoccupied. Today, when she gets ready for bed, I still read a short book with her or tell her a story, and she falls asleep by herself. Her entire way of carrying herself has changed a lot. She isn't as shy, and she's less fearful of loud noises.

"Shortly before Nina was born, there were fireworks in our town. The night before I gave birth, I went up to our roof terrace and watched beautiful fireworks. That's when my water broke. This could be connected with the fear that she brought with her into this world. Things are much better now. She can watch fireworks and enjoy them. She manages loud noises and being around wild boys much better.

"It's good that her father is very involved with the family. He is often at home because she still needs one of us to be with her all the time. She wants to know when Papa is coming home and when Mama is coming home. We have a much better understanding of who she is, and she senses this. We have more confidence that we're doing the right thing.

"I'm working on forgiveness, and the Reading has given me more strength and a clear focus for this work. The opportunity to look back at past lives is so helpful. If we accept these various levels of consciousness, we can resolve them and let them go. The clear pictures and messages in the Reading are a wonderful gift and have helped me a lot. They move people, and internal changes take place.

"I have talked with my husband about our daughter's past life. He didn't immediately respond the way I did; I had such a strong reaction. Yet, he is open to the idea of reincarnation. The story carries more weight because it doesn't come from me but from someone else. For this reason, he pays more attention to these messages. It was very powerful for all of us."

There are no great discoveries and advances, as long as there is an unhappy child on earth.
—Albert Einstein

For Your Toolkit: Owning the Situation

When you (or your child) are stuck in a pattern that is distressing you, try the following: Find a quiet place to sit, where you won't be disturbed. Focus on your breathing for a few minutes, until you feel quiet inside. Now imagine a situation, perhaps an extreme one, where the pattern you want to change is holding you in its grip. It's OK to make a situation up, don't worry about that. As the picture becomes clear, let the vision begin to move and unfold, allowing yourself to feel the emotions that are stimulated. Imagine! Follow it until it feels finished, then sit with it and observe yourself with this new information. This process is called "owning" the situation. Once we own it, we can change it and then move on to resolve it. We are no longer powerless victims, but creative, powerful people who can find a way to bring healing into the situation.

Have you "owned" your home? The hotel room you're staying in? The family you have adopted? Your relationships? Your in-laws? Just saying, "This is *my* home," and walking through and claiming each room, will allow you to relax and be more fully at home. Even in a hotel room, saying, "This is my space" will help you find peace there for the duration of your stay. Telling in-laws, partners, and our children, "I'm so happy you are my family" will be healing for everyone. Your life is your masterpiece. Own it!

Chapter 6: A Spiritual Crisis

For Your Toolkit: Judging

(Iris, born 1960)

Iris first heard about Maitra through Karin. They had been part of a singing group for many years. She was a new client for Maitra. She was working as a healer, and, like Karin, she was a reflexologist. Iris didn't come to Maitra with a specific question. She just wanted to see her, so that Maitra could tell her how she was doing. Iris wasn't feeling well at the time, and she didn't fully understand what was happening to her. Her health problems were emerging and it felt like she had hardly any flesh on her body. She felt like she was just a skeleton, walking around, wrapped in a very fragile covering. Perhaps there was an explanation.

The following is a transcription of their Reading:

M: I don't know how you look when you feel well, but I'm aware that you have very little energy. Your face is pale. Tell me about your health problems.

I: I don't feel well. I'm very tired, and this has been going on for about two years.

M: What happened two years ago?

I: I began to have heart palpitations. I went to the doctor; she checked things out and there was nothing wrong with my body. But I still feel nervous inside.

M: Let's look at your relationships and see if we can trace this.

I: I haven't had a lover for the last ten years, I live alone, and I ask myself 'Why?' I ended the last relationship because I could no longer continue on my path through life with him.

M: Do you feel depressed?

I: No, not really. My father died a year ago, and after that, my blood tests showed abnormalities. My iron was very low. I don't feel depressed, but I don't feel well either.

M: When I said 'depressed,' I didn't necessarily mean that you are sad. It feels like you have very little energy. Can you tell me what you want?

I: I read about you and I have come here to find out what you could see for me.

M: So you want to know why you feel like this?

I: Yes.

M: What else do you want?

I: I want to know what you can see about me. If you can tell me a bit more about all of this, maybe I can understand better how I'm doing. This might help me with my relationships and my current health problems.

M: Let's put this aside for a minute, and tell me what you really want.

I: I want support on my path to better health and relationships.

M: Do you have friends?

I: Yes.

M: Do they support you?

I: Yes.

M: Imagine I am your fairy godmother and could wave my fairy wand and give you anything? What would you want?

I: I don't understand the question.

M: I wonder if you have ever really expressed what you want. Imagine, you can make three wishes, and I am your fairy godmother.

I: I want good health, a loving relationship, and a good job. Now I work part-time in an office, and I also work as a healer, i.e. a reflexologist. I want to work more as a healer.

M: Let's back up. Can you tell me your name and birthdate again?

I: Iris, 1960.

M: Now I can feel your energy. Do you know that your third eye is open?

I: Yes, many people have said this to me.

M: How long have you known that it is open?

I: Ten years.

M: When I tune into it, it's a bit painful. Are you aware of this? Does it make you happy or do you get scared when you see things?

I: It enriches me. It's positive.

M: When your father died, how did it affect you, and what did you see?

I: Nothing.

M: I'm going to describe to you the impression I'm getting—you aren't fully in your body. You have partially left your body, but I can't find a reason for this. Sometimes, when someone dies, others leave with them. But that doesn't seem to have happened to you. You haven't talked about any traumatic events in the last three years.

When I asked you what you wanted, I didn't feel much energy coming from you, even when you expressed what you wanted. It's almost like in-difference. Something has caused you to partially leave your body. It must have happened earlier. Under these circumstances, you aren't in a position to heal your health problems or to approach anyone you find yourself drawn to. You just aren't there, available to yourself. This isn't news to you, is it? You already knew this.

I: A year ago, I had a breakdown, when my father died. My body was still here, but it was like an empty frame. That's how it felt, and the rest of me was somewhere else.

M: Just now, as you're describing this to me, and telling me that you are aware of this, I'm feeling the most energy from you so far. Let's assume that you're now about 30% here. That might not be quite right, it could be a bit more, but that's how it feels to me. If I ask you, 'Would you like to be 100% here?', what's your answer?

I: Super!

M: Now you can feel the difference between your words and your actual condition. Your words say 'Yes,' but your energy doesn't. They aren't the same.

I: I can't understand it.

M: That's why I keep asking you to tell me what you want. Our desires bring us here so that we can satisfy them. If you don't have any desires, you don't have any reason to be here. It feels to me that you are in a spiritual crisis, stuck in a place of disillusionment. We do need to discover the reason for this. You're only half-alive now. Is it important to you to heal yourself? Can you commit yourself to this?

I: Yes.

M: No children, no family, no lover, no father anymore. Is your mother still alive?

I: Yes, I have a good relationship with my mother.

M: Would you want to live for your mother?

I: No!

M: I see your light body and I see that you are pushing it away from you, that you are keeping it at a distance. At the same time, you are beginning to open up the channels for healing. How long have you been doing reflexology?

I: Ten years.

M: Would you say that you are using your power and that it is available to you when you are working with a client? Can you feel that you have potentially more power to connect with others?

I: Yes.

M: I see your light body, but it's about three feet behind you. It is available to you if you want to access it. No karma says you can't have it, or that this would be a big problem. It feels more like this is just all too much for you. Bringing your energy (light body) more fully into your physical body would help you feel grounded. It will make demands of you once you feel your power. And then you will have to close the back door. The back door is now open: This means that you can distance yourself from your body at will.

At the moment, you aren't really inside your body. That's why you have so little energy. This crisis began when you started to get in touch with your healing power, but you pushed it away. You rejected it. If you bring all your energy inside yourself, you will feel grounded. Many demands will be made on you. People will want things from you. What have **we**, the people, done to you that you reject us? I'm speaking here about human beings, about all of us, about the human experiences that we all share. It seems to me that your crisis is twofold. To begin with, one part of you has rejected your healing power. You have pushed it so far away that you are not taking good care of yourself and your body. That's why you feel sick. Of course, you can choose to go back and pretend that you don't have this power. The second part of you thinks that human beings, in other words, all of us, don't deserve to benefit from your healing power. That belief comes from a past life. Then, it allows you to believe that we human beings, including you, don't deserve the help and healing that you are capable of giving.

There is a wonderful book, *Illusions: The Adventures of a Reluctant Messiah*, by Richard Bach. He writes about a man who has the gift of healing and can teach others how to reach enlightenment. But he doesn't want this. It's too much responsibility and he didn't like people putting demands on him. You're also like this. This is you. You have all this light within you, and all this power that you could use for healing, but when you began to feel it, you pushed it away.

Now I can see that something is shifting a little bit inside you. Finally!!! You're not easy. Becoming aware of what you're doing is sometimes all it takes for you to make a different choice, for you to be able to say, 'Wait a minute, I don't want to do this.' It isn't easy to learn from you what you want because you have so little energy.

I don't know why the Akashic Records, that give me access to past lives, in your case, are so reluctant to open up to me. I have a feeling that you aren't sure that you want me to access them. Do you want to know the past life that will help you to understand this dilemma?

I: That's the reason I'm here. I want to understand it and I know that this is a spiritual crisis.

At this point, Maitra tells Iris about one of her past lives:

"Let me see what this is all about. I see images of lots of activity. Everything is frantic. You're on a big ship. You are a physician, but not the ship's official doctor. You are just a doctor who is on the ship with other people. It's World War II. This is a group of Jewish people who are looking for a place to land. They are refugees who escaped from Germany.

"People on the ship are ill. Whenever the ship approaches a port, the authorities there won't let the ship land because they are afraid of the illnesses that the passengers will bring with them.

"You are one of the privileged people on the ship. There were maybe twenty or thirty rooms on board for wealthy people, and you were one of them.

"There are hundreds of people below the decks who have only a little bit of space, and they can only lie on the floor. People have spread their clothes out all over the floor so that they can lie on them. It was really bad if someone got sick because there wasn't any place for them to go, where they would be isolated and wouldn't infect other people.

"You had already gone through a trauma earlier when it was discovered that you were part-Jewish. You were in a high position in a large, famous hospital in Berlin. In the early years, when the Nazis began to round up the Jews, you would hold your breath, hoping that you would be safe in this very prestigious position. You weren't only the director of the hospital, but also a professor at the university that was associated with this hospital.

"One day they came to get you. I see total pandemonium in the hospital. All the nurses and the other doctors were enraged. You were so beloved and so well-respected. Your position was secure and you were a mentor to many of the doctors working under your supervision. And you have published many articles.

"When the men in the black uniforms came, some of the doctors tried to stand between you and them. The nurses cried; it was pure chaos. You called everybody over to you and said, 'Don't worry, I'll get this straightened out. Don't be upset. Just continue to look after our patients, and I'll be back this afternoon.'

"They brought you before a military judge. This was the only concession they made for you because of your high position. It wasn't part of the court system, but it also wasn't like an officer's trial either. The judge had a lot of papers that confirmed your high position, competence, and popularity. The judge said to you, 'Look, I'm really not supposed to do this, but I will give you and your family twenty-four hours to leave the country. If something should happen to you and this becomes known, I don't know you!' You looked into his eyes and saw that he was one of the few in the Nazi Party who had any compassion. He said, 'Don't try to take anything with you, not even a bag of clothes. Gather together all the money you can and get out of here. This is all I can do to help you.'

"The next thing you learned was that there were people who worked within this system, but against the Nazi Party. There weren't many of them, and they didn't know each other. So what happened next was that they helped you and your family board a ship. Nobody was supposed to know that you were a doctor. But one of your children, your twelve-year-old son, was up on the deck with some friends, and he told them that you were a doctor.

"Word got around, and the captain of the ship came to you and said, 'Look, you've got to help us here. We don't have any medical personnel on board, but we have many people who are ill. We desperately need your help. This is terrible. We'll never be able to land anywhere if we can't say that we are free of disease.'

"You rolled up your sleeves and went to work. And your wife and your eldest daughter, who was fifteen years old, also wanted to help. You felt the illness was too contagious, but they both insisted on helping. For about a month, or maybe a bit longer, you tried to save as many people as possible. Above all, and you said this to the captain, what was most important was to stop the spread of the disease.

"You found a way to separate the healthy people from those who were ill. But then your wife and daughter came down with it and were very sick. So you went to the people you had been helping and said, 'I don't want to leave the sick people alone in that section of the boat, but I need someone who can look after my wife and daughter. I will supervise, and I will do everything I can to make sure that nobody else gets sick.'

"And do you know that not one healthy person was willing to come forward and help you? So you had to decide whether to stay with your wife and child and try to save them or continue to work in the area with all the sick people and try to save as many of them as possible. You didn't want to take your wife and daughter to the area where the sick people were. It was too dangerous. You stayed in your cabin with them, mostly, but still managed to help with the others. But when both members of your family died within twenty-four hours of each other, you just gave up. You did make an offer, saying that, if somebody was willing to take your place, you would give them instructions. Nobody came forward. You didn't want to continue to help other people who didn't have the courage to help you. You withdrew to your cabin and locked yourself in there with your two remaining children and just waited it out.

"More than half of the people on the ship died. When the illness had run its course, and all the bodies had been buried at sea, the ship was finally allowed to land. You landed somewhere in South America. You lived there for a few years after the war, but you were very disillusioned by the feeling that you had sacrificed yourself for people who were unwilling to help you.

"This feeling has remained with you into this lifetime, and it is very strong, even though you have tried to move beyond it, and are beginning to do another kind of healing. In the process, you've gotten in touch with your powerful healing energy. However, you are rejecting this ability to heal again. Your challenge now has to do with forgiveness. You need to forgive all the people who turned their backs on you, out of fear, in this past life.

"Because you overcame your fear, and your wife and daughter also conquered theirs, you couldn't understand why all these other people refused to help you. Now that you have come up against this problem again, we will see if you can accept other people as they are. Some are strong enough to risk their lives, while others are not. It seems to me that this is your moment of truth."

Iris thanked Maitra for sharing this past life with her and concurred: "I am now experiencing, with other people, the same situation in my present life and it takes so much energy out of me. I can now put many things together. Just yesterday I told someone that I'm sure that I was a doctor in a past life. I didn't know how to ask the question at the beginning of the Reading."

Maitra replied, "You were very disconnected from yourself, and now you are finding yourself, reconnecting. Your light body is beginning to merge more fully with your physical body."

Iris' Transformation

In the follow-up conversation with Iris, she described how her Reading gave her the tools to turn her life around:

"I felt a strong resonance with the past life that I learned about from the Reading; I had a sense of 'Aha, that makes sense!' And now I understand a lot more. I also know why so much of it seems familiar to me. I had many moments like that, and this has continued since the Reading.

"Before I sought advice from Maitra, I wasn't feeling well. Through the Reading, I received much powerful insight, and I listened to the recording of our exchange over and over again. This felt very good, and I understood more and more of the connections. I was familiar with many of these feelings before the Reading, but I couldn't say where they came from and how I knew them. This has confirmed my belief that we are here on earth for a reason. Things unfold according to a pattern or a plan. The Reading also showed me where I was in life at that time. It grounded me again; it brought me back to earth. I relived the story as a whole, again and again, every piece of it, with all the emotions tied to it.

"From this moment forward, I knew that I could free myself from the past, from everything that had taken place. I can let things go. I carried this great disappointment with me from a past life in which people hadn't helped me, even though I had helped them. And I also felt guilty because I, a doctor, ultimately refused to help others. In my current living situation, I am on a path to helping others, without feeling 'I have to.' This sense of 'I have to' belongs to a past life. In my current life, I am not a doctor, and things are unfolding very differently. This discovery has freed me from enormous inner pressure. I can now understand that these feelings are rooted in the past, and they can no longer cast a shadow on my current life.

"I don't have to get involved in things because I feel guilty. I don't have to live my life as a doctor or a therapist or some other profession if I don't want to. I can now make decisions freely. It's also becoming clear to me why my therapeutic work sometimes stalled.

"Over the past year, I have slowly begun to let go of my work as a healer. I have come to a final decision about this, with some sadness. As a student, I remember that there were a few situations when an instructor had to push me to finish my degree. It was as if there was a brake inside of me, keeping me from finishing this course of study. It was related to resistance and, once again, to the feeling of 'I have to do this!' It felt like I had to 'work off' something. So I completed the course of study to become a reflexology therapist and had a very successful practice for a few years until it ended.

"Now, after the Reading and what I learned from it, I can better understand why my career as a therapist didn't work out. I know that I don't necessarily have to follow this path. The burdens of the past had put a certain pressure on me. In my current life, I am free of this enormous responsibility and of the feeling I need to be a doctor. This has given me a new sense of freedom.

"I specifically decided to change my life to fulfill my allotted tasks. Everyone has their reasons why they have been put on this earth. That's my personal belief. I am busy with all the tasks that I have, and I work on them until I have solved all the challenges related to them. If I had not wanted this, I would not have been incarnated (born) into this family and this group of health workers where I am now. I find meaning in all of this.

"Already as a child in school, and in my relationships, I experienced situations that awakened in me a strong feeling and confirmed to me that everything and everyone is connected to everything else and is one complete whole. This sense of belonging is my truth, and it gives me a foundation and a good framework, even if there are moments of emptiness. I know there is something that is still to come.

"Even as I now follow my intuition, I can confirm that my life has a divine plan; this pertains to my life as well as that of others. I repeatedly find confirmation for this view, depending on the extent to which I can embrace life. When I notice that something doesn't quite fit, I can work on it and change whatever must be changed.

"I'm beginning to feel like myself again; my intuition and my bodily sensations are returning. I can listen to myself better and my connection to myself has been restored. I lost my way, and the burdens of this previous life still had a firm grip on me. I can retrace these connections. Putting all the pieces together has greatly enriched me and has simultaneously given me much relief."

> **Where love awakens,**
> **dies the ego, the**
> **dark despot.**
>
> —Rumi

For Your Toolkit: Judging

Choose a person, family or otherwise, toward whom you are carrying anger, resentment, and/or blame. You've been punishing that person by withholding your love or approval. You've said the words "I forgive you," but inside, you feel that what they did, or didn't do, just isn't forgivable.

Now imagine this: The aspect of you that is judging is sitting high on a bench, overlooking a courtroom. Below is a prisoner, the guilty party, i.e., your family member. The blaming part of you is the judge. The open-to-healing part of you (the heart) is the advocate for the guilty party.

The next part is best done out loud: The Judge (the blamer) gives the name of the prisoner and clearly states the offense in detail. The Advocate (the heart) pleads for letting the prisoner go, saying enough time has been served. Now the Judge must decide if the offender needs to serve more time or can be freed. A witness can be helpful if you wish. Be radically honest with yourself!

Remember, forgiveness doesn't mean that you have to like the person.

This tool can be useful whenever you find yourself punishing someone by withholding love or approval. Think about this—you can be angry at someone and still keep your heart open to them.

Chapter 7: Headaches, As Far Back as I Can Remember

For Your Toolkit: Superiority/Inferiority

(Helen, born 1958)

Helen, a meditation teacher and masseuse, came to Maitra because she had been having headaches since childhood. The following is a transcription of Helen's initial Reading:

H: I've had bad headaches ever since I was three years old.

M: What happened if you got angry when you were a little girl?

H: I wasn't supposed to get angry.

M: Were you afraid of what would happen if you got angry?

H: I don't think so; it doesn't seem that way.

M: Did your mother get angry at home? Did your father get angry? What would happen if your father got angry? Did he yell? Did he throw things around? Did he hit things or people?

H: My father could get angry at a situation, but not at a person. My mother would then say to him, "Don't be so angry!"

M: Were you afraid of your father when he got angry?

H: No, but I could feel how insecure he was. I was much more afraid when my mother got angry. She would blame me, and then stop paying attention to me or even looking at me. Cold anger. Withdrawal of love. She treated me as if I didn't exist.

M: Can you feel this in your body?

H: Yes, I can feel it. It's like a pattern throughout my life—this withdrawal—I can feel it moving through my whole body, down my legs, to my feet. It is connected to feelings of rejection and the withdrawal of love.

M: When I looked at you, I saw a red fist at the back of your head. I think you were so afraid of anger that you became afraid of your anger. Your mother's anger was cold, and she would close herself off from you. Your father's anger was hotter and he would say things that weren't nice. He probably didn't aim his anger at you most of the time. This led you to fool yourself into thinking that you weren't afraid of anger. You became disconnected from your anger and fear. It was like this in your family: The feeling in your household was, "You better be careful what you say."

How do you feel if you want to say 'No' to something?

H: It's still a problem for me to say 'No.' It wasn't a problem when I was a child.

M: I can see that all of this anger, and all of these 'Nos' got stuck in your neck and at the back of your head. I'm going to suggest a couple of things that you can do on your own. If you don't feel you can get through this on your own, or if you don't get any results and relief by the end of the year with these methods, then you can go through the Quadrinity Process course [a personal growth retreat] at the Hofmann Institute. You need to do some work to release your emotions. That was the first thing that I noticed about you. Everything is still inside of you and that is the cause of your bad headaches. Intellectual work isn't going to change this. You need to get in touch with your feelings so that you can begin to shift them.

I also suggest you do one thing daily, five minutes a day for two weeks, in a private place, where you won't be disturbed: Stand up and say, 'NO! NO! I don't want to hear anything! NO! I don't have any time for that! NO! I'm not doing that now!' Say it like you mean it, and feel it in your body, as strongly as you can. You can begin with three minutes and work up to five. In the past, every time you didn't say 'No,' or 'I don't want to,' the feelings went inside of you and built a reservoir. This exercise will allow you to release some of the negativity in this reservoir. And if you want to continue doing it at the end of the two weeks, then do it for another week. Your energy is all stuck here, in your neck and your head (See also Chapter 11, "Saying No,").

There's another thing you can do. You can write everything down in the form of a letter, for example, and express all your feelings in it, and burn it when you are done. The letter is for you alone so that you know what you are feeling. If you write a letter to your mother and tell her what she did to you, and how it felt when she cut herself off from you, what's important is that you release some of your feelings. It's better not to send these letters to anyone. It's better to burn them. They are just for you to release some of your feelings.

I want to tell you about something else, about what I can see in your relationship with your mother, why she acted the way she did with you, her coldness, and the closing of her heart. Your mother had the same experience with her mother, and back through the generations. This is the family legacy. If you can break this pattern, you will heal and change the pattern for the entire family.

The Buddhists say, 'When you free yourself from a pain that is causing you to suffer, ten generations back and ten generations forward will benefit.' I have an image of the Russian nesting dolls, the Babushkas. In your family, disconnecting from your feelings is a defense mechanism. It was your mother's way of defending herself against her feelings when she got upset. It would be good if you could break this pattern in yourself before she dies. It would help her a great deal. And there is your grandmother, who is also apparently somehow connected to all of this. You are the first one who is trying to break this pattern. The others all just thought, 'I have to live this way. Nobody can help me.' But you said to yourself, 'I need help, and I'm going to find somebody to help me.' This is wonderful for your daughters. You have already begun to break this pattern by saying, 'I need help.'

Often these deeply embedded patterns in the generations of the family are karmic. Let's see if there is a karmic pattern between you and your mother.

The following is Maitra's description of Helen's past life:

"I see servants in the royal house in Scandinavia—the house of the prince. Your mother had a very peculiar position. She was the bastard child of the prince. Blessedly, he didn't push her out into the snow. He took her into his house. But then she had this very strange position. She wasn't included in the royal family, but she wasn't a servant either. For example, where could she eat? The servants ate in the kitchen. The family ate in a big, gorgeous dining room. There was this kind of funny argument going on all the time between the members of the family, whether she should be included in the dining room or whether she should eat with the servants. Your mother got very confused; sometimes she was invited to eat with them, and other times, for some reason, they said, 'No, you go eat with the servants.'

"You came into the household as a nanny. When the children got older, the parents did a very unusual thing: They sent you away to school to learn how to teach children. So now you have an equally strange position. Now you have some education, so that means you are not one of the servants anymore. Neither are you a member of the family. The way it developed is that you and the bastard child (your mother today) became close friends and you ate together in a little alcove between the dining room and the kitchen. Sometimes the family would eat breakfast in there. The two of you ended up sitting together in this little alcove, and then there was the question of whether the servants waited on you or not. You had a kind of shared dilemma.

"When your mother was eighteen or nineteen years old, the question came up for her, 'Who would she be married to?' Because her position was in some way almost undefined, they couldn't propose marriage to a titled person, but they didn't want her to marry a chauffeur either. This was a subject of great discussion among the family. Finally, they arranged a marriage for her with a very wealthy man; actually, the royal family was always consulting him and he was giving them money.

"He was also in a peculiar position. He was included in a lot of activities because he had so much money, but he wasn't of royal blood. It was an advantage to him to marry her because she had royal blood, and it was an advantage to her because he already had a position with the family that was more 'in' with them. Now there would no longer be a question with whom she would eat. She did marry him, and she was quite pleased.

"After she married him, she thought she was too good for you. She felt guilty about it because you were her only friend, her friend when she really needed one. There wasn't anybody else. Now she was dressed in fancy clothes, attended holy days in Rome, and when she came into the house for dinners and events, she would see you but would just turn away. You were so hurt every time she did this, and she felt so guilty because deep down in her heart, she wanted to acknowledge you. She was trying so hard to be proper, and proper noble women didn't associate as friends with the servants. If she showed her feelings for you, it would be like saying that she wasn't a part of that other group."

Maitra and Helen talked about the past life and its implications for the present. Here is a transcription of their conversation:

M: Both of you have come together in this life because you want to resolve this. She wanted to make things right with you. But you said to me that you weren't wanted, even when you were born. You could feel her tremendous ambivalence about wanting to have you as her daughter so that she could love you. For her, this was almost a step down—a step down, because her higher position in the other lifetime was so tenuous. It wasn't solid, and anything she did could jeopardize it, especially if she did something wrong.

This is why she would shut you out as soon as she would start to have negative feelings. And then she would remember that she loves you, and she would try to come back and make things right. Your mother still needs to feel superior.

H: Yes, that's exactly how she is.

M: But she can't quite pull it off. I don't think you have much of that attitude in you. You don't want to be better than other people. Being born in this past life to a mother who wasn't married to her father, the shame had stayed with her from the past life, and she wanted to be acknowledged as a well-respected, equal person. The shame of being a bastard child remained a very confusing problem for her and it carried over into this life. She wanted to keep the peace at all costs. Rocking the boat could spell disaster.

That's how it was for your mother with your father. When he got upset, it was her job to calm things down and not to pay attention to what he was doing, even if he was doing things that weren't nice. This fits her idea of how a person of nobility behaves. You are with her now because she felt guilty and she wanted to connect to you, and sometimes she did, and sometimes she fell short of her goal. Can you sincerely say to her that you love her? If you ever get to the point, through this healing work, where you feel that you can sincerely forgive her, it would mean a lot to both of you.

H: I could say it to my mother-in-law, but not to my mother.

M: Don't say it to your mother unless you mean it.

Helen's Transformation

A few months later, Helen shared some of her insights:

"It was wonderful for me to meet with Maitra. I felt as if I was part of a community, and I am still moved when I talk about it today. It felt as if we were together, building up a wonderful energy, and that we could transform the world with it. That helped me a lot. The pain that I was feeling, felt real to me. The Reading confirmed to me that my headaches were real; sometimes I doubted this and thought that I was a bit crazy and only imagining them. This encounter with Maitra grounded me and I felt understood. This Reading convinced me that I am OK the way I am.

"It also helped me a lot to see the beginning of my relationship with my mother. I had felt these feelings for years and they fit her character—her superior, somewhat condescending manner. Through this new understanding, there arose in me much sympathy for my mother's current living situation. I can retrace better why my mother sometimes showed so little empathy and could scarcely show any feelings toward me.

"My mother is ninety-three years old, and her mind is perfectly sharp. As her only close relation, I am fully aware that I could determine her life. I talk to her every day, and I have to take care of her. I feel responsible for her. But sometimes I have mixed feelings about taking care of her. Through this healing process, I have grappled with this situation intensively. We discuss together the various issues in her life, and I like to support her while she's making decisions, and also afterward.

"Although I recognize that I was dependent on her in a past life, I am not reversing this situation in the current circumstances. It is important to me that my mother, even in her old age, can lead her own life, and freely structure it as she wants.

"Before the Reading, I couldn't imagine that I would ever say 'I love you' to my mother. I always had a feeling that, as a baby, after I was born, I was traded with another newborn. However, because I was born at home, that kind of exchange was impossible. The feeling that she wasn't my mother, and the wish for a different mother, accompanied me throughout my childhood and teens. I remember several situations where I lacked any connection to her, and I didn't feel like I belonged.

"To express my love to my mother, I need to value myself and feel this consciously. Today I have a stronger connection to her and I can say to her, '*I love you.*'

"I can now, more consciously and actively, better control my relationship with my mother. This feels very freeing. I confront my feelings of anger toward her again and again.

"The exercises that Maitra suggested, such as hitting the bed with a tennis racket or kicking a cardboard box, are very good for me. By allowing myself to connect with my strength, this anger can symbolically be transformed from a negative energy into a neutral one. Then I can work through current issues and observe real changes in myself.

"The Reading gave me access to these feelings and guided me on the path to feel my anger and release it. I can now allow myself to retrieve these feelings and understand the connections. Today I understand the origin of this anger, and this allows me to heal it.

"The headaches aren't all gone yet, but there are periods when I am free of pain. I am working on freeing myself from certain sequences and patterns of thought such as the negative and self-fulfilling prophecy, 'That will give me a headache again.'

"By listening several times to the live recording of the Reading, I have inferred larger and deeper levels of insight.

"I saw Maitra for the first time at the Reading. I didn't know her beforehand. She is an extraordinary person. It was just wonderful to laugh with her, and it opened my heart. A deep trust developed between us, and I could set aside my fears and barriers. She told my story with much empathy."

Mothers of daughters are daughters of mothers and have remained so, in circles joined to circles since time began.

— Signe Hammer

The thing about mothers, I want to say, is that once the containment ends and one becomes two, you don't always fit together so nicely... The living mother-daughter relationship, you learn over and over again, is a constant choice between adaptation and acceptance.

—Kelly Corrigan

For Your Toolkit: Superiority/Inferiority

Superiority and inferiority are opposite sides of the same coin, so to speak. When one is present, look for its sneaky opposite (perhaps not as conscious). Both are states of separation. We suffer because we immediately feel isolated when we feel either of these states. The challenge is to get reconnected. If we feel inferior, we could say to the other person, "I'd like to learn how you do that" or the appropriate equivalent. Acknowledging the feelings, even if only to oneself, will often get us connected again: 'Wow, there I go again, feeling less than.' If you feel superior, offering to share or teach a skill can reconnect you. "Would you like me to show you how that works?" Start where you sense there is a grain of truth in the feeling.

If the feeling is overwhelming and there's nowhere to go with it, start by naming it for yourself: "Yes. That's me too" (See pp.16&17). Examine your history. Perhaps you had a sibling who was so much smarter than you and it's still painful; facing and accepting this will let you move on to a deeper self-acceptance. The fact that someone is smarter, more beautiful, or richer than you, for example, doesn't mean they're better; they're just smarter, prettier, etc., and *there will always be those*. Self-acceptance brings the gift of being at peace with yourself and acceptance of the differences in others.

Just as one drop of water in the ocean is not superior or inferior to another, humans are not. Just different, and differences—diversity—can enrich us, enlighten us, give us pleasure, and make life interesting and exciting. *Vive la difference!*

Chapter 8: Hiroshima: A Trauma Beyond Trauma

For Your Toolkit: 1) Who am I? 2) Lifting Your Spirits

(Ruth, born 1967)

Ruth, an elementary school teacher and mother of three, came to Maitra, hoping that she could feel better about her place in the world. She doesn't feel at home with herself or in this world. She has the feeling that she is just going through the motions, that she is not truly living. Her parents and others expected things of her, and she did them. Then she would feel dependent on others, and that she was living for others so that they would like her. She feels at ease when she can help others when others approve of her, and when she knows what role she should play.

While Ruth was telling Maitra about her concerns and how she was feeling, Maitra saw the same image three times. She wanted to go inside (alter her consciousness for the Reading) and take another look to make sure she was seeing correctly; it was so shocking.

Here's the past life she uncovered:

"During World War II, you were an English woman living in Japan. You were afraid all the time because you weren't able to go home. They didn't allow anyone to leave. It truly was a hell of a war. You were married to a diplomat and, earlier, when he was leaving Japan, you couldn't find each other. You had friends there and they helped you. But you were one of many people who died when the atom bomb was dropped on Hiroshima.

"When the atom bomb exploded, your physical body vaporized. There was nothing left of it, in any form whatsoever. Your etheric body was also torn to pieces. The etheric body is invisible to most people. It gives life to the physical body. We die when the etheric body leaves the physical body. This is what happened to your body at that time: It was totally vaporized, just as when a tea kettle boils and you can only see a little bit of steam in the air.

"Because your etheric body was torn to pieces, you couldn't hold yourself together. You knew that you were no longer whole. Even though there was always a certain amount of consciousness still there, there wasn't any way for you to find yourself. You floated for quite a long time, for several years, in our terminology. Somehow or other, the pieces of your etheric body began to float back together. That's when you began to seek a path forward, and you have been continuing on this path ever since. You were so afraid. You couldn't see that there was help available to you. You couldn't recognize the angelic beings nearby who wanted to help you recover.

"Finally, you began to connect with yourself and to know that there is an 'I.' But there was no 'I' there, and no body. Who am I? You looked around and saw your mother, your mother in this lifetime, and she was praying for a little girl. And you just jumped straight into this baby body, inside your mother, with this thought: Now I can find a path to myself.

"Everything was very strange when you were born. You didn't feel like you were anybody. It felt more like, 'What am I doing here, and who are these people around me? What should I do next?' There was a very profound sense of disorientation. Finally, you began to get oriented. You would touch a chair, or somebody would give you a little toy and you would touch it, and you could engage with it. For example, here is the teddy bear, and I am touching it.

"In this life, you have learned to define yourself through things and other people, but you haven't yet reached far enough inside of yourself to be able to say, 'This is who I am.' You are still so unformed. You have started to look around, and you are beginning to say, 'I'm not like other people.' To a certain extent, this is true. Very few people have experienced such all-encompassing trauma. It is a trauma that is beyond trauma. There are no words to describe it. Not only did your physical body disappear, but your etheric body was also in minuscule pieces. You couldn't form an identity.

"Because you were in a state of panic when you became part of your family, you didn't know how to orient yourself in your physical body in the way that most children do. 'Who am I?' became the underlying theme, the unwritten keynote of your life. You don't have a sense of who you are. You are still trying to find yourself after the trauma that was caused by the bomb.

"You didn't consciously choose your family like most of us do. You can imagine it like this: You're running down a long hallway and you're afraid of what's behind you, and you're looking for a safe place and you try door after door after door, hoping to get in. But they are all locked. Finally, one door is open and you just rush in, with no idea what's inside. You only know that it feels safer than before. And then you begin to learn what you have gotten yourself into. You don't know what you should be doing. As I said earlier, you're beginning to look around and touch the things and people around you, and formulate your thoughts according to what you see. This gives you enough information to live your life: I have a body, I can sit in a chair, I have a mother. Sometimes she likes me, sometimes she doesn't like me that much. She seems to get upset about things. I don't know what upsets her. You try to find out what upsets her so that it stops happening.

"The teaching of a spiritual teacher by the name of Ramana Maharshi is to ask yourself, 'Who am I?' When you ask this question for the first time, you will answer it in this way, 'I am a woman. I have a name, I have blue eyes, I have red hair, etc.' He goes on to say that when you get to the place where you say, wonderingly, 'I don't know,' then you're beginning to wake up. If you begin to explore things from this position, by saying 'I don't know,' then the universe can begin to teach you, and then everything, and everyone becomes a teacher who helps you to know yourself.

"In a certain way, it is to your advantage that you don't feel comfortable with who you are; you won't feel like you have to give anything up. You can begin from the most powerful position: As Ramana Maharshi says, you are in the most powerful position when you have to say, 'I don't know.' That's where you are. That's where you've been living. From a spiritual point of view, it's a wonderful place to be. But when you compare yourself with other people, it doesn't feel so good. When you learn to stop comparing yourself to others, you will begin to appreciate it."

Maitra asked Ruth how she felt after hearing this. What follows is the transcript of their conversation:

R: Many of the things that you have told me are entirely true. I was in Japan last year and we visited Hiroshima.

M: Amazing! How did you feel while you were there?

R: I also asked myself this question. It was just very interesting for me to be there.

M: I can imagine!

R: I found it very challenging to see all the suffering there.

M: You didn't suffer to the extent that many others did. You were destroyed so quickly. For others, it was crueler; they were far enough away from the bomb that they weren't destroyed like you were. You were utterly destroyed. Your suffering was not physically painful; it was psychologically and spiritually painful. I would imagine that anyone else who was near the center of the bomb would have a similar sense of disorientation and would be unable to fully reconnect with their body.

R: Why does the universe allow us to return to earth, if the soul isn't 'repaired' yet?

M: The universe doesn't have intention. I think you are now really beginning to find yourself and be connected to yourself, and you are learning to take care of yourself. You will discover that you have an enormous capacity for compassion, and you will embrace that next. You experienced one of the most unspeakable events in human history. And when you have healed and recovered from this, you will understand all suffering.

R: I am searching for myself; how can I find myself?

M: It would be good for you to read Ramana Maharshi. He never wrote anything, but other people wrote down most of what he said. He looks like an innocent child, even in his seventies and eighties, and he has so much compassion. How would it be if you asked yourself every day, many times, 'Who am I?' 'Who am I?' Each time you ask yourself this question, let the answer arise from within and keep in mind that your primary focus is to become fully connected to your body. So, if I ask you now, 'Who are you?', what comes to mind?

R: I don't feel as constricted, as burdened down; I feel lighter now.

M: And you're less afraid because you now have an explanation for why you've been feeling that way. Ruth, who are you?

R: I don't know yet.

M: Who are you?

R: I can't feel an answer rising from within. I only know how to respond by listening to others who say that everyone is a part of this world and belongs to it and that it's right for me to be here. But I can't feel it.

M: When I ask 'Who are you?', you could say 'I feel cut off from myself.' 'Who are you?', 'I'm looking for my way home.' 'Who are you?' 'I don't know yet.' 'Who are you?', 'I am a seeker. I'm looking for myself.' 'Who are you?'

Can your husband get involved in this? Does he understand you at all?

R: Yes.

M: You can have him ask you this question three times a day. Have him surprise you with it, 'Ruth, who are you?' And then stop, and reach inside, and see what arises.

R: I don't know if I can bring him into my personal development. He doesn't know that I'm here today. It's all very esoteric to him. This isn't his world. But it's fine with him that I'm here. He wouldn't object if he knew.

M: He's quite sensitive.

R: I told him once that I don't feel at home with myself, that I don't have a good sense of myself. And I asked him if he could understand what I meant. He answered, "Not really, but I can feel that what you're describing is not a good feeling."

M: I'll leave it to your intuition to determine if you want to ask him for help. I can see that there are still pieces of you floating in the ether. I will now ask you, 'On a scale of 1 to 100, how much of you wants to be in the body today? If at least 51% of you didn't want to be here, then you wouldn't be here. Can you agree to this 51%?'

R: Yes, because I have to. I'm here. I can't just die.

M: No, you can't. You brought yourself here. Beginning at 51%, how much of you wants to be here?

R: I wish I could say 100%. I think that would feel best.

M: That's a beautiful goal because hardly anyone alive is at 100%. We are all somewhere in-between, and it can change daily. That you want to be here, that you have decided that you want to be here, that's a very big step. You can ask yourself every day, 'How much of me wants to be here today?' I think the answer might already be a bit different from when you walked in the door.

R: Yes.

M: How much of you wants to be here now? Do you remember that you were already very afraid before the bomb exploded? You had no idea that such a thing existed. You were afraid of the Japanese. Not of all of them, because you had Japanese friends. But you remember several people talking to you in a very unfriendly tone of voice. You went into hiding, and your friends protected you. You were already feeling out of place before the bomb was dropped. When we die, we carry with us whatever death is to us, and, how we feel when it happens, continues to affect us. I think it was very courageous of you to go to Japan recently and look at the effects of the bomb on the people there.

R: It was chance, and I didn't know anything about it.

M: I think it was a part of your healing; by going there, you could see that it was real. When you were vaporized, you didn't know what was real. To go there and have this experience helped you to reorient yourself, and probably opened up the path for you to come here today and experience what I have told you. And, by the way, you spoke fluent Japanese in that past life.

R: I have been to soldiers' graves and historical battlegrounds in France, and it was even more difficult to feel the history there and come to grips with the fact that so many people had been killed there.

M: Can you see how important World War II has been for you? Your instincts keep taking you back there, and you keep trying to understand what happened to you there. I think you are doing a very good job of reflecting on what happened to you; only a tiny part of humanity would have had this experience. Every time you say, 'I want to be more present,' you are embracing a bit more of yourself, and pulling it further inside your body.

Do you know the meaning of the word 'annihilation'? Not many people are familiar with this word. To be annihilated means to be completely wiped out, like when a bomb is dropped on a little village and it is wiped out. But you are here now, and you dare to come to terms with this throughout your life, and you know what it means not to feel at home. When you look around, many people feel this way, not everyone, but many. Some people care about this. Others don't. But this feeling is so much stronger in you. If this feeling of being at home with yourself wasn't familiar to you, you wouldn't miss it. You know what this feels like. You've been misaligned and it is difficult for you to get back to yourself. Amazingly, you went to Hiroshima.

R: I'm surprised that I didn't feel more. I would have expected that I would have been very sad there if this story of my past life were a reality. Or else I would have had to leave the place.

M: What happened to you there was more than a feeling. You felt compassion for the people there who were hurting. When you get better connected with yourself, you might shed a few tears. Imagine the shock of what happened to you. It's not only like dying, it's more than that. Now, you are here again. You have your body, and you have people who love you.

R: I'm excited to see what will happen next. I feel like things are getting sorted out.

M: You already had most of the pieces of what I have told you, but you needed to be able to see the whole picture.

Ruth's Transformation

In the following interview, two years later, Ruth describes how she found peace within herself:

"When Maitra spoke, I didn't feel like I was hearing anything new. She didn't say anything that frightened me or anything where I thought 'that can't be right.' There were also moments when tears immediately welled up, because, at those moments, I had the feeling, 'Exactly, she's truly speaking to me from her soul.'

"She would tell me a story that exactly fit me and the way I was feeling. Previously, I had never been able to see a past life. The lost parts of my soul, that she talked about during our one-on-one meeting, gradually brought me a lot of inner peace. I did find the way she told the story frightening, and I imagined myself somewhere in an in-between world, running down this corridor and checking every door to see if it would open, to escape from this dilemma and the many feelings that had paralyzed me until one door did open, and I could enter it and escape whatever was so threatening. This impressed me. I thought to myself, 'Yes, that's exactly how I feel sometimes.' And I can fully feel these pieces of my soul that have now come back to me. In a certain way, I am beginning to feel whole again.

"Earlier, I would orient myself, and identify myself through others. I do this much, much less now. I will be in a situation now and just say to myself, 'This is how I'm going to do this,' and I don't second-guess myself anymore. It's OK the way it is. This helped me the most.

"I felt very well for a while. When I got home right after the Reading, I had a strange feeling that the things in my apartment no longer fit with how I was feeling—as if the change that happened to me in that one hour had not also happened at home. When I returned home, everything in my apartment was still the same as earlier, but something was very different in me. Then I took a walk in the woods and I felt better. That was a very interesting experience for me.

"Since the Reading, I often take a pillow to embrace myself; this gives me a strong feeling that 'Yes, I am put back together again.' This is a soothing feeling each time. It has helped me feel secure and at peace with myself. In the last weeks, I have felt less of a need to do this.

"I needed to acknowledge that I have been out of touch with my inner core and my soul for a very long time; and, that I have merely existed for more than sixty years and have been constantly searching to find ways to endure and therefore survive.

"Now, two years later, these pieces of my soul are returning, and they also want to be included and expressed in this life, although I haven't yet integrated everything. For example, I might want to be funny, and I dare to tell a joke, and then others might react with discomfort, and others might react with, 'Do you find that funny?'

"In such situations, my doubts arise, and I think, 'Maybe I shouldn't have said that.' But I know that somewhere down inside me is a witty person who wants to come to life. I am not yet confident in all situations and sometimes still lack joy in life, yet I am feeling better and lighter.

"My soul is screaming for something new. I have a sense that things are progressing. I hope that the sadness that I sometimes still feel, will get lighter. I want to feel a sense of joy for life more often, and I want to feel more excited about things. I'm happiest when I run into a student on the street, and the child calls out to me and greets me with great excitement. I am pleased when others notice me favorably. When this energy comes from outside of me, I feel good. I still don't feel much inner joy. I would like to have an idea or vision of the future. What do I really want? What excites me? What do I want to experience? I can't get a feel for this.

"I know that everything lies dormant inside of me. If I engage in meditations that lead me inside, I sometimes still become frightened of opening up these doors to the soul, and of just taking things as they come. I'm afraid of change; I need to feel secure. If I open the doors to my inner soul, I'm afraid that change will bring chaos, even though I know it might be better if many things change. I'm afraid that I lack courage. But I am taking small steps, and am slowly moving forward.

"Gradually, the old defense mechanisms and armor are falling away. And I know that this is what's most important. It's also important to me to feel free to talk about all these things, to understand myself better, and to be able to make myself understood. But I also know that it's better not to talk about everything with everyone. If you have been affected by a death, most people show sympathy and you can talk about your experiences with it. But, if I talk about a past life, a subject that is foreign to most of my friends, then I have to decide with whom I can talk about it. But I have one friend who is open to talking about this. Many people don't ever think about whether they had past lives; perhaps they aren't interested in this subject and don't want to know anything about it. If I nevertheless want to talk with them about it, I'm afraid that they will turn away from me, if I tell them about my experiences.

"I like to be open to changes, yet I also need stability in my life, at home, and in my friendships. I don't want to risk too much there. I don't want others to think that I've become very strange, and I don't want them to turn away from me. I'm also somewhat afraid that my husband will suddenly have enough of me if I continue to move in this direction, and that it will become too much for him. Then I get the feeling that if I continue like this, the relationship might fall apart. My husband isn't interested in past lives; he has no concept of what comes after death or between lives. But I know that my husband doesn't limit me. I can now take more responsibility in shaping the relationship and our life.

"I have always lacked a basic love for life; I could never really feel it. I have often felt sad and melancholy and I wasn't aware of any event that weighed on me. I also have days when I feel very heavy and cry a lot. I hope that this sadness will someday fade away. I would like to be able to put it aside."

What am I doing here anyway?
It's a lifetime kind of question
Because
As soon as I find an answer
It's no longer true
Because
it turned to ashes the next moment
And
a new one started to rise
and the circle goes around and around.
Sometimes gladness is the answer,
then sadness comes into sight
Love keeps reappearing
Welcome, Welcome come the sighs
This phoenix is familiar
it has become my friend.
I'm getting less particular
With my judgments: good and bad
I let it—all of it—go—Yes, I can
Let it flow.
A whisper rises from the earth
"You are"
I am?
"You are"
From the sky, a breezy sigh
"You are"
My heart, a drumbeat—I am
Yes. I AM
It's enough.

—Maitra

For Your Toolkit: 1) Who am I?

The sage Ramana Maharshi himself never wrote anything, but other people wrote down most of what he said. He looked like an innocent child, even in his eighties, and was said to embody compassion. His teaching is called the no-teaching teaching:

A laundryman in India, on his way to the village with his donkey one day, found a baby lion whose mother had been killed. The laundryman adopted the little lion and brought him up with the donkey. One day the laundryman was spreading the clothes to dry on the rocks in the sun. The teenage lion and the donkey were grazing peacefully in a nearby meadow, when along the river bank came an old lion, who gazed with astonishment at the donkey and lion eating grass together in the meadow. He went over to the young lion and said, 'What are you doing, eating with your dinner?' He led the young lion over to the river bank, where he could see himself reflected in the water, and said, 'You are not a donkey—you are a lion! Wake up and roar!'

This is Sri Maharshi's message to all of us—wake up and see who you are!

What would happen if you tried his method?

Ask yourself every day, many times, 'Who am I?', 'Who am I?', and each time you ask yourself this question, let the answer arise from within. Keep in mind that your primary focus is Self-Realization*. When you exhaust all the descriptive words, age, gender, family, career, etc., and you only say 'I don't know,' you have begun to realize all the fallacies that you thought were you. Asking yourself, 'Who am I?' isn't really about finding an answer. It's about dissolving all the false premises that we have identified as ourselves. Then what's left is a new beginning: the possibility of self-realization. We can 'Wake up and roar'!

For Your Toolkit: 2) Lifting Your Spirits

Do you have days where you are 'down in the dumps?' Days where nothing seems to work and you can't pull yourself out of a mild depression? Think of it this way: You need some attention from someone who loves you unconditionally, and that someone is you. You can learn to better manage your energy and your emotions; one way to do that is to recognize what you need and provide it for yourself. Give yourself a hug when you need one. Take yourself for a walk in the sunshine when you need a lift. Move yourself into a different mood through exercise or yoga. Take a nap in a comfortable place, inside or out of doors; it will refresh your brain and help you see things in a more positive light. Read an inspiring book or some poetry that you like. Go visit a child. Get a massage. Have lunch with a friend. Take a hot bath with candles and lovely scents. Find what comforts you, what is healing for you. Practice the 'Inner Smile': Imagine each organ of your body smiling, one by one (this is a Taoist teaching).

Make a list of the things that soothe you, give you a lift, and be sure to look at it when you are down. Commit to meet your own needs and value the balance of work and play; that will help you move toward your potential.

Chapter 9: Recovering from Enslavement, Loss, and Powerlessness

For Your Toolkit: Ritual

(Mary, born 1978)

Mary, an artist, a student of shamanism, and a social worker came to Maitra after hearing her give an evening talk about karma, hoping for some insight into her situation. Mary's housing situation was unstable. She sensed that her future was somewhat uncertain, because of where she was living. The house was falling apart; nevertheless, she was in the process of settling down there. The owner lived next door. Mary described the problem in detail:

"My landlord has lived there his entire life, and I have a feeling that it's difficult for him to change anything or let things go. I don't understand my role in this living situation, and I want to know if I have a future there. It does feel like my home. I even have a sense of responsibility for this place. I can't get a clear answer from the owner as to whether I can make it my permanent home, and even possibly buy it. I live in the house with my partner and he is also somewhat unsure whether it's the right place for us. I would also like to have children, but my partner can't fully commit to that. He's hesitant to start a family. There just isn't enough clarity about our current living situation."

Maitra immediately saw the problem as stemming from another lifetime:

"Ever since you entered the room, I see this black, African woman, again and again. This is a past life, perhaps going back three or four lives. You were the midwife in your village, and you had a very secure role and job in the village. You had a wonderful husband, four children, and a fulfilling life. People displayed their wealth in their jewelry and clothing. Yours were the most splendid; your clothing had magnificent patterns, and your necklaces had rows and rows of beautiful beads. You would even wear your jewelry to bed. You were very proud and happy, and you would sing all the time.

"Then there was a tragedy. People arrived who made other people into slaves. They were also black. They came to your village at night. At sunrise, all the villagers were sitting together in the middle of the village square, their heads bowed down, and their hands bound together. Then the intruders looked at each of them, deciding who they wanted to take with them, and who was worth the most money. You were one of the first to be chosen because you looked strong and healthy, and because they saw all your jewelry.

"They took your husband and children, who were the kind of people they wanted— strong, healthy, powerful people. Before anyone could protest, they had taken more than half of the villagers. Only the aged, the sick, and people who were crippled and could no longer do much work, and very young children were left behind. The elderly were left behind to look after the babies. Everyone else was lined up in a single, dense row. From the beginning, they were very careful not to let members of the same family stand together. If there was any indication of a close relationship, you were separated. This event is very relevant today.

"You were taken to a market and sold to white slave traders. They put you on a ship that brought you to the West. It could have been North America, the islands off the Atlantic Coast, or even South America.

"Earlier, you had a very happy life and then, all of a sudden, everything in your life was taken away from you.

"From then on, life was unpredictable and difficult. You were alone and at the mercy of other people."

Maitra went on to point out how some of the issues from the past are relevant to Mary's present life:

"I think some of the memories of this time are now coming back to you because of your current situation. You are looking for security so that nobody else can come and tell you what's going to happen to you. You're also ambivalent about having children, as is your partner. If you had children, this fear would increase.

"This past life was so hard for you because you were separated from your children. You were taken to different places and you never saw them again. The hardest thing for your husband was that he felt so powerless. And you lost your sense of home, your place in the community. But the worst thing was the loss of your children. Now you are trying to find a little place that feels like home, a place that nobody can force you to leave. You know that you feel safer now, but that you won't be safe until nobody else can tell you what to do. Your pain comes from your attachment to having your place, and all the mixed feelings that go along with that. Your partner was your husband in this past life. His fear of having children is based on his concern that he won't be able to protect them. This is the effect of the past life on him. You have come together again to heal. Now the feelings are coming up that will allow you to heal."

What follows is a transcript of Maitra's conversation with Mary:

M: Let's look at your landlord, the owner of your house. Does he visit the house?

Ma: In the beginning, he came over often, but no longer. It feels like he wants to control things.

M: I can see that he likes having you there. He's afraid that if he sells the house to you, he will no longer be welcome. Now he has reasons to visit. He likes to check on the house and the yard. Do you sometimes invite him inside?

Ma: Yes, when neighbors also come over.

M: Do you like him?

Ma: Y-e-s, I can somewhat understand why he behaves this way.

M: You know, he is very lonely. You probably sense that he's seeking you out a little bit. Be yourself around him. But tell him if you like him. Then he might be able to let go of his need to control everything.

Ma: For me, it's also a question of trust, and whether he can trust me enough.

M: Do you have the confidence in yourself to know that you like him enough not to slam the door in his face if he sells you the house? It would make him feel good to know that he could continue to be close to you when he felt like it. But you can't pretend, you have to be honest with him. Let's think about it this way: If he were your grandfather, would you be friendly with him, and would you let him know that you love him?

At the same time, though, you can set some boundaries.

Ma: Then I could be friendly with him, but I still feel insecure because I don't know what he would do or what's going on in his mind.

M: Look, he's getting older. He just wants to have a family and other people around. In the next weeks, imagine him to be like your grandfather. And ask yourself, 'What do I want to do differently?'

If he were your grandfather, you would love him, but you wouldn't want him to run your life. The difference is subtle; I think he wants family and connection. You have to decide what you want. Then he will feel more able to negotiate with you. He is not going to ask you to leave unless there's a huge problem. He likes having you there. For him to feel safe enough to sell you the house, he needs to feel more secure. Would you invite him in and cook him a meal if he were your grandfather?

Ma: I would go over to his house and visit him. It is difficult to reach him. Often I don't see him for quite a while, even if I go looking for him.

M: You have reached out to him and done your part. He knows that you went over to his place. He wants to be closer to you, but he's afraid. If he were your grandfather and you saw him, what would happen to your energy? What happens when you see somebody you love?

Ma: I would open up my heart and let him get closer.

M: I don't want you to manipulate him. I want you to be genuine. I just know that if he felt closer to you and had more confidence, he would be ready to sell the house. He is not hurting for money now, but it would help him if he could sell the house—especially if he ever gets to the point where he has to move to an expensive home for the elderly. If you just open up your heart a bit more to him, I think things will get a lot better. Your trust was broken in that past life. Everyone in your village was happy, and you were also happy, you had something to offer, and you liked to offer it. You trusted life, and then disaster came.

Ma: I feel like I am the keeper or the guardian of the place. I am the one who has connections with everyone there. In a way, I am already taking care of this place.

M: Anything is possible. You feel quite secure where you are, even though you don't see it this way. The owner likes having you there. I think he trusts you more than you realize. That's why he doesn't come around as often anymore. When you are walking around in the next weeks, think to yourself that he's like a member of your family, and see how it feels. Maybe you will take care of him later if that's what you want.

Ma: There are still unpredictable things.

M: I had a teacher once who called this *the fear of the imagined future.* Don't worry about it too much until it happens. Do you see how you are always worrying a little bit about the future as a way of protecting yourself? That's because of the tragedy that happened to you in that past life.

Ma: That's true. I'm at ease in the present. When I think of the future, fear arises.

M: Yes, the moment you start projecting into the future, you get frightened.

Ma: I have the feeling that I have to accomplish something big to be somebody. I have high expectations of myself, and then I start asking myself if I will be good enough at what I'm doing. And I lose my sense of ease and joy. I will soon have an art exhibition with my father, and these feelings are coming up now.

M: That experience of having everything taken away from you is still inside you, and you remember it. Now, be brutally honest with me, are your paintings wonderful? Do they say what you want them to say?

Ma: I'm not so sure. I'm just not sure if I'm truly expressing what I want in this exhibition. But when I feel free to do as I please, I feel good about what I am doing.

M: I'd like to ask you something. What is your degree of satisfaction with yourself? Is it about 50-50?

Ma: I am very aware of this issue, and I want to make changes so that I can get away from the part of myself that I don't like.

M: If you are a slave, can you do things to please yourself?

Ma: Not really.

M: You have to please your owner, or else you will be sold to somebody else. You still have a dark shadow from that lifetime, and it sneaks up on you when you have an upcoming exhibition, like now. To heal this shadow, I think it would be good for you to host a small ceremony or ritual. You need to create your emancipation papers. You need to burn your slavery papers; they tell you that you owe everything you have to someone else. To establish your freedom, you could go back and look at some of the records of the slave owners, at the bills of sale. Or at the records that say a person once belonged to somebody else. These are called emancipation letters. Examples are available online.

Emancipated slaves, free people, only needed to please themselves. That's why I asked you that question. You are doing quite well with this. You are pleased with about half of what you are doing. So, go and get your emancipation letters, and then take the paintings that you don't think are quite right, and put them in front of you, one at a time, and ask yourself, 'Now that I am free, can I save this painting? Is there a small change that I can make in it, that will make me happy?'

If there isn't, take some white gesso paint and paint over it. If you can't save it, paint over it and make it into a new canvas. Now, as a free person, you don't have to please anybody else. It would be amazing, in this ceremony, if you put chains around your wrists and broke them; or, find another ritual that will symbolize this freedom to you.

You already know the secret of all the great painters. They didn't paint to please somebody else. They painted because they had something to say. It was important to them to express themselves. Do you know that Van Gogh only sold one painting in his lifetime? He wasn't even considered a good painter until he died. And now his paintings sell for millions.

So, you want to please yourself. Pleasing yourself doesn't always mean that a painting is beautiful. It means that you said what you wanted to say. The point is that you are not a slave. I can still see so many small places inside you where you aren't quite free. This continues to have an impact on you, and you are therefore a bit insecure.

Ma: Yes, I often have the feeling that some things are forbidden, that I am not allowed to do things that I like to do. I can't do them because I am blocked.

M: Your future looks good. You are willing to view this man, the owner of the house, as possibly being a part of your family.

Mary's Transformation

In the follow-up conversation, about a year later, Mary spoke about what she had learned from the Reading:

"I'd like to set down my roots again in this place where I live. Through the Reading, I became aware of my uncertainty and insecurity, and the fear that I could once again lose everything. The past life called forth a deep response in me. Throughout my life, I have often felt that my hands are tied together and that I really can't take action. Earlier, it always seemed to me that I was blocked whenever I wanted to do something, for example, in my orientation toward healing and shamanistic work, or other projects in my life like artistic production. I still have an inner feeling that I shouldn't be doing such things. This plays out on various levels in my life, in my living situation, and in my desire to have a child.

"Maitra urged me to view the owner of the house like a grandfather, and I have embraced this idea and way of thinking. In the meantime, the relationship has changed in a very positive way. Shortly after the Reading, I suddenly realized it would be very good if I could address him by his first name, and now we are truly on a first-name basis. It happened spontaneously one evening when a lecture was being given at my sister's house, and everybody there suggested that we address each other by first name. He's now also on a first-name basis with my partner.

Based on his age, he could surely be my father, yet the idea of looking at him as a grandfather gives me a certain distance and a good feeling.

"He doesn't have such a good reputation with everybody, and sometimes he can be a bit snooty and very stubborn. Now it bothers me if someone speaks badly of him. I also feel closer to him now and try to point out his positive qualities. Thanks to him and his mother, this village with its old houses wasn't just torn down and replaced with new buildings. It is still a green spot, like an oasis. I sense that I now defend him more for his role in this. I can also feel that he trusts us more. He seems very open to new things. When I'm at home, I now trust that he would ask us if he wanted, or had to, sell the house.

"I planned this ritual, this ceremony, that Maitra had suggested to me for my birthday. I took time to prepare the space for the ritual, and I found an old carpet from my ancestors and I used it to fill the fireplace. This also gave me a connection to my origins.

"It was also very important to me to have witnesses there. I invited some very close women friends to join me. The black midwife in my past life was very happy and sang a lot. I felt a strong inner need to sing because I also had this debilitating inner voice saying: *You know that you can't sing*. My sister was such a good singer that I always held back because I didn't want to embarrass myself. So, I incorporated certain songs into the ceremony that had to do with freedom and emancipation. In addition, when I was painting and drawing for the exhibition, I always listened to these songs, sang them, and internalized them for the ceremony.

"A part of the ritual was for me to dance my way to freedom. Before I began to dance, I told the story of this past life to everyone who was there. Telling the story was a very powerful experience. The story felt very clear to me and once again touched something deep inside. It was easy for me to tell this story. Before this experience, I didn't know that I could tell stories so well. In the end, I told them that this was one of my past lives.

"This ceremony included a fire, the story, the dance, the singing, and above all, the knowledge that I was able to free myself from this old experience, from the memories of this tragedy, and the slave within.

"Organizing and leading this ceremony has strengthened me enormously. The ritual has had a very powerful effect on me. I no longer have the feeling that something is being taken away from me. I have become much more productive and can create things from within. I permit myself not to create for others, and I am able and must continue to do this. Instead, I express myself as I see things.

"While leading the ritual, I got in touch with a very strong inner power. I sensed that this was a gift that I should use more. I want to stay in touch with this power. I felt very empowered to do this. I am interested in shamanism (such as a medicine-man or spiritual healer) and have done some training. My heart is fully engaged in this. I need to reconnect people with nature. This also flows into my work with children. The shamanistic path to healing helps me to continue on this path.

"I can also feel the karmic connection with my partner very deeply. The Reading confirmed my feelings that we had this family in a past life and that this traumatic separation was very difficult for everyone. This familiar feeling was always there; it wasn't foreign to me.

"I am looking forward to the exhibition. My father is also artistic, and we are doing the exhibition together. He approached me and asked if we might want to exhibit together. This made me very happy. I feel that he acknowledges me, in my way of being, and in the work that I do. We can now relate to each other on this level. The experience of this exhibit has made me more authentic, in the sense that I can communicate the language of my paintings and objects in a way that I feel them. I accept my way of expression and see myself reflected in it. I no longer have to hide. Everything can be the way it is. I accept my way of perceiving and feeling things.

"Imagining the landlord as my grandfather was a key to understanding the entire situation. Viewing him as part of my family has changed many things. If anyone speaks ill of him, it hurts me. Even though he's a bit of a character, a closeness has developed between us. In the beginning, I was very distant.

"The memories of the trauma of this past life prevented me from engaging in many things. As a slave, I couldn't experience and practice many of my skills and gifts. The Reading spoke to me about several things that I was feeling before our meeting. It was a confirmation, and I felt a deep, inner resonance. I now feel much better and freer."

The most beautiful thing we can experience is the mysterious. It is the source of all true art and science. He to whom the emotion is a stranger, who can no longer pause to wonder and stand wrapped in awe, is as good as dead—his eyes are closed. The insight into the mystery of life, coupled though it is with fear, has also given rise to religion. To know what is impenetrable to us exists, manifesting itself as the highest wisdom and the most radiant beauty, which our dull faculties can comprehend only in their most primitive forms—this knowledge, this feeling is at the center of true religiousness.

—Albert Einstein

For Your Toolkit: Ritual

Perhaps there is something in your life that you would like to change, something you would like to let go of? As in the Reading above, you can create a ritual to help you move in the direction you want to go. Rituals can remind us that we are already free, that we are making choices that limit us without being aware of it. Our unconscious beliefs about ourselves (such as Mary being a slave) can block us from reaching our potential. For example, you might want to develop your ability to express yourself more clearly, whether it be painting or writing, or simply communicating better. Your Ritual could be a celebration of creative expression, including many ways of expressing yourself—be sure to have friends present to support and celebrate with you. Let it include the expressions you are most afraid of having people see—when you are the most vulnerable. Anger, tears, and joy may all have their place in your poetry, your song, your Ritual. Strip away the public persona and let the authentic You have his/her voice. This is an opportunity to conquer any fear you have of what others might think, or embarrassment over 'being seen.' Take your freedom! It's yours!

This is what Rumi meant when he said, "Run from what's comfortable. Forget safety. Live where you fear to live. Destroy your reputation. Be notorious. I have tried prudent planning long enough. From now on, I'll be mad."

Chapter 10: A Fear of Public Speaking

For Your Toolkit: Addressing Fear

(Jack, born 1970)

Jack, an M.D., and also a healer and teacher, had been studying with Maitra for a few years and is struggling with skepticism regarding past lives. Jack was a student of Maitra's Lotus Group, which studied reincarnation. He came to the Reading because he had a lot he wanted to say, but he had been unable to conquer his fear of public speaking.

He also wanted to clarify the issue of why he was afraid to speak in front of a large group of people. He didn't have a problem speaking in front of a small group or a one-on-one conversation. But as soon as he was standing in front of a fairly large group of people, he wasn't able to speak or think clearly. He wanted to be comfortable standing in front of large groups of people and sharing his experiences with others, but he still got so anxious and uncomfortable in these situations.

Maitra had immediate images of a past life:

"I assume you know about the Inquisition. It was a court. There were three judges and three examiners, and afterward, there could be torture. You were a monk in a brown robe. You were a simple man; you had grown up on a farm. You loved animals. You were part of a bargain struck with God. Your father wanted something and he promised God that, if it was given to him, he would give a son to the Church. You were the youngest son and probably a lot like you are today, more of the type to become a monk than your brothers.

"You were about fourteen years old and your father came to you and said, 'I promised God a son, and you are the one and I think that you will do the best job.' He tried to make it sound like a good thing. You said, 'But I don't know what to do.' And your father reassured you, 'They will tell you what to do, don't worry.' You went along with him, and when you got to the monastery, you discovered there was time to do a lot of the things that you liked to do. On the farm, there was never time to read, draw, and just hang out with the animals.

"Because this was a working monastery, they grew their food and also had animals. You could choose what you would like to do each week to help out. You realized that it suited you; it was very good for you.

"You began to discover that you could heal animals. You learned that if you put your hands on them in a certain way, they really loved it and they felt better afterward. Although the results were not dramatic, certainly time after time, there was confirmation that they were feeling better.

"The other monks knew what you were doing; you were the youngest, and they just thought that it was God's work. They didn't make any fuss over it. There was a little bit of curiosity here and there, but not much other than that. Then you grew up and you were assigned to a healing center, a clinic where people came who had problems.

"One wing of the monastery was in a separate yard, and people would come and bring their children; pregnant women and the injured came for help. It was a form of medical help, but not the way we do it today. Herbal remedies mostly, sometimes setting a bone, cutting out a splinter, those sorts of things. You soon realized that what you could do with animals, you could also do with people.

"One of the older monks said to you, 'It's fine, you can do that, but don't ever talk about it. Because, if you talk about it, they will get scared, and if they get scared, you can't help them. So just do it, but don't talk about it.' And then he commented, 'just like you couldn't talk to the horse about it, just do it the same way.'

"And you said to yourself, 'Well, that's funny, I do talk to dogs and horses,' but you understood what he meant, and so you went ahead with seeing people. It was a rotation. Nobody was there all the time, but everybody was expected to put some time in there.

"It was the most significant way in which you had contact with the outside world from the time your father brought you there. You liked it. You liked seeing children, and you liked being able to help people. It was very satisfying. You continued to have a kind of innocence or naïveté about you. At a young age, you didn't have any real worldly experience, but you were extremely curious.

"You were full of questions for the other monks who were there for entirely different reasons. You had been told that you weren't supposed to ask such questions, but you couldn't resist. This went on for several years.

"I see you now, probably in your forties. You are wearing small, round eyeglasses that don't help very much. You carried yourself similarly to the way I see you today. You are full of goodwill. There is warmth in you when you sit down and introduce yourself to a person. People immediately feel at ease with you and can talk to you about their needs.

"There was a rumor that men were coming from Rome. They called them inquisitors or judges. You were quite a long distance from Rome, but still in Italy. This visit was a strange occurrence, something that had never happened before. They were coming as representatives of the Pope, who wanted to know what was going on in the far reaches of the country. Nobody had any idea of what this was all about, nor were there any details that would have given rise to any fear in you. No one had ever told you that you had done anything wrong.

"When they arrived, they were welcomed and offered the best that the monastery had to offer, the best rooms, and a comfortable bed for each visitor, in contrast to the monks, who slept on thin pallets on the floor. They planned to be there for a couple of days, walking around and seeing what everybody was doing. They walked inside the buildings, examined everything, and made some notes, and you thought that was going to be the end of it. But then they said, 'Well, we found some discrepancies, so we want to start examining people.'

"What was the meaning of all of this? They didn't seem to want to tell anybody what this was all about. People began to worry.

"A special room was set up with a table for the three judges. They wore black robes, special ones, unlike anything you had ever seen. When the judging started, people were brought in one at a time. Everybody in the monastery had to be there to watch, every single person, including the kitchen help and the gardeners.

"Many people went into the examination room before you, many of the monks and the abbot. But when people came out, their faces would be either very white or red. They looked very upset, but they didn't want to answer any questions about what was going on in there. In the days that followed everyone was subdued, very quiet.

"You were the last person they questioned. They asked you about other things, but they mostly asked you about what you were doing with the people in the clinic. You didn't think much about it, although you did remember at one point what the monks had told you earlier —that you shouldn't talk with others about what you were doing because people wouldn't understand it and would be frightened. So, you didn't talk about the fact that when you lay your hands on people, they would feel better.

"You just talked about mundane things and the advice you would give others about how to keep things clean. You were feeling a tad guilty that you didn't tell them about the other thing, but you knew intuitively that you had to keep it to yourself.

"Let me back up a little: They started questioning the monks. All of a sudden, the monks were talking about you, saying that they thought you were touched by God because people would feel better when you lay your hands on them. You were just shocked that they were talking about this because they had told you earlier not to talk about it. But lo and behold, almost every other monk was questioned about this, and every single one of them said the same thing. It became clear to you that they had been talking about it for a long time behind your back because they recounted stories of all the different people that you had helped.

"You just hadn't realized that the monks were watching you; you were still rather naïve. The monks, somewhat in awe of you, were aware that people were being healed. They had never treated you any differently, so you hadn't noticed this. You didn't know that you had so many admirers who thought you were special.

"The three judges are now standing at the front, they are asking the same questions over and over again, and they are getting the same answers. And, although the men are answering these questions somewhat reluctantly, they don't suspect that this is going to end badly. Everything that was happening was a big surprise to everybody.

"This questioning went on for several days and some men were found wanting or lacking in something or other. They were told that their punishment would be announced later. But even though people were serious, there wasn't a tremendous amount of fear. I don't think anybody had any idea of what was coming.

"The judges went through the whole group and when they came back to you, they asked you whether what people had been saying about you was true, and you said 'Yes.' Then they asked why you had lied to them before, and you said, 'I was told it would be better not to talk about it because it would frighten people, so I just thought that it was better not to talk about it here either.'

"Then they started using the word 'Devil,' saying that the Devil is devious, the Devil is secretive, and the Devil doesn't want you to talk about his works to other people. Then they started talking about conspiracy, that there was a conspiracy among all the monks in the monastery to hide what you were doing; the fact that they felt it was necessary to hide it, meant that they knew that the Devil was behind it. Yet, they let it go on anyway.

"You were starting to shake. Your mind was not able to grasp what they were saying because there was nothing in you that knew anything about the Devil. He wasn't any part of your experience. And when you looked around at the other monks and saw the fear on their faces, you knew that it was the same for them. They didn't know anything about the Devil either. Two of the older monks tried to stand up and say, 'How could it be the work of the Devil if it helps people? How could this be?'

"These two monks were sharply reprimanded, and every single monk who had supported you in any way was tortured until he admitted that he knew it was the work of the Devil. Then the torture would stop, and they would come out and be treated, and their wounds were bandaged.

"Every day you were sitting in the observer's balcony, and watching and hearing the things going on below you, and you slowly began to realize that it was all happening because of you because you were laying your hands on people so they would feel better.

"And you started to think, maybe they're right. In the face of all these other people coming around to this point of view, you began to doubt yourself, and said to yourself, 'Maybe they're right, it is the work of the Devil.' And then, as this was going through your mind, you would remember a little girl who was crippled, and after you worked on her three times, her foot came around to the way it was supposed to be, and she could walk and play and run and laugh with the other children. And then you asked yourself, 'How could this be the work of the Devil, whose acquaintance I have never made?'

"By the time the judges turned to you, you were thoroughly confused, and you felt like you couldn't even speak when they asked you the same questions again and started to hand down your sentence. And when they would say to you, 'You knew what you were doing was the work of the Devil,' you would say, 'No, no, no, I didn't know.' They sent you away and told you to come back the next day. And then they started to torture you, and by the end, you said, 'I guess I didn't recognize his face, so when I was doing it, I did it without knowing what I was doing.' They were finally satisfied because you admitted that you had done it, even if you didn't know that you were doing it.

"By the time the judges left, some people had been permanently injured. Some people could never walk quite right again, or their hands were in pain all the time. There were different punishments, like the man who yelled at them, saying that it wasn't the work of the Devil, and had his tongue cut out and could never speak again. And there you were, walking around, trying to understand how this could have all come about, and wondering what it had to do with you. In some way, you could never quite take it in that all these people had been hurt because of you. And you couldn't admit it to yourself, and you couldn't deny it. It was all in the realm of the unbelievable, and there wasn't any way for you to understand what had happened. You could only think, 'What did I do wrong? How could all these people think that I did something wrong? How could I be so fooled to have done the work of the Devil? How could this have happened?' You went through the rest of that lifetime thinking about this.

"Afterward, the other monks never had the same feelings of happiness and trust and were never as close to each other. You all continued to live together, but in a state of isolation from one other, yet still trying to be kind to each other and going through all the motions of running the place and growing food, and all that sort of thing. The clinic was closed and never reopened."

Maitra then goes on to explain the effects of that trauma. A transcript of her exchange with Jack follows:

M: You never trusted yourself fully again in that life. Many lifetimes have passed since then, and you have been slowly rebuilding your ability to trust yourself. In this life, you are still working on this. Whenever you remember that room again, you know that it wasn't only about you. It was also about the people who suffered, you thought, because of you. You weren't the only one at risk, but you felt in some way responsible for the suffering of all the others in the monastery.

Logically, if you can get some objectivity, and can look back at it today, you will see that you just got caught up in a juggernaut, like a big stone that's rolling down a hill and gets faster and faster and picks up things while it rolls, and nothing can stop it. That's what was happening with the church at that time. That juggernaut, called the Inquisition, was rolling and rolling, right through your monastery, and it devastated everybody there.

Because so much of the focus was on you and what you were doing, this experience has stayed with you. It serves as a warning, 'Be careful, don't let people see you.' And it all comes back to you in certain situations, like whenever you have to take a test. Or your mind almost comes to a full stop, when people might be judging you. You have managed many situations in this life very well, and you've made much progress, but it's not quite complete. You haven't forgiven yourself yet.

Now, when this fear comes up again, you can say to yourself, 'It's a memory, it is not happening today. Even if people knew about this today, the worst thing that could happen is that they might think I am a little weird.' In reality, people might distance themselves from you a bit. There is no Inquisition today. But, as you know, some people are still afraid of things they can't understand.

There is still a lot of fear around us about such things. This still happens today, and it is the same for anybody who is on the leading edge of change. If you're in a leadership position, gradually your self-confidence, your clarity about what you are doing, and your certainty that you have nothing in you that wants to harm anybody gets transmitted, and you find yourself more and more able to be at ease with what you are doing.

J: Is it possible to get rid of these fears?

M: As more and more people experience healings, there is less fear about it. Our fears can settle down, too, because consciousness is changing. I can't tell you what will be gone tomorrow, but I can tell you that consciousness is changing, and I see changes in how they depict healers and psychics in movies and on television. It's completely different than it was even ten years ago. Earlier, there were always conversations where someone made fun of healers and psychics and thought they were just weird and crazy. This is all approached in a much more serious way today; healing is viewed as one of many possibilities, and our gifts are more respected. It will take patience, and being able to recognize that a lot of your fear comes from the memory of this past life in which you not only suffered but believed that other people suffered because of you. You see yourself as connected to people and you don't want to be the cause of anybody's suffering.

Karma comes from intention. If we intend to hurt somebody, and then we hurt them, we have to be karmically responsible for it. If we do something, not meaning to hurt someone, but we do hurt them, we are not karmically responsible for their misinterpretation. We *can* try to correct it. Sometimes the best we can do is let it go.

Jack, you surely have some patients who can easily handle what you tell them, and some who can't. You tell the people who you think can handle it, 'I'm getting some information and I would like to give it to you.' If you still feel insecure, what's the worst thing that could happen? You're still afraid of being wrong and you are afraid of what other people think.

J: It makes me sometimes speechless.

M: Ask yourself, 'Is it as true as I know how to make it? Is my motivation to help others clear?' If you meet those criteria, now it's just you alone deciding that you're going to take the risk to go to another level of this work. It sounds to me like you are trying to move to a new level. When you're there, you will even be able to speak to people who don't know anything about what you are doing in your work. But this is who you are. So just try to find the courage, from moment to moment, to be who you are. This is the same for all of us, except that, as a doctor and healer, you may have more to lose, but you also may have more influence. People do listen to you; it's your assignment in this lifetime.

One more thing: If your fear were a dog, what kind of dog would it be?

J: It would be a big one who shows his teeth and moves around a lot, with long hair.

M: And if you had a dog like that, and it kept getting in your way so you couldn't move the way you wanted to, what would you do?

J: I think I would change my position. If I stood like that, I would make myself smaller and wait to see the reaction.

M: You are paying attention to the fear, so I suggest, that you train your dog. When he walks up to you and won't let you do something, you say, 'Sit, lay down, I don't need your help right now.' Because your dog (fear) is here to help you, he's trying to warn you of something, but you get to decide if it's something to be afraid of or not. You get to tell the dog when you want him to do his job and when you don't. So, when you're afraid, you can look at the dog and say, 'OK, sit.' You choose to master your own emotions. You choose to become the master of the dog, rather than having the dog be your master. Do you see what you have been doing? You have been making yourself smaller. You have given too much power to the dog. Now you can become the master of your fear, rather than letting it block you.

You are going to become famous or very well-known, and this is already beginning to happen, so it is time for you to get that dog well-trained and master your mind. This is probably the biggest challenge that any of us have. Our minds can get out of control very fast, and take us —who knows where? Fear is a contraction, and when you contract, everything shuts down. As you get more control over your fear, you will be able to relax and open up more and more and trust that you can manage whatever is coming into your mind.

This fear is an image that anybody can relate to. You don't have to worry about your brain. Your brain is fine. There is no deterioration. Fear has been causing your mind to go blank. It's the synapses that aren't responding. Saying things out loud helps a lot, I've discovered. When I say something out loud that I want to remember, sometimes two or three times, it sticks. This is a way of giving your brain instructions. Your biggest challenge is fear itself. If you can play with my dog idea and can get some level of control over that, you will do a lot better. If you look at it logically, you already know that there is nothing to be afraid of, but your feelings still get in the way. So, appreciate that dog! He is there to protect you, and to help you, and that's what he wants to do. You can tell the dog what you need, such as 'I don't need your help right now; *lie down*!' That is self-control. Self-mastery.

Jack's Transformation

Jack described how the Reading affected him in the following way:

"I just listened to this story and found that everything sounded very exciting and interesting, but I didn't feel that much resonance with it. Nevertheless, I felt something very special after the Reading and the description of the behavior of these monks and all these terrible events. I noticed that I sometimes still behave in the same way in my life today. This produced a powerful response in me to this past life. I could feel how careful I am, that I don't promote myself very much, and that I don't broadcast my psychic abilities, my spiritual orientation. My colleagues in medicine scarcely know me. As it is, I'm a bit of an odd bird.

"I reveal a lot about myself, and word gets around. They talk about me at the beauty salon, and that I sometimes do psychic healing with people. On the one hand, it doesn't matter to me, but on the other, there is still some fear. This fear is evident in a feeling that someone could turn against me, above all because, as a doctor, I don't always use traditional medicine. My rebelliousness is a part of this. I'm aware that I'm going against the main-stream. Consequently, a part of me wants to be noticed as little as possible by my colleagues, even though I stand out because of the way I work and act. My work is already outside the norm. It has certain structures, but Maitra also found it amusing, because she said I look and dress very conservatively, though deep inside I am a revolutionary. And I have to say, she hit the nail on the head. It is 'packaging' so that I can go through life without being noticed, although deep inside, things work very differently.

"So, what did this Reading offer me? It removed some pressure. Everything didn't change all at once. I still have a problem standing in front of a large group of people. But my perspective has changed. It's as if I can look at this situation from a larger dimension. For example, if I think back to an earlier time, or reconnect with feelings about taking an exam, I can say that the stress I feel today is based on an earlier experience. That's very comforting. My goal is to put aside this fear completely. This is also the reason why I seek help on this issue at all levels. It is now much less of a problem for me to sit across from somebody or be the leader of a group. But as soon as I stand in front of a large group of perhaps 500 people and I begin to feel that I will be criticized or people will respond negatively, and I can't avoid the situation, the fear returns, 'Will I lose my footing?' The fear returns that I won't be able to think clearly, that I will lose my connection with myself and stand there speechless.

"I was never enthusiastic about the idea of a past life, although I've known for twenty years that such things exist. I have always avoided trying out anything with my patients on this topic, or working with it. I had a problem with this earlier; I didn't want to enter into these concepts. I found it un-comfortable. Because I always had the question, 'If information from a past life exists, what would I do with it afterward?' If a patient couldn't come up with any connection to specific information, I would ask myself, 'What kind of weird stuff have I been talking about?' But now, feeling much stronger,

I realize that I can perceive my own past lives and those of my patients now that I am becoming increasingly sensitive, and am learning how to cope with things differently. I am also able to explain these issues differently. I don't yet know how my patients will react to this, but through the experience of this Reading, I can make peace with the topic of past lives.

"I can see today that problems in my current life might be connected to patterns from a past life. Because I work in the medical profession, there is still a certain expectation to be scientifically accurate. By looking at the Akashic Records, I am entering territory that appears incomprehensible and downright whacky to many people. To be sure, I can't produce evidence, and others can say that I am a total fraud. So there still is a certain insecurity and I feel more susceptible to being attacked and more vulnerable.

"Previously I didn't have a good approach to the subject of reincarnation and past lives. It would sometimes happen in my practice that something pointed to the idea that it could be a matter of a past life. Through my work with Maitra, I'm more confident about things I feel internally, and I have clear images of them inside. This has given me new permission to embrace this awareness and trust what I can see. The more I allow this to happen, and use it with my patients, the more I trust the images that appear to me.

"My main problem, fear of speaking in front of a group, is not yet completely resolved. But it will be. I suspect that it is connected to how much more open I can become and how my perception of myself develops. In addition, there is the question, 'What do I have to say to groups of people?' Emotionally, I see myself giving lectures or talking about certain topics that I receive intuitively and want to share. I see myself going in this direction. Then it is a matter of spiritual, and also medical topics. Fundamentally, it's a matter of good health, a zest for life, how we function, and our belief systems. It is a matter of questioning all of our patterns of belief and how we can change them.

"The prayer of Niklaus von Flüe feels extremely powerful to me. It is a guiding principle for me. It is a matter of removing our ego as far away as possible so that it no longer stands in the foreground and we can act from a very different position.

> *My Lord and my God,*
> *take from me everything*
> *that keeps me from you.*
> *My Lord and my God,*
> *grant me everything*
> *that brings me closer to you.*
> *My Lord and my God,*
> *free me from myself to give my all to you.*
> —Niklaus von Flüe (1417-1487)

"There are many different lifetimes that confirmed to me that I had previously lived as a friar, a priest, a monk. I was familiar with herbal medicine. I have a great attachment to Italy and I recognize that I am drawn to a quality of monasticism and the ascetic life. But I have no desire to live in a monastery today.

"Taking exams has always been difficult for me and caused me a lot of stress. So I concluded from the State Examination that I didn't want to become a medical doctor, but I continued in this field. Then I worked for three years at the Faculty of Medicine. I supervised students and worked a lot with lecturers, and I had to evaluate them based on student feedback. I was continuously in the presence of so-called authorities. At the beginning, I didn't understand why I was there, but it had to do with reducing my fear of people in positions of authority, even though my education was not authoritarian. While there, I was dealing with about seventy professors daily. In the beginning, I barely had the courage to address them. In the end, I said to the Dean, 'If you don't give me a class schedule, then I will do it myself.' I surprised myself because I would have never dared to speak to the Dean like that earlier. Through this experience, I was able to greatly reduce my fear of people in authority.

"I had put all these professors on a pedestal. But through daily interactions, I had gotten to know them from a different perspective. I was deeply disappointed by many of the professors. It wasn't directly due to their interactions with me, but because they had terrible interactions with each other. There was a lot of envy, even gloating. I never considered that kind of thing worth striving for or something I would consider desirable. It was all too much about power. Afterward, I couldn't look at the professors in the same way. Of course, there were some wonderful people among them. Yet many of them were seeking power. The memory of all these experiences and issues also helped me to process the traumatic events of this past life relating to the Inquisition. I no longer put these people on a pedestal."

My Heart
My Heart and the Heart of the Universe are one Heart
Beating, steady, under all the earth's chaos
Under all the doubt and self-doubt
Through all the sorrow and illusion of loss
Under the fear of Freedom
I am nourished.
I am illuminated.

—Maitra

For Your Toolkit: Addressing Fear

Go back and review the part of the Reading about imagining your fear as a dog. Begin by naming your fear: Is it public speaking, as with Jack? Or social situations? Physical challenges, such as scuba diving? Violent people? Dogs? Snakes? Spiders? Letting people down? Losing someone you care about, tests, dentists? The list of things we can fear is endless.

Imagine your fear as a dog that is trying to warn or protect you. Is it a big dangerous dog? A small, yappy one that gets tangled in your feet? If it were a real dog, you would quickly see a need for training and would want to make it clear that you, the master of the dog, will decide whether the danger is real or not. Telling the dog—your fear—to stay or lie down and stay out of your way will signal a step toward mastery over your emotional body. The mastery of your fear can open the way to experiences that were closed to you previously, both within yourself and in the world.

Putting your fear into perspective can change your perception of the Universe from varying degrees of dangerous and frightening to a wonderland of possibility, full of synchronicities and miracles. Then, when something comes along that threatens us, we are not crippled by our fear; we can deal with the danger and ask for the help we need.

Mastering our fear doesn't mean we never need help; mastery means we know when we need help and we're not afraid to ask for it.

Chapter 11: Entering a New Relationship (Bonnie and Keith)

For Your Toolkit: Saying "No"

(Bonnie, born 1954; Keith, born 1947)

Bonnie, a medical technician, now retired, came to Maitra with a question about relationships. She was having difficulty ending her last relationship. She said she needed time until she felt OK about it being finished. She has found a new partner with whom she feels very comfortable. But her previous partner won't let her go. She continues to feel responsible for him because he would get very depressed. They decided to remain friends, but it wasn't working.

What follows is a transcription of Maitra and Bonnie's conversation:

B: I would like to tell him that it is completely over, but I can't get myself to do it.

M: Why?

B: I'm afraid for him, concerned about him.

M: Let me have a look to see if he is really that unstable. When I split up from my first husband, I was having a hard time like you are, unable to finalize things. I was concerned that he might have a breakdown. So, I went to see the psychologist with whom I was working, and he said, 'Have pity on this guy, he will never find anybody else if he keeps hoping to be with you.' And I said,

'But I still love him.' He said, 'Be kind to him, tell him you don't love him anymore. Set him free.' I followed his advice, and it was the best thing I ever did. He was re-married again within a year, and he stayed with her for forty years.

In a way, it's not that helpful if you try to protect him by not telling him the truth. He keeps hoping and hoping that you are going to change your mind. It's useless; you are not going to leave this new man and go back to the previous one. Tell him, with kindness, 'It's over. I have a new friend, I am not going to change my mind, and I want you to look for somebody else and be happy.'

B: I've already told him this, but he says that he is too old. But that is his problem.

M: When he calls you on the phone, as soon as you hear his voice, just very gently hang up the phone, not with anger, just to say 'No.' If he comes to your door, don't open the door.

B: He writes a lot.

M: Send it back. Every time you read a letter from him, you get his hopes up again. But if the letters come back, and they haven't even been opened, he will say to himself, 'I think she means it this time.'

B: Do we have a karmic connection?

M: Of course. Do you need to know more? You are finished with him.

B: That's right.

M: Have you been writing back to him when he writes to you?

B: Sometimes.

M: Write one more letter, only one, and say, 'It's over. It's enough. I won't accept your letters, and I won't talk with you on the phone anymore.' This will allow you to be available to your new relationship and it will set him free to find someone else.

B: I'd like to find out if I know my new partner from a past life.

M: That's a better one to look at. What is his profession?

B: He's an artist and he teaches art.

M: He's doing a very good thing by letting you into his life. It's just the medicine he has needed for a long time. In his last relationship, he felt it was not worth the effort. He thought it was better to just concentrate on his work and his students, but that left him feeling very sad. So, one day he finally said to himself, 'You know, I guess it's time.' And there you were. It's very nice for both of you, I think. You are not living together yet. It looks to me like you will. Did you live with the other man?

B: No. He didn't want to live with me.

M: He didn't want to, he didn't want to, he didn't want to, and now you are here. With your new man, it's not going to move fast either. He has got a bit of his agenda. On the other hand, I think he is ready for something more. As he slowly becomes aware of this, you will be ready. I don't see anything standing in the way. You seem to be very open with each other, and it will go as far as the two of you want to take it. It's not always smooth. You move to a certain level of intimacy and then it sits there for a while. Then you both realize that there is more there, so you take another step. And then it moves, and then it stops for a little bit and then it moves again.

You haven't opened up the door to your creativity yet. I have the feeling that you're going to want to open that door, now that you are with him. I can't guess what form it might take. It probably won't be the same as what he does, but when you feel the urge, take a step and see if you like it.

When you begin to experiment with your creative process, you will have another way to connect with him. It looks very good. So try things out. If you want to try painting, go ahead. If you want to get some clay and make a pot, try that. Sculpture, dance, music ... there are lots of ways to express the creative urge. You have been putting this off. You let the previous man stop you. Your new partner will celebrate when you find a way to express yourself. It might be something to do with textiles, batik, or color.

B: My dream has always been to draw pictures in children's books.

M: GO! Find a story that you like and experiment with it. Art is an interesting thing. Some people don't start until they are eighty years old, and then they discover that they can do something wonderful. Grandma Moses is a famous example in the United States. She was seventy-eight when she started, and she became very famous. It's not something that is limited by one's age or experience. It will be a nice addition to your relationship, another connection, between the two of you. Maybe you're going to write the book, too. Do you have some stories in you?

B: I had a few, but they disappeared. Maybe they will come back.

M: Now let's look at your past life. But before I go into it, can you tell me what you are afraid of? There is so much fear in your heart. Are you afraid of being happy?

B: At the moment, yes, because I have never been used to it. I haven't felt I deserved much happiness.

M: What would have to change for you to feel that you deserve it? How can you earn it?

B: I don't know.

M: Do you think that most people deserve it?

B: I think it's in the past lives, maybe you have to earn credits?

M: Well, that's true, it's what they call merit. So imagine you get to play God for a minute. I am going to give you that power. How many people that you know deserve to be happy?

B: I would grant it to everyone.

M: You would? What's so difficult about that? If you are giving it to everyone, what happens when it's your turn?

B: Then I could give it to myself too.

M: Then maybe you deserve it too? Yes? We have some strange programming in us, don't we? How do we learn to deserve to be happy? I think it's important to be happy because, when we are happy, this happiness spreads to people around us.

You are still questioning whether you deserve it or not. You just have to keep watching yourself and catch yourself when you are withholding it. We all know that we're not going to be happy every minute of the rest of our lives. 'Shit Happens!' as we say in the States. Things come up that are difficult and we lose touch with our happiness a little bit. If we know that we deserve it, and it's ours, then we keep coming back to it, and in the moments when we lose it, we know that it's going to come back. Do you know the quote, 'This too shall pass?'

B: That's comforting. I have a feeling of deep intimacy with my new friend, even though we haven't known each other for long. We get along very well.

Maitra, who had had several sessions with Bonnie when in Europe during her annual visits, replied to Bonnie's earlier question about whether she had had a past life with her new partner:

"I see a big workshop. It was during the Renaissance. What I'm calling a workshop is a church. They are putting paintings on the ceiling and the walls of the church. There are two or three people making sculptures, and you and this young man, who is now your new partner, are helpers. You are both running around from morning until night. So much is going on and it's so exciting and you are both so happy to be there.

"You became very good friends in the first months that you were there. There is an interesting little tidbit to add. Most of the people they hired as helpers were men or boys. You decided that you wanted to be there, but you were a girl. So you decided to pretend to be a boy. This made for some uncomfortable moments.

"Normally, if two boys had to pee, they would go outside and find a spot, and they would pee together. But you never wanted to go with your new friend. You always said that you didn't have to pee right then. Finally, he realized that you were being weird about something, and he said, 'What's going on with you? Do you have some kind of injury, or is something wrong with you?' You said, 'Promise not to tell anybody?' He replied, 'Sure, no problem.' You said, 'I'm a girl.' He responded with shock, 'WHAT?' You said, 'You notice that they don't hire any girls, so what could I do?'

"You showed him how you had wrapped your breasts. You were fourteen years old. You were big enough to look like a girl when you were trying to be a boy, so he was a little bit dubious about this. He said, 'You better show me the rest.' And you pulled your pants down and he saw that you didn't have a penis. 'Oh, my God,' he said. This was amazing. You see, he felt very happy and comfortable with you because he thought you were another boy. Of course, when he discovered you were a girl, he went back in his mind and remembered things that he had said, that he wouldn't say to a girl, and you both just laughed and laughed.

"You remarked, 'It's the price I pay.' And he said, 'Well, I don't think you are going to be able to get away with this for very long. As you get older, it's going to be harder.' And you replied, 'Well, I will deal with that when it happens.'

"Soon after this exchange, he became an assistant to one of the sculptors, which is quite different from just being a helper. It meant that he would be learning how to make sculptures, and, as he got better at it, he would be trusted with making some parts of the model his teacher was working on.

"Up to this point, you hadn't even dared to let anybody know that you wanted to do something more. But, all of a sudden, he was promoted. As an assistant to one of the sculptors, his job was very different and very intense. The two of you could no longer run around together and do whatever you wanted. You decided, 'Well, if he can do it, maybe I can too.'

"You went to one of the artists, who was painting the ceiling. He agreed that you could help him. This meant climbing up high. The ceilings in those churches were many meters high, and every once in a while, there was an accident. You were well aware that this was quite dangerous. And they weren't painting the walls anymore, the walls were done. There was only one choice of going all the way up if you were going to help. In the beginning, you were mostly carrying things up, carrying up paint and brushes, carrying up rags to clean up spills, and lots and lots of climbing. You knew that it would be a long time before you would be trusted to hold a brush in your hand.

"The painter, the one you were assigned to, was abusive. He had a temper, he liked to get angry, and he yelled at the person who was helping him. Everything had to be perfect, or else he would make you go back down and do it over again.

"At that point, you were also learning how to mix paints, and you had to get just the right color that he wanted, or it was down and up again, and he was yelling at you the whole time. You knew that he was doing this because he was the only one in this big, huge church. He was always yelling. You just accepted his habit of yelling abuses after a while.

"One of the other painters had been keeping an eye on you. He suspected that you were a girl. He came to you and said, 'Do you want to work for me instead?' You looked at him and said, 'He will never let me go. The only way I can get out is to quit the whole project. That's what happened to his previous helpers. They were just finally fed up with the way he acted, so they looked for a job somewhere else.' This man said, 'Leave it up to me.'

"The man with the bad temper was a good painter. So he had a job, but people knew who he was and how difficult he was, and they also knew how to manipulate him. The new man, who liked you, made a bet with him. If he won the bet, he would get to take you as his helper. He won the bet. He signaled to the painter you were working for, that you were his now.

"The other guy got so angry that he almost knocked you off the scaffolding. You were hanging onto the scaffolding with one hand, scared to death. Somebody helped you and you didn't fall, and you went to work for this new guy.

"Then there was another problem. Whenever you could find a little bit of free time, you would visit your friend. His job with the sculptor was very different, and nobody yelled at him. The man, for whom he was working, was very intense and very intent on the work he was doing. As long as his helper was there when he needed him, he was happy.

"Another friend, Fernando, an assistant painter, was very sympathetic to you for the abuse you had been getting from the first guy.

"When you told him that you had a new boss, he said, 'Which one?' When you told him, he said, 'Oh no.' You said, 'Well, why? He is nice. He helped me. He got me away from that other guy.' Your friend said, 'He is a womanizer. He uses one woman after another, for sex.' You said, 'But he doesn't know that I am a girl.' Your friend said, 'Oh yes, he does, he knows you are a girl.'

"Of course, this man now had power over you, which is what your friend was telling you. He knew your secret and he knew that you didn't want anybody to know it. This meant that he could make you do things that you wouldn't have done otherwise. This period was very difficult for you. You kept trying to protect yourself from him, and he kept trying to catch you alone. He let you know right away that he knew you were a girl. He said. 'You can't fool me. I'm an expert on women.'

"Your friend was keeping an eye on you. Several times he would show up right at the time when you needed him. He would invent something, and your new boss was becoming aware of what was going on.

"Finally, your friend decided to help you. He went to the architect, the person who was in charge of it all. He told the architect about you. Before Fernando told him, he said, 'Do you know who __________ (your name) is?' He said, 'Yes, I know who everybody is. I know how everybody is doing.' Your friend said, 'What do you think of the job he is doing?' And the big boss said, 'He is one of the better ones. He is always doing a little extra to please. We are lucky to have him.' Your friend then said, 'What would you do if I told you it's a girl?' The boss said, 'Are you telling me it's a girl?' Your friend said, 'Yes.'

"Your friend had decided that the only way to protect you was to get it out into the open. When he tried to talk to you about it, you said, 'No, don't tell, don't tell.' He thought and thought about it and decided that it was the right thing to do. He knew it was a risk but he also knew that you were a very good worker. He got the big boss to reconsider, and the boss let you continue working as you were. You didn't know whether to be mad at him or grateful; actually, you were both. You were mad at him because you had told him not to tell anyone. On the other hand, it was getting harder and harder to cover it up and now you could just relax. Because it was known, Fernando spoke with your new boss and said to him, 'Don't you dare touch her!'

"It turned out OK. Your new boss was able to keep his hands off you, mainly because he wanted to keep his job. And you were able to learn about painting. You never got past the beginning stages, because it turned out that your friend was talented as a sculptor, and when things changed for him, they changed for you.

"He was offered a job at another project where he could do a lot more of the work. When he left, he said, 'I can't promise you a job there, but I want you to come with me to a different city.' You asked, 'What do you mean? What are you saying?' He said, 'I know that I don't really know what I'm doing, talking to you like this, but I love you and I don't want to leave you.' 'You just said, Oh!!' You went with him and you ended up getting married, you had a baby and you didn't do much painting anymore. He continued and progressed well in his work.

"That was that particular past life. You do have other lifetimes with him, but this one is probably the most relevant to the present, and it recognizes your shared history. It had many satisfying challenges. You learned how to make paint from nothing, which was what everybody had to do at that time. You couldn't go to a store and buy it. You had to learn how to make it, and you did.

"And your partner is also doing some sculpture in the present?"

Bonnie answered, "Yes, my new partner is making sculptures. It is so interesting that he still has the desire to protect me."

Bonnie's Transformation

Several months later, after some soul-searching, Bonnie talked about the Reading:

"I was amazed, and it was very exciting for me to hear about this life in Italy. Earlier, I was always fascinated by Renaissance art, sculptures, paintings, frescoes, etc., and it moved me to learn that we had this life together at that time.

"As a woman, I was hidden in this male role because I wouldn't have been tolerated as a woman. I see parallels to this today. I felt, especially at the beginning of my new partnership, that he would protect me in certain situations. This is something intimate between us, and the story from my past life confirmed this for me. This pattern continues to exist between us and is sometimes apparent.

"I still find this situation very special, in which I disguised myself as a man, to be accepted in a man's world. When I was about ten years old, I had already reached puberty and I found it very embarrassing that I had breasts. The change was very noticeable, and considered 'precocious,' as one said at the time. There was then a phase in about third grade when I wore suspenders under my pullover so that one couldn't see my breasts as well. I experienced this once before—this feeling that I wasn't able to do what I wanted to do with my woman's body.

"My partner is, of course, an artist and he paints a lot, and I am still interested in art. This is something that we have in common, a foundation for our relationship with each other.

"The Reading gave me confidence. At the beginning of this new partnership, I often felt insecure because I wasn't sure how important I was to him. So, this Reading helped me to see our common interests, and I know that they will last. Knowing that we were previously a fit, gave me a very good feeling. In earlier relationships, I often felt insecure, and oftentimes disappointed. This explains why the Reading was a real help to me.

"Previously I had a male colleague at work and the clients had the feeling that he had a different status, even though he hadn't even finished his education. Just because he was a man, he was viewed differently, and the boss supported him more than us women who did the same work. I observed this over and over. This is still very much anchored in human thought. Maybe I notice this much more today due to the insight I gained in this Reading into my past experiences. I can let things be the way they are. I can assert myself if necessary."

In another Reading with Bonnie, she came with questions about her connections with Russia; both she and Keith had felt drawn to that country and she had the feeling that she had lived there. She wanted to find out if they had known each other there. Here is Maitra's explanation of why that feeling was so strong:

"This is what I'm seeing: It shifts back and forth between a city and the countryside. You are a man, and you are a musician. Your father has a large piece of property out in the country. Some of it is farmed, and he has horses and cattle. He has a vineyard. You are his second son.

"Your father also has property in the city. He is a businessman. He wants to raise his two sons to take over the business. The older one, that's your older brother, has shown interest in his business in the city. He is away at school, learning how to run it. He is very determined to please his father. And he is also your mother's favorite.

"You came along, four years later, and you are a rebel. You don't want to please anybody. You are just interested in the things that you want to do. They don't have anything to do with business. Your father wanted you to learn how to run the farms and manage all the different agricultural and animal projects that he has going.

"For a while, he had some hope for you because you showed a lot of interest in horses. You liked to ride; you were good at it, and you were interested in breeding horses. You found this fascinating. When they would bring in a stallion from another bloodline and put him with the mares, your father would think, 'Well, over time he will become interested in the farms too.' But you didn't. You weren't interested in managing the horses either. You were interested in the horses, but that's not the same thing as running a horse ranch. You liked to play music, and you liked to draw, paint, and read.

"You were not interested in money in the way your father wanted you to be. You wanted to have enough money to do whatever you liked, but you didn't think it made that much difference where it came from.

"Your father's sister was dependent on your father. She had had an early, tragic marriage in which her husband was killed when they had only been married for a few months. She moved in with her parents and they had taken care of her ever since. Now your father is taking care of all of them. She was always around when you were growing up, and she was the only one who was interested in the things that you liked to do.

"She encouraged you to do the things that you found interesting. Your father thought she was betraying him. As a result, he was always threatening to kick her out. You always went to her when you were feeling distressed. She was the only one who understood you a little. Your father was so disappointed and so angry at you. Your mother also thought that you should listen to your father.

"When you were about seventeen years old, you decided to run away from home. Your aunt helped you to steal some money from your father because he wouldn't give you any money unless you earned it.

"From his point of view, since you weren't interested in running the farms, you should have to do the dirty work, if you wanted any money. He never gave you enough money to be able to save. So, you told yourself that you needed to leave and that you were going to take enough money to live on for a while.

"It turned out that you became a street musician in this big city, and you were amazed at how much money you made. You just put your hat out and played, and people came and threw money in the hat. I don't think anybody was more surprised than you at how much money you made.

"You were able to send the money back to your father that you had taken from him three years earlier. This was the first contact you had had with him since you left. You wrote him a letter, telling him that you were making your way in the world and supporting yourself and that you were able to pay him back the money you had 'borrowed.'

"Your father was shocked. He had pretty much given up on you. But now he was curious: 'Were you lying to him? How could you be making money playing that stupid instrument?' In truth, you were very good at playing this instrument.

"He found out where you were playing, in a park, at that time. He went there without telling anyone and watched you play. He said to himself, 'Well, he is really good. He could do better than play in the streets.' He was amazed, and he came and spoke to you. And then *you* were amazed. You couldn't believe that your father would do such a thing. He had such strong ideas about what you were supposed to do, and when you didn't do them, you thought he didn't want you as a son.

"You had just accepted this. So here he was, and you were saying to your father, 'Can I buy you dinner?' You didn't take him to a fancy place; instead, you took him to a very simple, little place that had excellent food. Of course, you knew all these places. He said to you, 'You are not the son I thought I wanted, but I have come to realize that you are my son. I am delighted to see you doing this work that makes you happy.' So, in a funny way, you were accepted back into the family.

"This is an interesting saga. Later, you had a son. Your father helped you; you were playing in concert houses and other places, making much more money. You were able to marry and have a family. Your son loved to go out to the farms. He said to his grandfather, 'I want to learn how to do what you do.' Things came full circle and your father's wish for his family was realized.

"This story has a happy ending. It has a little bit of everything. It took place in the eighteenth century—a time of horses and buggies. It is my impression that this all happened in St. Petersburg. It's a beautiful city with many statues and fountains and water running through it. There were magnificent homes and municipal buildings there. This was the scene of your music career."

As the Reading finished, Bonnie was excited and wanted to know if her partner was there. The transcription reads as follows:

B: Did my current partner also play a role in this?

M: Is he Russian?

B: No, but we are fans of all things Russian!

M: Was he your father in the lifetime we just saw?

B: That's what it felt like.

M: Yes, he was your father. He discovered that he really loved you, even if you didn't conform to his ideas. You were his major teacher in that life. He had strong ideas of how things were supposed to be, but he was willing to change.

In a second interview with Bonnie, after a holiday in Russia, she had a lot more to say:

"As I was traveling through Russia, I immediately felt comfortable. Arriving in this landscape felt like coming home.

"I was happy to hear that I had lived in Russia. It appealed to me that I was a street musician. Unfortunately, I no longer play an instrument, but I like street musicians best of all nowadays. I prefer to listen to them than to a professional orchestra. The Reading explained this to me. I just like folk music and, most of all, Russian music.

"I always enjoyed and felt drawn to street music and above all to Eastern music. The instrument that I played at that time was a typical Russian instrument. It might have been a balalaika.

"Already as I child, I would often watch *Doctor Zhivago*. When I was seventeen, this movie came to the movie theaters, and the theme song was played on the balalaika. I loved this melody so much that I bought myself a phonograph and listened to this music over and over again. After seeing the movie, I wanted to learn Russian because it had moved me so much. I could have studied Russian in school, but I had no gift for languages. The Slavic languages appealed to me so strongly. This might explain why my first husband was Czech, although I think Russian is even more beautiful.

"Last autumn, I was given a balalaika by a Russian choir, with whom we had organized a concert. This made me extremely happy. In the beginning, I tried to play it myself, but I needed somebody to teach me. When I have more time, I would like to learn to play it.

"My willfulness and independence in this past life have left an impression on me. I followed my path with all the consequences. It was moving to see how well it turned out. There was a reconciliation with the father and that was very beautiful.

"There is a connection between my current partner and the father in the past life. I had the feeling that this could be the case because my current partner is very tolerant, and he lets me live the way I want. He's accepting, something that I'm not very good at. The restraint and tolerance that my father finally had in his past life fit well with my current partner.

"There is another past life in Russia with Keith, that I was able to access through Maitra. It might be beneficial to verify certain details."

As the relationship between Bonnie and Keith developed, more shared past lives emerged. In a subsequent Reading, with both of them, Maitra reported:

"Now I am seeing a very mountainous area with a river down at the bottom of steep cliffs. Your current partner is an architect. He was sent out from the city to survey the area because they wanted to build a road with a bridge across the chasm. This was a very radical idea. Nobody believed that it would work. He went there and said, 'It can work. We can make it work.' He had some new ways of looking at how to build this bridge because it's very dangerous to build a bridge across such a deep chasm.

"When I look at these pictures, I can't see how they did it. It was so high up above the river. He had some ideas on how it could be done. When he went back to the city, he presented them. It seems this was really like a dream come true for a lot of people. If this road could be built, it would tie together two parts of the country that had been isolated from each other. It would open up all kinds of things. This company decided to give him a chance and see if he could make this happen. They risked a huge amount of money on him. He came to live in this village where you lived.

"At the time, you were a pretty, young widow, thirty-two years old. Ironically, your husband had been killed in an accident in the same area, where the cliff drops off and the water is far down below. He was killed while they were trying to build a walking bridge across it. A few times, over the many years, there had been a small, swinging bridge, but sooner or later it always fell. He was one of the people who was trying to put it up again, but they were never able to do it.

"This other man (Keith, your life partner today) came into the village, and he needed a place to stay. Ever since your husband died, you had been struggling, with no real source of income. You were taking in washing for other people, doing mending for people, anything you could do to make a little money. At the point when this man came along, you were thinking that you were going to lose your house. You hadn't been able to make enough money to keep everything going.

"Suddenly, here is this man, saying, 'I need a place to live and maybe I can bring some other people here who need a place to live. This project is going to take several years.'

"You asked, 'What project?' He said, 'Well, we're building a bridge across the river.' You just laughed ruefully, and said, 'That's been tried before, but if you want to try it too, I'll rent you a room.'

"You had five bedrooms, and if all the bedrooms were filled, you would have more money than you could imagine. The men said that they would stay there for several years. You didn't think for one minute that they would. You thought that they would try it and would soon be gone. But he moved into your house, as did the others.

"He was the only one there for a couple of weeks. He was still doing a lot of survey work. Then the other workers started to come in. It gave a big boost to many people in that village. In the two weeks when he was alone in the house, the two of you discovered that you liked each other and that you could meet each others' needs in certain ways. In the beginning, it was practical. As time went on, you came to love each other.

"The bridge took twelve years to build. Many people died in the process. Every time there was a big setback, he would find a way around it. It was as if everybody in the village was watching everything that he did. People came to visit you who had never visited you before. They wanted to have a look at this crazy man. They could see right away that what he was trying to do was impossible, but he was doing it anyway. Then they started to build the road on the other side and that took many more years.

"This little town began to grow. Houses started to be built, and businesses started to open. Financially, you were doing very, very well. Eventually, the two of you got married.

"You didn't know what was going to happen when he finished his work, but you thought it was OK if you had to move and go somewhere else with him. After some time, you no longer needed to rent out rooms, but you continued to do it, though only for people you liked. Your little rooming house became a meeting place for people who wanted to discuss new ideas.

"You had a good marriage with two sons. You and your husband became very popular in the village as 'the crazy man who did the impossible and the widow who married him and had two sons.' In that life, you liked to cook. But you especially loved to have everybody sitting together around the table. His arrival brought the whole town to life."

By now, Bonnie was making many changes. Her ability to make discerning connections was growing and she enjoyed the process and sharing her insights:

"Keith, my partner, was a visionary architect. Although everyone said that it was impossible to build this bridge, he didn't give up and he managed to build it. I also see some parallels to our current life because he is always persuaded of things that I think won't work, and then he says, 'Yes, that will work.' And then it always does finally work. I tend to be the person who raises many objections when it comes to making something happen. Then he says, 'Yes, it will work,' and then he just does it. He's very persistent. My partner's confidence reassures me and then I can put my doubts aside. With this attitude, it's possible to accomplish a lot more. It would be exciting to find out if this bridge is still standing, and where it is. This must be a very strategic and important connection.

"At that time, we had many guests. We continue to do this today, and both of us enjoy being with other people.

"I've read many books about reincarnation. Because I have learned more about this through the Readings, I have a sense of security in this life. For example, I don't consider it an injustice if someone has a lot of money or is successful. Today I look at it this way: One has been given a certain task that is to be mastered. Because people have such different paths in life, it isn't a matter of having to emulate others. Even if things don't look so successful from the outside, things can be in order. I don't simply see it as an injustice if others are having an easier time than I am. I don't think about it that way. Perhaps I had or will have that kind of experience, and everything will balance out. This gives me the feeling that things are fine the way they are, and that's OK with me.

"If I think about dying, the thought comes to me that I have already experienced it several times. With this in mind, I am less afraid of it. For me, this is a big relief. It will surely be different when it gets closer, but my basic attitude toward death has become less fearful. In the Readings that I listen to from time to time, new levels come to the fore, and while I am listening, I hear things in new ways.

"The Readings also helped me when my children were young. Because I had a lot of problems with the children, when I learned about their past lives, I was able to view them differently and respond appropriately. Taking all this into account, I can understand many things from a different perspective."

Since this was a Reading involving both of them, Keith also had something to say:

"This resonated with my life as a builder of bridges. I am sometimes still tempted to do crazy things. Earlier, I had lots of these kinds of ideas, especially in the arts. But I couldn't carry them out for financial reasons. I became an art teacher and worked in this profession. I wanted to make very specific figures and sculptures out of plastic fibers, but I gave up on it. I've always had a very strong relationship with the construction industry. My mother came from a family of carpenters. I had a connection to this craft, though not quite a direct one, because I didn't get to know my grandfather until I was sixteen years old. His family had thrown him out because of his second wife. I lacked a direct connection to his work as a carpenter. However, he built many things. He built chalets and was a successful man; I feel connected to him, and I later studied draftsmanship. I have always been interested in architecture, and still am today. It isn't at all foreign to me. I designed and built my entire house by myself.

"Through the particulars in the Reading, I noticed how things became familiar that were previously totally foreign to me; for example, learning Russian seems possible to me now. This is also the case with my relationship with Russia and how it has changed through my real encounters on these travels with people, with the landscape, and with the entire culture. Because we grew up in the Cold War, as a little boy, I was afraid of the Russians; it was said that they were dangerous and mean. At that time, for me, the Russians were the embodiment of danger. We were told that one can't trust these people at all.

"Then one goes to this country for the first time as an adult and has a different experience. When I experienced the people there, how they live, their society, and their family structures, I discovered that everything that I was told earlier wasn't true. Our society changed dramatically due to the '60s movement. These observations were very revealing to me. I experienced so much warmth and kindness. Initially, they are a bit reserved, but once you have made friends with them, you will experience their warmth."

May we all learn to recognize what has the ring of truth for us — and may we have compassion for ourselves when we can't integrate it as quickly as we'd like to.

—Maitra

For Your Toolkit: Saying "No"

Are you as comfortable saying "No" as you are saying "Yes"? Can you be honest when you don't want to do something? There is a belief in early childhood education that if children don't have permission to have boundaries when young if they're not allowed to say "No," they won't be able to say "Yes" to life, and they will be unable to trust themselves as they grow up.

If this is your story, you may have a bag of unsaid "Nos" that you are carrying around. Your challenge today is to begin to empty that bag. Try this exercise: For ten days (not necessarily in sequence), find a private place where you can yell and scream, if necessary. Then for 3-5 minutes each day, say out loud, with feeling: 'No, I don't want to,' 'No, I don't have to,' 'No, you can't make me,' 'Stop it, I don't like it when you do that!' or whatever phrase best speaks to your situation. You may find that you want to shout or hit something (your fist on a pillow or a tennis racquet on the bed?) You will begin to clear your bag, and also familiarize yourself with emphatic boundary setting. Soon it will be easy to say "No," without apologizing, explaining, or shouting! You have given yourself the right to say "No." You are free to be you.

Chapter 12: Conquering One's Fear of Death

For Your Toolkit: Fear of Death

(Keith, born 1947)

We met Keith, an artist and middle-school teacher, in the previous chapter. On this occasion, he came for this Reading with two questions. His first question concerned his health. He also wanted to consult with Maitra about his current life. He was sixty-eight years old and had stopped working a year earlier. Six years ago, he had a heart attack, and two years ago he had heart surgery. He is feeling pretty well, although he sometimes still has pain in his chest; he assumes that it's a result of his surgery. The doctors say that everything is in order. He has pain when the weather changes. But that's not his most important issue. He regularly wakes up at night with very bad night sweats. He can't completely relax, and he feels very tense.

Here is a transcript of his conversation with Maitra:

M: You were born after the war. Was your father involved in the war?

K: Yes, but he didn't fight on the battlefield. He was a soldier in the Swiss Army, at the border during World War II.

M: You strongly identify with your father. As a child, you wanted to be like him. I don't know why you didn't want to be like your mother because you were closer to her when you were small. Yet I feel all this energy that was focused on your father. Your father carried tremendous tension and stress from the war, plus he felt fear most of the time.

Your father was very courageous. I say this because he didn't want to get out of bed in the morning, but he got up every day and did what he was supposed to do. You were tuned in to him, thinking, 'I want to be like him. I want to help him.' And you acquired from him the habit of carrying debilitating tension in your body. Is your father still alive?

K: He died very early, when I was twelve.

M: You carried this tension for your father. These memories are somehow visiting you in the night, these memories that you took into yourself to try to help him. How did your father die?

K: He had leukemia.

M: Was that listed as the cause of death?

K: He was sick for three years, without being diagnosed, because they didn't know enough about diseases of the blood. We lived as a family for three years with my father's illness.

M: You were nine when they diagnosed the leukemia?

K: Yes. In the end, he died of a brain hemorrhage.

M: It was a stroke that killed him in the end. The way he carried this tension also contributed to his death. I think you are right to be concerned about this tension because it puts so much stress on the body. It's not an accident that, when you learn what it feels like to relax, you realize that you don't want to be like your father in this way. You could feel the tension in him and you wanted to be him. For him, it was such a wonderful thing to have a boy. I don't know if he ever told you that.

K: We were three children; I was the youngest and his favorite child.

M: It was so wonderful for him. You wanted to help him. Sometimes you couldn't, but your natural response to seeing someone suffer is to want to help them. Your father was suffering before he knew that he was ill, because he couldn't let go of his tension. Since the war, living was like being at death's door for him. May I follow the topic of your father a little bit further? I'd like to give you more information.

I am happy to report that, even though he spent a long time being so afraid of death, when it finally happened, it was so beautiful that he felt guilty about it. He thought that he shouldn't enjoy it because it meant he had to leave his family. He had always been afraid that he wasn't good enough, even though he always pushed himself to do what he thought he was supposed to do. And, especially when he had fear, he had to push himself hard.

So, the first thing that he was told by the light beings or guides who came to help him after his death, was that he should be at peace, and that he had been a good man. They told him that the pain was behind him now. For a long time, he stayed close by, watching over his children, trying to be there for his wife, until his guides finally said to him, 'It's time to go now.' But he had stayed close by for several years, knowing that it was the right thing for him to do.

Your father's fear of death is part of what you took into your body. Maybe you are conscious of this? If you can free yourself from this tension, if you can let it go before you leave your body, then the whole process will be beautiful like it was for your father. To clarify, death is not close to you right now. You still have some years, and you know this, you can feel it. You can learn to relax more, although you may need to get some help with it. You can learn. It was out of love for your father that you took it on. Now, out of love for yourself, let it go.

It's rare to see someone as affected by the war as you, given that you were not even born during the war. You were very much affected by the war because of your identification with your father. I think it's true that the war killed him, indirectly.

K: I think my health problems are also related to my stress. I feel that I am on the way to overcoming my fear of death.

M: Yes. I think so too. What was your profession?

K: I am an art teacher for young adults. When I was teaching, I didn't have time to do my own artwork at home. I always wanted to paint or sculpt, but I became an art teacher to earn money.

M: So, one thing that you are afraid of is that you won't have time to express what you want to say.

K: Yes, but when I am painting and drawing, I am always in a state of tension as to whether it is good enough. I am afraid of negative criticism, and I don't feel free to do what I want.

M: This is another piece of the puzzle that you took on from your father. You are your own worst critic. For whom do you paint?

K: I paint landscapes because I like landscapes, and I paint for myself. And, I have another wish. I would like to contribute more toward world peace through my paintings and sculptures, and I think that love between people is the basis of peace.

M: When you are talking to someone, discussing something, are you able to express yourself the way you want to?

K: I sometimes hold back.

M: If you realize that you are holding back, what do you do? Are you aware of what you are doing? Do you acknowledge the limits you are placing on yourself? Ask yourself, 'Is this what I want to say?' You have been imposing restrictions on yourself that aren't real or necessary.

K: Yes, that's right. The pressure was always there, already when I was a child. I felt it in school due to the religious restrictions. And, working as a teacher, I was also in a system with some restrictions.

Keith's Transformation

Keith came to the interview with new understanding that he wanted to share:

"My father's early death had a major impact on me. As I result, I lacked many things. I was always aware that I never had my own father introduce me to life. In this regard, I learned from the Reading that even after his death, my father was around the family for a long time and looked after us. I found it very interesting to learn this because my sister once told me that she had a vision of him after his death. In the vision, our father told her that she should be calm and that he was doing very well. This was soon after he died, that my sister received this message. She only told me this a short time ago. She said that she didn't feel that she could tell this to anyone at the time because people would have said that she was crazy.

"I myself never had perceptions like that. At the time, I was twelve years old, and my sister was sixteen years old. I only realized recently that she had a much more intimate relationship with our father than I did. When I was nine, my father became ill so I only knew him as a sick man. As a child, I wasn't mature enough to understand. It was therefore surprising to me when I realized my sister had a totally different view of my father than I did. That greatly moved me, and helps me make connections and understand them much better.

"I was brought up a strict Catholic. My father was sick; we prayed for him for three years, and then he died. Then I said, 'This just can't be the way things are, that everyone in the family prays for him all day—in the morning, the evening, and I don't know when else—and at the end, he nevertheless died. Where is the dear Lord, the Lord God, in all of this? I don't believe any of this.'

"I slowly grew up, read various books, and shoved this religion aside. I shoved aside anything and everything that had to do with religion. I didn't refuse to go to a wedding or funeral; I wasn't that radical. But once I was at a funeral or a mass, I found what the priest was saying was irrelevant to me.

"It was simply repellent to me, in a strange way. This punitive God was alien to me. I rejected him and I didn't want to know anything more about him. So I left the Church.

"I remember how I suffered greatly as a child under these rules and commandments. We were told that there were so many things that we mustn't do. Of course, this inhibits a child's curiosity and love of life. I experienced these prohibitions and commandments as much too restrictive.

"The Catholic Church speaks repeatedly about religion as a comfort. I always felt ambivalent about this. People become fearful from looking at certain images, like those of hell. This is not soothing. One can't really feel supported by them. These religious images caused me a lot of stress as a child. To be sure, my father was religious, but he didn't force it on me in a strict way. That came more from my mother, and it often troubled me and made me afraid.

"The Reading was able to show me a connection between my physical difficulties and the night sweats that were related to my father. My father was posted on the Rhein border, where he endured extraordinary hardships; as a result, he was very fearful. He carried this trauma inside himself. Later, this made him sick and led to his death. I wanted to help my father, so I approached him with this attitude, but I also took on his fears. I'm still working on letting go of what I absorbed from my father. I'm learning to be more easygoing. Sometimes I'm still a bit stressed. I get in situations in which everything is speeded up, but this doesn't happen without a lot of internal stress. Yet, my goal is to approach life in a more relaxed way and to really enjoy it. I'm often just at home and working in the house or the studio. I have lots more plans and they keep me on the go.

"When I listened to the tape of the Reading again, most of all I took in the story with my sister very deeply. At first, I didn't pay that much attention to my father's fears. Yet, after listening to the CD again, I really became aware of them. I could now understand a lot better the connection between my own stress and the heart attack, and my fear of death and my tension. The Reading calmed me down a lot. Feelings about my own death receded further into the background again."

Keith was interested in learning more about his connection to Russia (see Chapter 11), and he wanted to know from Maitra if he had other lives there.

"The first thing I see is a man with an accordion, standing in a big square in the middle of a beautiful city. The sun is shining, lots of people are around, and people are dancing to the music. You were kind of a piper, playing music in public places and lifting the spirits of the people around you. People liked you; I see them calling to other people to join in the dancing and enjoy themselves. You had a little cup, or a hat, in front of you where people could make donations. That's one part of your Russian experience. I should say, that's one lifetime in Russia. You were an itinerant musician, maybe even a gypsy. You had a little dog who accompanied you, wagging his tail.

"I see another lifetime in Russia. You were painting pictures on walls, sometimes on ceilings. You were always in demand; you were very busy. Perhaps some of your paintings can still be seen in big buildings, where the very wealthy people lived.

"You were very popular. They paid you a lot of money to do these murals. You could never keep up with all the people who wanted your work. It always felt like you were painting what somebody else wanted, not what you wanted to say. I don't know exactly how this translates into the present situation—this feeling that you were very successful at painting what others wanted you to paint, but, for yourself, you were never really happy and satisfied. In fact, you became wealthy, not only because your clients paid you very well, but because you were also given gifts by these extremely wealthy people.

"If your patrons gave you a piece of property such as a house, it caused a conflict for you. You were torn between always feeling that you couldn't express yourself in your work and making so much money that you couldn't stop. Memories of Russia are a bit of a mixed blessing. Both of these two lifetimes were very good ones, but, running underneath the good feelings, was this feeling that you weren't doing what you really wanted to do. You frequently felt frustrated.

"You were there when the royal family was assassinated, but you weren't close to them at that time. You had retired to the country home that had been given to you. You spent the last years of your life trying to do your own work, but you were never successful.

"This lifetime, right now, is your time. You have the opportunity, finally, to express yourself without external constraints—you are free!"

Keith's interview continues:

"The second part of the Reading focused on my artistic work, on my painting. The issue involved self-criticism and why I never feel free when I paint, which means I have to make such a big effort. I am taking time for myself now, and have been able to develop some ideas, without lowering my standards. I'm learning to approach everything in a more relaxed way, and to feel confident in the process. Earlier it was always linked to the question, 'Do I even know how to paint? I don't know how!' Now I have the clear feeling that I do know how to paint. When I do something new, I don't always find it that easy. But now it feels different when I do it. I feel good about this.

"I wanted to know if I have a relationship to Russia. I was also concerned about learning whether I knew Bonnie, my partner, in Russia. I wanted to know if we had a personal relationship there. This past life showed her as a street musician. She played gypsy music on an accordion. I still like this kind of music; I especially like Russian folk songs. They have a different quality than our own folk music, and today there are such amazing musicians who play this very special music.

"In our childhood, my sister learned how to play the accordion, but I didn't have the patience to study and practice that kind of instrument. I was allowed to play her accordion; she showed me how, but I had neither the concentration nor the will to study it. I couldn't master the finger dexterity.

"From the past lives in both of our Readings, I see Bonnie and me as potential musical friends. This is an exciting overlap. According to one of the Readings that Bonnie, my partner, received, I was also a fresco painter in Russia. It makes me happy to know that there are past lives in which we created projects together. Perhaps this information will become even more meaningful in the future; I do have a sense of 'WOW!'

"If I think about death, I don't know what comes after life. It simply remains open. Perhaps I will know this later. I just take things as they come, with no definitive ideas. If I think about life after death, it feels free and easy.

"I realize that I don't have to accomplish everything right now. There will be more opportunities in the future. This removes the pressure from all the things I still want to do.

"I had never been involved in past lives before I went to this Reading. Of course, I don't really know if it's true. I wouldn't say that I believe all of it. For me, it is simply an interesting way of looking at things that provoked in me this feeling of 'WOW!' Earlier, I would have rejected it and said that this doesn't exist, and that would have been the end of it. Today, I find it very interesting to broaden my point of view, and be able to say, 'It's possible.' I keep my eyes open and make an effort to remain a little more sensitive.

"The view that past lives could exist is a much more open position, and I can understand that one repeatedly has tasks and challenges that one has to master. I came into contact with this perspective through my partner. She had always been involved with this, and had told me about it. For my part, I wouldn't have gone to a Reading on my own, but of course I didn't know anything about past lives. My perception of reality was expanded through the Reading, and it has made my life calmer."

Bonnie and Keith moved in together a short time later.

Be grateful for whatever comes.

—Rumi

For Your Toolkit: Fear of Death

If you are fearful when confronted by death—your own, or that of others—you will benefit by learning as much as you can about it. Once again, go toward the fear, into it, instead of avoiding it. The problem with avoidance is that the whole issue then goes underground and compromises your aliveness. A teaching common to all the major religions is that until a person faces his/her death, they are unable to fully live.

Here are some ways to do that:

- Watch *What Dreams May Come*, a movie starring Robin Williams. It is based on teachings from all the major religions, and illustrates beautifully what happens after death. You can also find Richard Matheson's book by the same name, and it has an extensive reading list at the end.

- Ask permission to attend a dissection class at a nearby university, to fully appreciate the miracle of life after you have seen a lifeless body.

- Volunteer at a local Hospice Center; being present when someone leaves their body can be an extraordinarily beautiful experience.

- Meditate on the title of the book *How to Enjoy Death: Preparing to Meet Life's Final Challenge Without Fear* by Lama Zopa Rinpoche. Find the courage to read it.

- Write your own obituary. Brag a little.

- There are many people who have had a near-death experience, and then written about it. Read some of those books; they will help reprogram your brain to accept the inevitable.

Franklin D. Roosevelt said it:

The only thing we have to fear is fear itself.

Accepting that you will die, will free you to enjoy and cherish your life.

Chapter 13: "I Know World War II Inside Out"

For Your Toolkit: The Long View

(Dylan, born 1964)

Dylan is an executive at an IT Company. His wife was studying spiritual teachings. She got to know Maitra and attended one of her Lotus workshops, and also had a private Reading. In the Reading, she learned, among other things, about one of his past lives, which Dylan could listen to on a CD. He had never been very interested in this earlier. If anything, he actually considered it nonsense. Today, he says he would still put it in that category, but he will take a look at it, depending on what he thinks of the person. He states that he can certainly believe in reincarnation as a possible reality, although he doesn't consider himself a very spiritual person. He just wants to keep his feet on the ground. He says, "Reincarnation isn't as important to me as it is to other people, like it is to my second son, for example, who is very interested in it."

After Dylan listened to his wife's Reading, he made an appointment with Maitra to further explore his past life in Germany during World War II.

A transcript of this Reading follows:

"You were put to death in your past life. What I am seeing is that you were one of the German officers who tried to assassinate Hitler. You were among the first of many people who complained that Hitler was crazy, and that he would drive the whole country crazy. You were trying to bring a different leadership to Germany before it was too late. More than once, you had to pull back because things were so dangerous.

"I don't see how many of you were involved in this attempt. I call it an 'assassination attempt' because I think that's what it was. You were all caught and executed. Today, you are very laid back. You want to be safe. You have your judgments. You see things that are going on in politics that you are critical of, in the exact same way as you were critical of Hitler. Your decision to participate in the assassination was an honorable thing to do.

"In the end, the world's judgment of the men who tried to assassinate Hitler was very favorable. That was such a courageous thing to do. You should be proud of yourself. You risked your life and everything else for something you believed in.

"You are not carrying the energy of failure. You are carrying the energy of, 'I don't want to go through that again.'

"No revolution is necessary where you now live. That is why you chose to come back to Switzerland. You are watching the world. You are not only informed about World War II, you stay informed about world politics today. But you are somehow hiding your intelligence. You don't want to be very visible because your past life was such a bad experience. You have earned the right to hide a bit.

"You stood up, and you were counted in the most horrific world experience we've had to date. You gave your life for it, so you get to have a rest if you want one. What has remained with you, as a result of all this, is a lack of confidence. You should soon be able to let that go. The reason for your ambivalent feelings is that when you were a part of that plan, you put your whole family, and everybody you knew, in danger. Many people suffered because of your idealism.

"I think you remembered some of that life, enough that it has impacted this one, because you wanted to bring all that knowledge back into your conscious mind. Maybe you haven't yet fully connected with the role that you played. But now that you know this, you probably could even go back and identify which one of the conspirators you were."

Dylan's Transformation

Dylan describes the affect that the Reading had on him as follows:

"After I received the past life Reading, for a moment I found it rather funny. I gave myself time to take it in, and there was a lot that I could explain to myself about how I see myself, what I'm like. There were parallels to my character.

"When I'm in a group of people, I like to stand on the sidelines. This is the case more in private social situations than at work. I like to start by just observing things. I reject all forms of hierarchy. I had a very authoritarian father. When I was sixteen years old, there were young people protesting in Zürich and I was heavily involved with them. I knew a lot of people who were activists. I wasn't directly active politically in the existing groups, but I always participated in demonstrations and events, and I knew the people. If we went out to demonstrate, we always took lemon juice with us to protect ourselves from tear gas. I spent a lot of time at the Youth Center, a place where young people could meet and exchange ideas. I was tuned in to these events. As a teenager, I sympathized with the anarchists, although I don't feel as strongly about that today. But I am still against hierarchical systems. I'm also uncomfortable with it in business life. However, if a person has something to say, I'm interested in it. Now I have an explanation for why this is the case.

"Ever since I was a little boy, I was interested in war. I know World War II inside and out. As a child, I had already begun to read books about it. I can imagine that it's connected to what I experienced in the Reading. After I received the Reading, I didn't focus on it right away. Then I became somewhat curious as to exactly who this person was. When I began to look at the pictures of the people, I began to be interested in knowing who I was: 'Which one could be me?' Everything has been documented—for example, which men were shot at the time—and I have an emotional connection to a man named Beck. I wanted to know how he had lived his life, and his path to this event. He should have committed suicide, according to the records, but he was shot instead.

"In the past life, I also killed other people. I know this, and I would do it again if I were in a situation in which I had to protect someone I cared about. What I experienced at that time must have been hell.

"I always considered Hitler to be a despicable man. I was very interested in everything that happened at this time during World War II. I don't understand it and I hate the things people did to one another. I don't know today if I would come up with another plan to blow Hitler up. It would be presumptuous for me to claim that I would do it again.

"I resist situations in which humans control things so much. I also find nationalities bad, although I am happy to live here in Switzerland. I reject all organized religions. If it involves concepts made by humans, I find it difficult. I don't believe that religion makes people better.

"Deep down, I'm an anarchist, but I'm now old enough to know that it doesn't work. Here, in Switzerland, we are in the fortunate position that we can in fact live a bit anarchically. As long as you follow certain rules, then you can do whatever you want. I can now well imagine that my attitude is connected to the past life experience.

"The people who were part of this conspiracy were also within the system. They had been followers for years and many of them didn't want to be involved in what we did, but they did it because they rejected Hitler's mindset, and because they were afraid they were losing the war. We made the attempt only because one man took responsibility for carrying out the plan; he wasn't necessarily cleaner than anyone else. These were all officers with careers in the army.

"Hitler had already taken Beck aside, before the war. He wasn't actively participating in the war, yet Hitler took him aside and said to him, 'If you start a war with me, you will lose!' Beck wasn't fundamentally against Hitler, but he viewed things differently. Everyone who was a part of the assassination attempt was involved in their own way in all of the events and effects of this war.

"Six or seven of these officers were executed in a backyard in Berlin. I was one of this group. The events depicted in the Reading can be checked with the historical documents. For me, this is all very exciting and convincing. I can believe in this. Perhaps I will go at some point to the place in Berlin where I died, to see how I respond to it.

"I was also a soldier here in Switzerland in the present time. I completed my RS (Volunteer Recruiting School), and then 3 weeks of annual service, until my first son was born. These experiences were catastrophic for me every time. I already had weeks of sleepless nights before I entered the Army.

"I told my sons that they should consider very seriously if they wanted to serve in the Army. Neither of them enlisted. The issues in my life, and especially this whole aversion to hierarchy, surely has something to do with these experiences from this past life. This was all very troubling for me, but I can deal with it today.

"Things are going well in my professional life. There aren't any hierarchies in my current work so I work very well. Of course, there are gradations similar to hierarchies, but it isn't played out like it was during the war, and things function extremely well.

"I am in an executive position at work and have a lot of responsibility. If I look back now, I realize that I was able to resolve many conflicts at work after the Reading. My interactions with others have changed a lot. I am more open and active at work than at home.

"I like to relax at home and hang out on the sofa. I don't like to take center stage in my private life. Many things were put into perspective. I feel these changes and the Reading resolved something in me. It's not as if what was shown in the Reading is now a defining event, but it did say that I chose to live in Switzerland because it offers more peace of mind, and that I'm now living here in order to rest and relax. With this, I can tell myself that when I decide to relax at home, it's OK.

"I am much more self-assured today and I can understand and appreciate my position at work and my competencies, and apply them. My former rebelliousness is no longer a problem. Today everything has become more natural. By accepting myself and my relaxed way of handling things, I can affect things a lot.

"I meditated a lot earlier; sometimes I still do, although I don't think the channels are completely open. I'm not drawn to group meditation. I would also never seek someone out whom I didn't already know a little bit. I have to feel secure in order to be able to believe and trust them.

"I also got to know Maitra in person. I feel her presence very strongly. She radiates tranquility to me and I can feel it. The peace that I felt in her presence is very beautiful and has left an impression on me."

**The intuitive mind is a sacred gift and the rational mind
is a faithful servant. We have created a society that honors
the servant and has forgotten the gift.**

— Albert Einstein

For Your Toolkit: The Long View

Sometimes we can see and understand things better when we take the long view. In 1977, when I was part of the Family of Man group in California, we were shocked when our teacher, Marsha Mossman, stated that Hitler did more to expand our consciousness than anyone else in modern times. 'How can that be?' you ask. Hitler did it by exposing that aspect of human nature that wants to destroy anyone different from ourselves, be it due to race, color, language or culture. He caused an international repudiation of that intolerant, destructive part of ourselves, and humankind rededicated itself to making room in our hearts and minds for our differences. As a whole, we humans discovered the importance of our capacity for compassion, perhaps even an appreciation for the magnificent diversity of humankind.

Unfortunately, we didn't learn our lesson well enough, so now in the twenty-first century, we must take a refresher course. We still struggle with such things as racism, divisiveness, deceit, greed, and hatred and fear of those who are different from us. Too often our leaders turn out to be representative of the worst in us rather than the best. Too often we are appalled to see that we are repeating the failings of the past, instead of learning to do better.

It can help to view the repeated crises as healing crises, by recognizing them as a signal that change and healing are underway. Although we cannot yet see it, we are progressing as a species. We are becoming kinder to one another, more compassionate. Change is slow, with many backward steps, but in the long view we are progressing toward unity—the recognition that we are a world family.

For a better understanding of the long view, read *Sapiens* by Yuval Noah Harari.

Chapter 14: Why Was I Born into This Family?

For Your Toolkit: The Hypnagogic State

(Wendy, born 1964)

Wendy, a graphic designer and a true Swiss farm girl, who became a healer, came to Maitra with the question, "Why was I born into this family?" She thought that her family hadn't taught her much, other than to work hard and enjoy good food. She had to take responsibility for herself very early. This led to her question: "Why did I come here to this life?"

Wendy also wanted to know why she was unable to establish an emotional connection with her mother. In her view, throughout her life, she has had to repeatedly start over from scratch. For example, she lost nearly everything in a house fire in 1996, when she was in her early thirties. The only things left were some of her clothes. She laments, "This is the story of my life."

Maitra recognized a karmic situation in Wendy's view of herself as powerless; this is the past life that emerged:

"I see a lifetime in Japan. It was in the 1700s before the white man was welcome. Your father was disgraced, and the only honorable thing he could do was perform hara-kiri. He had to kill himself. This was not like suicide in the West; it was honorable to do this. It could save your family. It's what you were expected to do if you disgraced yourself.

"Your mother was left with four young children. Your father did whatever he could to ensure the family's survival after his death, but not everything he had set up in advance worked out. For example, he had friends who agreed to help the family, but these friends were not always available.

"You were the oldest daughter. There were three girls, which was a problem because girls were considered second-class citizens, and then there was the youngest child, a boy.

"You were the smallest of the girls who were all near your age. You were twelve or thirteen years old, in puberty, when your father died. Your mother realized that it was too many children for her to support and that she needed to find placements for the two oldest ones. You were very pretty, though small. You weren't strong enough to be a servant. It would have been a loss of face for the family if you became a servant, but you would have done it if you had been big and strong.

"Your mother went to the geisha's house, and she told the geishas that you were sensitive, pretty, and delicate and that you could be useful to them. She told them she hoped you could someday be trained as a geisha.

"She brought you to them, into a room where there were five or six women, geishas. They walked around you, and you felt that they were looking at you as if you were a piece of meat. You were frightened when they started to take off your clothes. They wanted to see what your body looked like. You were used to taking off your clothes at home with your family when you went into the bath. But you had never before taken your clothes off in front of anybody outside the family. Your mother was standing across the room, hanging her head down, crying. When she looked up at you, her look said, 'Let them do what they want to do.'

"You were standing there, feeling very alone, because your body was just beginning to mature. Your breasts were starting to show, you had pubic hair, and you were self-conscious, even with your family, because it was all new to you. There you were, standing naked with all these women, and they were all looking at you, and they were asking you to squat down and put your arms out and take all kinds of positions.

"Finally, one of the women took out a feather which she had hidden in her kimono. She pulled out this feather and she tickled you with it. You were so surprised that you started to giggle. Then she started to giggle. Then all the other women started to giggle. And your mother didn't know what to do, and finally, she started to giggle too. That broke the tension enough for you to relax and realize that these women were not your enemies. You didn't understand why they were doing this, but you started to feel that it was OK, anyway.

"You were accepted by the geishas. In the beginning, you were more like a servant. You ran and got them cups of tea, and you cleaned their shoes. It wasn't hard work. They didn't make you do the heavy work; they had other people already doing the difficult jobs. You were a little helper. When they were getting dressed, you would help them dress and make sure that everything was in place. You put fresh flowers in their rooms every day. You prepared flowers for their hair, all kinds of things like that. As you got to be a little older, around fifteen, they started to casually say things to you: 'This is the way geishas do it. This is the way we sit. This is the way we stand. This is the way we hold our fans. Most importantly, this is the way we pay attention to men so that we know what men like and how to dress to please them.'

"You were surprised to learn that they had to read every day because geishas had to be informed about history, about government, about current news. They had to be able to hold a conversation or follow a conversation that the men were having, and if the men looked at them, they had to have something to say. You realized that your mother hadn't known any of this about geishas. These were things that most women didn't have to know, but the geishas had to be intelligent and informed about current events because their task was to keep men happy. This was very interesting to you. They were not prostitutes. They sometimes did have sex with men, but it was a very respectful arrangement.

"Sometimes a man supported a geisha and asked her to leave her profession, and he might buy her a house to live in. That is what happened to you. You showed great talent for pleasing the men, perhaps because you were a bit psychic. You could 'read' the men and you could also 'read' the other women. You knew what they needed, what they wanted, and what made them happy. You knew when they were feeling upset about something.

"One of the men, a quiet young man, was taking over his father's business, and he was considered to be very young for this. He was probably in his late twenties. But most of the men who gathered here in this geisha house were older, in their forties or fifties. He was impatient with the formality. He was practical, and he wanted to get down to business when he met with other men. The custom was to go through a ritual discussion of the weather, the news, and other topics before they talked about business. He got very impatient, and you were aware of this, so you drew him over to one side and invited him to talk about what he wanted to talk about. He valued this about you.

"He had a wife and two children already, but his wife—it was not that she was intellectually inferior—didn't consider it her place to discuss these kinds of things with him. She was very traditional, just waiting to be told what to do. She didn't offer her opinion. He liked the fact that you were not only interested in what he had to say, but you had an opinion too. You could respond in ways that surprised and delighted him. He told you that he wanted to buy you a house, which he did. He put it in your name, but he also left his name on it. He said, 'When we are both older, in a different time of life, or if I ever have to go away from here, I will remove my name. But for now, we'll leave it this way.' You said, 'Fine.'

"Some time went by, maybe a year, and he got into a power struggle with someone else in his business, and he was murdered. His business was taken over. His wife and children had to go back to her family; everything was gone.

"While going through the papers, the people who took over his business found your house. They came and said 'You have to leave. It is part of his property, and we have taken over his property.' You said, 'No, look at the paper again. My name is on the paper too. It is meant to be mine. He gave it to me.'

"You were causing trouble, so they left, and two or three days later, your house was set on fire. That was the first thing that happened. You knew immediately that they were trying to make you leave. The fire was put out. People came from all around to help put out the fire. You went to the prefect—a police official—and he said, 'Well, the courts have to decide who it belongs to, or how it could be divided. It would be a good thing if you took care of that right away before they do something else to harm you.' He didn't offer to help or protect you. He just gave you advice about what to do.

"At some point, you went to see your mother. She was still caring for one child at home. And, she was still struggling. You said to her, 'I just want to know: If I have to leave my beautiful house, can I come to you, can I come home?' Your mother looked around and she said, 'No. I'm so close to losing everything myself. Unless you can bring in some income, I can't take you in, because I barely have enough for me and your little brother.' You went away feeling very dejected, not blaming your mother, but saying to yourself, 'Well, I should have known that I am on my own.'

"When you went to the court and asked for a judge to look into the matter, the authorities decided they didn't want to take on the case. The enemies of your partner had already murdered him; it was a common thing to do. Soon after, they got rid of you too. Most likely, you didn't even know them. In the night, two men came silently into your house and cut your throat in your sleep. You didn't even wake up. Then they took your house and everything else they wanted. There was nobody to contest it.

"When you became aware of your death, you said, 'OK. In my next life, I am not going to be dependent on other people. I am going to learn to be independent. I am going to overcome this feeling that other people can make decisions about my life.' Even the geishas were always pleasing others so that they could have a job, and they never felt that they had much power—not the kind of power that keeps you safe when there are problems. You were still depending on men to help you. After your man was gone, you were too vulnerable, unable to protect yourself."

After the past life, Maitra went on to explain how that experience continues to influence Wendy in the present:

"So, why did you choose your family? The culture here in Switzerland makes it much more likely that your family would help you if your life fell apart. Also, when the men in the past life blocked you when they made it hard for you, they forced you to become strong and to trust yourself more than anybody else. You still have that underlying current of fear that your life could all fall apart again. You don't trust yourself and your power well enough to know that, even if it falls apart, you can put it back together, even though you have done that more than once.

"Now you are working on building the confidence that will let you overcome your fear that you could lose everything again. If it happens today, you will save yourself again. You have the strength and you are beginning to know it. To go from being a geisha to who you are today, where you are becoming a therapist and healer, shows so many positive things about your progress.

"The kind of attention that you give to a man when you are interested in him is also reminiscent of a geisha's life; many of these things about you go back to the influences of this past life."

Maitra continued, "We are also here today to address your second question regarding the karmic connection between you and your mother:

"Now I am seeing Holland with the dikes and the tulip fields, and wooden shoes sitting outside of the house. They wore wooden shoes on the street, but they didn't wear them in the house. It must have been around the time of World War I. Your mother was born in 1934 in this life, so this must have been her most recent lifetime, possibly yours too. She was married and in her early twenties. Her husband (your father) was a soldier and he was gone, fighting.

"You were her only child, about two years old when your mother got pregnant again by a sailor. He was from Holland, home on leave. Her mother, your grandmother, came to babysit, and your mother went out with her girlfriends to the bars, to dance and to drink. When she got pregnant again, by a stranger, she went to someone who wanted to help her, although he had no medical training, and she had an abortion. She got an infection and she never fully recovered from it. She was weak and ill, and her immune system was compromised, and you ended up living with your grandmother, who was becoming senile. She forgot, for hours at a time, that you were there. She forgot to feed you, to change your diapers. She was a good-hearted woman, but her mind was deteriorating. Your mother (her daughter) was very ill; she was in a hospital by then. I don't see you living with your mother anymore. She had a massive infection in her body and was going downhill rapidly.

"This is your present mother, who, in this past life, was forced to abandon you because she was too ill. She was only twenty-three years old. She left you with her mother, who was unable to care for a two-year-old baby. You were crawling and you went out into the street. You were hit by a horse and a cart full of wood, and you were knocked unconscious. You weren't immediately killed, and someone picked you up. They took you to the hospital where you never regained consciousness. For a while, you were out of your body. You couldn't find anybody you knew, and you were such a small, little person. A loving being, an angel, came to help you and decided not to send you back because you didn't have anything or anybody to go back to, even though you could have recovered. You didn't have anyone who could take care of you. It would have been too hard.

"When it was time for you to reincarnate, you had unfinished business with your mother from when she became too ill to take care of you. In the past life, your mother died several months later and would not have been available to take care of you even if you had lived. In her lucid moments, your grandmother suffered from guilt because she hadn't protected you. Sadly, she wasn't lucid most of the time."

In this lifetime in Holland, the dynamics between family members became clear; this made it possible to give names to the lessons that were being learned. The following is a transcript of their conversation:

M: One of your sisters today, Mary, was your senile grandmother. Her mental and physical health were rapidly deteriorating at the time. She was only sometimes lucid.

W: I don't have a real connection with her. It is difficult to have a relationship with her. She lives with two dogs and only goes out with them, and is always talking about the dogs, although she has a family with two children.

M: Maybe she is still living in the other world of that past life. Also, your mother was full of guilt in that past life because she couldn't take care of you. Her fear of death today has to do with how she failed you. And this has caught up with her as she approaches death. She felt so guilty about getting pregnant with this child from an unknown sailor, and then having an abortion. The sailor, who was the father, didn't know anything about this. He left to go back to the ship and was gone.

Today, your mother is afraid of dying. She feels her death coming and she doesn't know what is going to happen. Even with her religion, she doesn't have peace. She wakes up in the night, afraid, and tries to pray; she is having a crisis of faith because she is finding that she doesn't believe the things that she accepted before. Some people would say, 'OK. What *do* I believe?' But not your mother; she thinks that there is nothing she can believe in. She's in a state of disillusionment. She is feeling more lost now than ever before because she has been pretending for a long time that death isn't real. Now, it is suddenly real. Death is coming, and what is going to happen to her? She thinks about all the mean things she has said to people. She knows that she has hurt people over and over again. Even when she tried to stop herself, she couldn't. The impulse was too strong in her.

It would help both of you, for you to visualize your mother and send her a blessing, such as 'May you find peace before you die. May you realize that you are loved. May you know that your children understand that you did your best.' This will help you neutralize some of the bitterness that you have about all of this, and help you forgive yourself for pushing her away. If she doesn't find peace before she dies, she will have a difficult time after her death. Show your compassion by sending her blessings. You can use a picture of her when you are giving her blessings. You can sing *Om Namah Shivaya* (a spiritual chant) for her too. She may not appreciate it in her conscious mind, but she will feel its energy at a deeper level. When you contribute to her peace, you contribute to your own.

W: My grandmother was harsh with my mother too.

M: Yes, when you can feel your grandmother's presence, then she has come because she wants forgiveness too. She has been shown how much harm she did.

Being born into your family, with this mother, resulted in you being empowered because they weren't taking care of everything for you. You had to develop strength, independence, and confidence in yourself. That wasn't an accident; it was what you wanted. You wanted to be free, to be yourself. The more they tried to stop you, the more determined you became to be yourself. You had to fight for it. You had to let go of a lot of things—what they thought about you, how they talked to you, the way they withheld love from you, all that. Now you are coming into yourself more and more. This is your backbone, your inner strength, trusting yourself, being comfortable with your power, and your confidence. When you get stronger, people can't push you around anymore.

That is when you are in your body when you are present and your power is there. It is tentative, you are still wavering a little bit, but you have gotten a lot stronger in these last years. Earlier in your life, you were apologetic, asking yourself, 'Do I have the right to be here, to take up space?' You came into this family because they had just what you needed, what you wanted to learn and develop in this life. It wasn't easy; you weren't happy, but it was what you needed.

Wendy's Transformation

In the follow-up conversation, Wendy describes what she learned from these two Readings and how they changed her life; she was able to give up blaming, which allowed her to move out of victim mode:

"My past life as a geisha taught me that I can't rely on others, that I am responsible for myself. I was always conscious of feeling alone. As a geisha, one is not completely free in society because the work and the duties are prescribed. I feel freer today. At that time, these women couldn't have a 'real' relationship with a man. To be sure, the men had relationships. They had families and were married. But they couldn't have the same relationship in their marriage as they could with a geisha. The geisha, however, didn't have any claim on them.

"I never experienced a real feel for a loving family. The Reading helped me; I can understand everything better. Today, in my work, counseling and supporting people through healing therapy, I am much freer.

"The only feeling I have left from my past life as a geisha, when I was murdered, is that of suddenly being out of my body, on the other side. I'm not afraid; I don't feel traumatized. It was simply the way it was. Death is like going to bed in the evening and waking up the next morning in another dimension. One of my teachers had a very nice way of describing this: 'Everybody knows that they will die someday, and it is very unrealistic to be afraid of it because death will come, even if one fights it. If we live in constant fear, even though we know that we will all die, it's a waste of our vital energy.'

"There are other parallels to my current life; for example, the first time I did Tai Chi, I had such a deep feeling that I had always been doing it, and it was so familiar to me. Also, as a geisha, one learned these dances whose movement sequences come from Tai Chi.

"I've also had more thoughts about my mother from the Reading. She was born into a family that was very prudish and thought about life in restrictive ways. In her life, one had to cook, knit, and weed, and one had to be quiet and pray. She was brought up with these kinds of rules and attitudes. At times, she punished herself. From my point of view, she didn't want to change or develop.

"Sometimes I have thought to myself that I came into this life, to this mother, to heal her, but she couldn't accept it. I chose to come to her again, and this mother-daughter relationship has been very strange. I never really sought physical contact with her, for as long as I can remember. I always kept myself at a distance. There was no emotional connection. I wasn't able to trust her, given her way of treating me. Her accusations are never-ending. She still criticizes me or makes harsh comments. That's all I ever get from her. There hasn't been any intimacy.

"When the Reading revealed this past life, I didn't have heavy feelings about death after the accident with the horse and cart. Nevertheless, memories from my childhood came back, when I often had breakdowns and fainted. There wasn't any medical explanation for this. Perhaps these were memories of this last death or attempts to leave my body, simply to help me remember.

"In my family of origin, I couldn't share ideas about my life, my changes, and my discoveries. My mother's attitude was very limited. I understand now that she has decided to stay stuck in this situation. Through the insights in the Reading, I gained the clarity to forgive and heal my wounds, and to bless her with sympathy. This has been very freeing.

"It's no longer about feeling guilty. I can let things be the way they are. I understand everything with greater clarity. The Reading revealed a lot about me, about my strengths."

> **Darkness cannot drive out darkness;**
> **only light can do that.**
> **Hate cannot drive out hate;**
> **only love can do that.**
>
> —Martin Luther King Jr.

For Your Toolkit: The Hypnagogic State

Do you have someone, a family member for example, from whom you are estranged? Do you feel powerless to resolve the situation because communication is impossible? You may be afraid that one of you will die without healing the situation.

All is not lost!

At night, as you're drifting off to sleep, between being awake and asleep, you go into a hypnagogic state. In this state, you can give yourself instructions to accomplish during sleep what seems impossible when you are awake. When you're in the hypnagogic state (also called Theta*), give yourself directions to go visit this person, during your sleep time. You can invite your guides, a healer, other family members, or a spiritual teacher, for example, to help. When possible, repeat this every night with a clear intent to heal the rift.

This technique can also be used to contact people who died before you could resolve whatever issues you may have had with them. It can also be used to improve relationships that are faltering; it can help keep a strong connection with someone who lives far away.

This is not a 'quick fix,' but over time—days or weeks or even months—it will make a difference, and you will come to understand and appreciate that you are not powerless in the situation. Perhaps the most important thing about it is that you feel empowered to do something to improve the situation. You are free to express your love.

Chapter 15: Disorientation

For Your Toolkit: Being Present

(Carla, born 1989)

After coursework to prepare for university enrollment, Carla studied very hard for the exams, which she found very intense; then she was without work for two months. She didn't have anything to do, and lacked direction: "I didn't know what the future would hold." She needed money, then did some advanced study because she didn't know where to go next.

After the exams, Carla went to Maitra for a Reading because she needed help to decide what to do next; she was disoriented. It was the right moment for her to receive counseling. This was the first time that she had been involved in this kind of Reading, and she didn't know if she believed in anything like past lives. Carla wanted to be creative, but she felt blocked. She wanted to know: 'Why is this? Where does this come from?'

Maitra answered her: "You are afraid of your creative power. I'm seeing a powerful past life that is gathering momentum in your life right now. Your soul recognizes that this karma is blocking you and wants you to be free of it.

"You were an art student, in Paris, at a famous art school. You were starting school against all odds because it was during the war and nobody knew what tomorrow was going to bring: Are the Germans going to come into France? Are the French going to stand up against them? What is going to happen?

"You were a boy in that life; you were so outspoken and passionate. You can see, what you have been holding back, holding back, holding back in this lifetime. In your last life, you were … WOW!!! Everybody would listen. You questioned what the Nazis were up to. It was 1933, and the Nazi Party is just coming into power. They haven't come to France yet, but there are many rumors about it. You keep hearing things but nobody knows what is going on in Germany and whether they are going to attack your country or not.

"You are in the midst of this craziness and you are determined that you are going to get your education. You start art school. Your parents in that lifetime are doubtful about it. They say, 'We are paying for this school and we can't see how you are going to make a living. Who is going to take care of you? What are you going to do when you are an artist? What makes you think you are any good?' and on and on. You say to them, 'Look, I have to do it. I don't know why. If you don't want me to study art, I'll get a job.' You knew your parents wanted you to go to school; they didn't want you to take a dead-end job. It was just that they didn't see any future in studying art.

"So you made a compromise, and you agreed to study something that would make money as well; you would enroll in the business school too. You agreed with them outwardly, but inwardly you were saying, 'I am not interested in business.'

"What surprised you was that, as more and more news came from Germany, you began to get interested in politics. You wanted to keep up with the latest news. So you started hanging out in the coffee shops, where the people interested in the possibility of war were hanging out, rather than at the one with the other art students. You gravitated to places where the possibility of war was being discussed.

"Some news came in, involving Picasso, one of your artist heroes. He had friends in Germany, and he gave an interview in a newspaper about what the Nazis were doing, about the concentration camps, the rounding up of people, about taking peoples' homes and all their money.

"You were upset by this, and you said, 'It has to be true. He wouldn't dare to say this, and the paper wouldn't dare to print it if it weren't true.' So, you went back to your art class and you began to paint. You were painting sometimes around the clock; sometimes you forgot to sleep or eat. The other students came and watched you. They couldn't believe what you were doing;

you were painting all these passionate, strong, bloody, violent pictures of what you understood was going on in Germany. You said, 'People have to know. They have to know.'

"In a corner of the classroom, you had a pallet on the floor which was folded up during the day. You slept there at night when you were too tired to go home. The room was never locked because you were there. People would come in during the night and watch you, not just students, but professors would come in too. Sometimes they brought their friends to watch you paint.

"The next thing I see is German officers who are living in Paris. Nobody knows what is going to happen tomorrow; everybody is on edge. Everything is up in the air. What are these Nazi officers doing here?

"A well-known man, who was anti-Nazi, came to the school and looked at your paintings and said, 'We have to show these; we have to let people know what's going to happen here if we let the Nazis come in.' You said, 'OK.' You were not thinking about what to do next. You were absorbed in the work itself, in the creative impulses that were pushing at you and keeping you awake at night and making you forget to eat, etc. You were in a creative fervor.

"Interestingly, what set off this creative fervor for you was Picasso, who was famous for sometimes painting for a week without sleep; he would just be mad with it. You were like that too.

"The show was in a small gallery, on a street where there were many galleries. The bigger galleries didn't want to hang these pictures; they didn't want to upset the Germans. The man, who was sponsoring you, didn't think it would be like that. He thought your paintings would shock people and make them think; maybe they would get people motivated to keep the Germans out of France.

"The show was hung. You were present; you were in your twenties, dressed all in black, and looking very young to be having such a show. You were probably about the age you are now. You were lost, you didn't know anything about what it meant to hang pictures; you just wanted to paint. You were feeling that somebody had to talk about the horror, but you weren't thinking about what would happen when you depicted it.

"It opened in the late afternoon, around four o'clock; many people were there and you sold five or six paintings in the first hour. People were impressed with your talent, your daring, your courage, and what you had to say.

They were excited and thought your work would be collectible. You didn't know about any of that; you just thought, 'Oh, people like my paintings, WOW!'

"About seven o'clock that evening, the owner of the Gallery came in. He had been in and out all afternoon; now he came in again and said, 'I heard that the authorities are coming and are going to arrest us—me, you, and your sponsor.' 'Who is going to come to arrest us?' 'I don't know.' 'The authorities.' Somebody else said, 'Get those paintings out of here. We are going to be in trouble.'

"It was only fifteen minutes later. You were all looking at each other and saying, 'What shall we do?' You hadn't decided to do anything at that point, and all of a sudden, there were many men in uniform in the doorway and at the windows, and they came in and took down the paintings, and put them in the back of a truck. Then another man, not dressed in uniform, but the one in charge, came in and asked: 'Who is in charge here?' The gallery owner came over and said he was the owner, and he introduced you and your sponsor. The man in charge said, 'You are all under arrest. You can walk out and get in the truck or I can bring people in and drag you out.' You three looked at each other, and then went out together and got into the truck.

"Before the truck even started, they separated you and put you in a different truck. No one would explain anything to you. The next thing you knew, you were in this dark truck and you couldn't see anything. It was black in there, except for a little bit of light coming in through a small window at the top, above the driver. You are thinking, 'What is this all about? What is going on here?' When the truck stopped, they took you out and put you in a shower room. They told you to take your clothes off and they took them away. You were terrified. They hosed you down with a fire hose, making you turn around, for many minutes, and then gave you a one-piece coverall to wear.

"You were locked in a cell where you couldn't see or talk to anybody. It was enclosed, except for a window where they could observe you. You didn't know how long you were there because you didn't have any way of telling time. You didn't have shoes or a blanket and you were cold all the time. After several days, finally, the guards came in and gave you some shoes.

"They said, 'We are going to take you to court.' When you arrived at court, the other two people—the gallery owner and your sponsor—were there. They did not let you talk with each other; then you realized that you were going to be tried separately. They gave you an attorney, but he didn't say one word to you; he just agreed to whatever they said. It became clear that the trial was a formality. You didn't understand any of it. They deported you to a German prison; this was something new for a French citizen. Later, it happened to many people, but it was something new at the time when it happened to you.

"They forced you to watch while they made a big fire out in an open field by the prison, and burned all your paintings.

"A few of your paintings were already sold when the men came to arrest you, so it's possible that two or three of your paintings still exist. I can't say what happened to them.

"After that, you were imprisoned in the concentration camp, where you died of pneumonia. You died of not having enough food to eat, not having warm clothing, and of being unable to get well when you got sick. There was no medical care. You died trying to catch your breath."

The Reading made it clear why Carla had to keep a lid on her passions. She feared discovering what she wanted to express in this lifetime; the cost of expressing herself might again bring suffering and even death—these memories, although they had been unconscious, were present enough to cause her much inner conflict. Maitra tied past and present together to help Carla find her way to freedom:

"This past life explains your fear; it's the reason why you are afraid to connect with your heart's desire. In that lifetime, you got what you most wanted—the opportunity to express yourself about something you deeply cared about. You were extraordinarily passionate about it and also became lost in it; it moved you so profoundly.

"Remember, today you sat down and I said to you, 'What moves you? What do you care about?' And you can touch that feeling a little. But to touch what's inside of you, the depths of feeling, the passion—it's much too scary, because it cost you everything, even your life, in the last lifetime.

"Everything was out of your own hands so quickly. All you could think about was painting. Getting canvases, painting them, putting them aside, and going on to the next one. You had a lot of friends who were in awe of you because you were so young and so passionate.

"Today, I notice that you say how young you are, that you are not ready to do this or that. I think it's a recall from this lifetime. You said, 'I was too young to have that happen to me. I was too young to be that passionate about what I was doing. I never had the chance to find out who I was, to grow up.' Your feeling is that in this lifetime, you're going to take your time with it, you won't let yourself be pushed or rushed into anything. You're not going to let anybody take over because that was what happened before. You were painting and painting, and suddenly everything was out of your control. You were in art school, then you had paintings in a gallery, then you were in jail, then in a concentration camp, cold and hungry. An early death. You felt you didn't have any say in any of it. All you cared about was expressing yourself.

"This time you don't want to do that. You want to cut off your passion, and your creativity, and give yourself time. Unfortunately, you can't forget what happened to you there. The memory is inside of you. It's just below consciousness, and it's saying to you, 'Not so fast, I need time to grow up and know who I am.'

"I don't know if you're a painter today, but your creativity is who you are. Your heart is in expressing yourself, whether it's art, such as painting again, or writing, or whatever. My suggestion after looking at this past life is that you try some different ways of expressing yourself and see what begins to loosen up that fear. Let go of thinking that these fears are predicting the future; they are a memory of a profound freedom of expression and the trauma that followed.

"There's a reason why you have been afraid to discover what you want, a good reason, but it's not who you are. Now you have to find out what you want to do. Maybe you're going to watch a movie about the Second World War and see if you can move some of that fear and sorrow that is stuck in you. Then your challenge is to find a way back to yourself again. You are not lost. You are processing something profound and traumatic; it's been mostly unconscious. Now it has risen into consciousness so you can see what you are working with. Since you see and understand what's been holding you back, now you can begin to see where you want to go."

At this point, Carla asked how a past life can affect one's current life.

"Whatever was unfinished, whatever feelings were still there, seem to carry over into the next lifetime. You didn't finish maturing in that life and you express that frustration today. You say unusual things: 'I'm young and I don't want to have a boring, full-time job, and that's all I do from day to day.' Most people wouldn't say that. From the perspective of the past life, it makes sense that you would say, 'I don't want to let that happen again, and yet I can't quite get hold of what I want.' It's your creativity, yourself, that you want.

"It seems to me you have conflicting desires. You fear the depth of passion that's in you, and so, the more you start to care about something, the more you're going to push it away because of what happened to you in the previous lifetime. You went with all your passion for what you wanted, and you expressed yourself, and then your life was over. You never saw the sun again."

Carla's Transformation

A few years later, when Carla was interviewed about the Reading, her passionate nature was beginning to show itself as she related the insights she gained from the Reading:

"The Reading released so much in me that it felt like it was true. It's as if it opened a new dimension in me so that it was very clear to me afterward. It made a lot of sense to me that we come back to life and bring stories with us that we haven't yet brought fully into consciousness in this life. Some things are somewhat inexplicable in our current life and have, in fact, a different origin. Then everything isn't so ego-oriented, and one gets a better perspective on issues that one is working on.

"At least, that's how it's been for me. I can now embrace certain issues as history, and not as 'I/ME' with all my failings in this lifetime, but rather as the 'me' who has certain difficulties. I can instead view these events as the history of my soul, as a history that seems complicated, and I have the power to heal it in this life.

"The theme of creativity was very important to me in this Reading. It was in part an issue of my wanting to be creative, of how I wanted to play that out, because I simultaneously felt blocked. Through the story of my past life in the Reading, I could understand these issues very well. I noticed that it related well to my previous life. Maitra gave me the advice to be creative so that I can heal from this whole story in the past life. Unfortunately, I got a job soon thereafter and didn't have the time to give my creativity enough space. But it wasn't that hard for me because I felt as if several of the blockages in me were dissolving, and being resolved.

"During the Reading, when Maitra was telling me about this past life, I had to cry a lot. I felt a strong connection to this story. It released something in me. Maitra told me this story of how my ideal life had looked. At that stage of life, my ideal was to be an artist; it appealed strongly to me. I was a painter in Paris, expressing myself fully, I had a focus, and my heart and soul were committed to what I was doing. That isn't the case at all in my current life. My energy is much more scattered. At one time, I'm here; at another time, I'm there.

"I could now somewhat let go of my ideal life as an artist that I was shown in the Reading. I'm not that person anymore. I can no longer enjoy or become passionate about something to the extent that I was able to at that time. This insight was very important to me. The story of the past life ended very abruptly due to this very fast death during the war. Because of the appearance of the Nazis, and the consequences of my passion, I still have fears in my current life about what I like to do best. I became aware of the fact that I'm afraid, above all, of everything important to me, and I want to heal this, remembering that it all happened in my last life. All this information made sense to me. I enrolled later in an art school to take a preparatory course. At the time, the Reading released a lot in me. For a few days afterward, I felt as if I were walking on clouds. I had the feeling that I could now understand a lot more. It was a really good feeling.

"I am now studying ethnology; this is also creative for me. Earlier, I imagined creativity to be more visual, that I would paint with paints and brushes. Now I am discovering intellectual creativity. This is also a part of me. Now I can study what interests me. I feel privileged. Now I can even make a film—I think this is fantastic. This will be my Bachelor's thesis. Art and science come together in ethnology. It's as if there is an opening here for scientific thought, in that one can integrate science and artistic films as a path to understanding ethnology. I am extremely interested in this. It's wonderful that I can do this at the institute where I'm studying.

"There was a chronological correspondence between my present and past life. When I died in my past life as a student, I was barely over twenty years old. I was the same age when I went to Maitra for the Reading. I was about twenty-one years old when I was deported by the Nazis. I've always had a very strong feeling that I won't get old. I've also often had the feeling that I didn't arrive in this world properly. Sometimes I have a feeling that I don't want to be in this world or this life. These feelings were very strong when I was young. Sometimes I felt a certain discontent, even mistrust. I had the feeling I was in the wrong movie, that I came into the world at the wrong time and wrong place.

"My real decision, and saying a clear 'Yes' to life, came after an accident in which I suffered a traumatic brain injury when I was twenty-four years old.

I felt at that time that my life hadn't come to an end and that I would go on living, that it wasn't over yet. I feel as if I'm really on a path now; before the Reading, I didn't trust life. Now my basic trust is very strong. Today, if I listen to the story of this past life again, I feel that I am at a very different point in life. It feels as if I have healed; it's far away.

**Let go of your cup of yesterday
so you may drink the glory of this moment.**

—Rumi

For Your Toolkit: Being Present

Being centered and grounded in one's body, Being Present, is one of the best-kept secrets for happiness and success in all areas of one's life. People report that this one tool can change everything for the better.

Try this grounding technique: Imagine yourself like a living vase, with the top of your head completely open. Visualize and feel a flow of radiant, golden light pouring slowly down into your body from above, filling your head, then your neck and shoulders, flowing into your chest and down into your belly. Feel the light filling every pore, flowing into your pelvis and hips, your genitals, and finally feel it flowing down into your legs and feet. This light is infinite and inexhaustible; it is the true nature of everything.

Now, imagine that you have long deep roots growing from the soles of your feet, about twenty-five feet wide by twenty-five feet deep. Let the light flow through openings (chakras*) in the bottom of your feet, down into your roots, and through them into Mother Earth. The Eastern traditions call this the 'Hollow Bamboo'—when the earth receives the cosmic healing light through you.

Now you have become a blessing to the earth itself; this will keep you present in your body. Practice it several times a day—it will become instantaneous—until it becomes a part of you and you only notice when it's momentarily gone.

When you finish the visualization, close the opening at the top of your head. The flow will continue.

Your Presence is the gift you bring—feel free to be generous!

Chapter 16: Understanding a Karmic Pattern in a Dysfunctional Marriage

For Your Toolkit: 1) Creating Balance 2) How We Learn

(Gina, born 1960)

Gina, a social worker, came to Maitra with a compelling question. Her marriage was very difficult; she had never been in love with her husband. She always had the feeling that there must be karma between them. She recently separated from him after thirty years. They have a son. Gina came to Maitra because she wanted to understand the karmic connection with her soon-to-be ex-husband, Don.

When Gina requested a past life Reading, Maitra immediately saw the following one, in great detail:

"Don was your beloved son many lifetimes ago, sometime in the hundred years after Christ's death. I am seeing you in Italy and you are a part of a Christian sect. It is a secret group. He was your only child; your husband was gone. Your husband left the sect—you and your son stayed. You were sorry to see him go but you didn't want to leave. At the point where I'm seeing your son right now, he was thirteen or fourteen years old and he had made some good friends outside of the Christian group. Your group was a secret because you were living and taking part in the outside community; you had jobs in the community, and people didn't know that you were in a sect. You lived in a big house, kind of a commune with a lot of other people who all belonged to the same sect.

"There weren't any children your son's age in the group. He made friends with some neighbor-hood children. They went everywhere and did everything together.

"He loved his friends. His heart was engaged. Then, one day they began to come into the house. Everybody in the house was a little bit uncomfortable with it, but they didn't want to say to the boy, 'You can't bring your friends into the house.' Icons and pictures that might reveal who they were, would be hidden. When the boys came in, there would be this feeling of everybody being very careful around them. Your son was oblivious to all the fear. He just wanted to be with his friends. He wasn't thinking much about it.

"One rainy afternoon, the children were let out of school early and they decided to come to your house. Nobody had any warning that they were coming and the adults were not at home. The boys came into the house and the things that would normally be hidden were out in plain sight. Your son was oblivious to this. But to his friends, it was shocking, and after they had been there for a little while, they made an excuse to go home. When they decided to go, he wanted to know, 'Why?' The other boys said, 'Well, we just remembered something, and we have to go home.' He was puzzled and hurt and didn't understand what happened.

"When he went to school the next day, his friends—there were three of them—

wouldn't speak to him. If they saw him coming, they would turn around and go the other way. He couldn't understand this. He tried to catch them and asked 'What happened? What did I do?', but they wouldn't talk to him at all. The three of them were together in this. It became more and more obvious. Then some things started to happen in the neighborhood. Neighbors suddenly weren't friendly to the people in this house. For example, people no longer wanted to share their tools.

"Suddenly the doors are closing all around you. You kept questioning your son: 'Did something happen? What happened?' He said, 'Nothing happened. I don't know what happened.' Finally, you got him to say what day it was when the boys were last there; they had come in the middle of the afternoon when nobody had prepared for them. You realized that the boys had seen some things that revealed who the group was, and now everybody in the neighborhood knew you were part of the sect. The residents began to discuss the necessity of moving away.

"The image I saw showed that his heart was twisted, that when his friends, whom he loved, turned their backs on him, he took it so personally that he began to be angry at everybody in the sect.

"First, everybody moved to a new place and that was hard enough, and then he was so angry and causing so many problems in the house that they finally asked you to leave, too, you and the boy. Now, all of a sudden, he is the one who is causing all the problems; he can't understand why they are kicking you out. First, he lost all his friends—they turned their backs on him—and then he lost his family. Although they were tolerant in the beginning, they decided that they just couldn't have him in this house; sooner or later they were going to have to move again because he was just impossible. He was rejected by everybody who he thought cared about him. In the end, you had to leave too. You took him to where his father was, and you said to his father, 'I can't deal with him anymore. He is so angry all the time. He alienates everybody, it's your turn to take him.' His father did take him, but reluctantly. (Maitra aside: 'My heart is hurting; I can feel the boy's heart hurting so much.')

"A few months later, you were shopping in the marketplace, and you saw your son with some boys his age, stealing food. When you tried to catch him and talk to him about it, he ran away from you. You went to his father's place immediately and said, 'What is going on here?' His father said, 'Well, I had to tell him to leave; he is living in the street.' At that time, he was only sixteen."

At this point, Gina is upset, nearly in tears from what she is hearing. Maitra continues to help her understand:

"If you still think you made the wrong decision about your son in that lifetime—he is your husband today—you haven't understood the whole situation yet. When you can understand the whole thing, you will realize that it was an experience that was beneficial to both of you. Then you can free yourself from this rigid 'right and wrong' thinking.

"Consciousness is moving beyond Yin and Yang, the black and white symbol of right and wrong, good and bad. We are beginning to realize that it's a dynamic symbol and that as our consciousness is raised, there is more and more gray, and less and less black and white.

"It would be good now for you to think about learning to meditate or call it contemplation, opening your mind so that your unconscious can reveal new understandings of the things you have already learned.

"You are beginning to have a deeper appreciation of who you are. My impression is that you have been pretty daring, and even though fear was sometimes there, you didn't let it stop you as many people do. Now you have to conquer your fear of indecisiveness, of not knowing what to do. And the fear is not going to come up in your mind, it's going to come from deep in your belly.

"Our pictures or ideas of how it 'should' be in relationships can get in the way. It keeps us from being present. Look again, at some of those places where you think you failed or you made a mistake. This time, look for the benefit in even the most difficult experiences. What did you learn? All progress is made by people who are willing to make mistakes.

"From your son's point of view (in the previous life), everybody in his life who he thought cared about him, rejected him, and he could never see what he did to bring that about. Today, he is your husband; you wanted to help him because you felt you had failed him in that previous life.

"The reason you think you made such a big mistake is because you couldn't achieve what you wanted to achieve, which was to help him understand how he contributed, unknowingly, to his own isolation. He still believes himself to be a victim. Today, he can't open his heart because it's twisted, the result of what he perceived as betrayal. He can't believe that anyone could love him, and he can't believe that he could love anyone. In a way, he plays a game with it, but you can't get through to him because he's not going to allow it. He is unhealthy; he has such a strong neurosis.

"Your son of this lifetime is OK today. He has a big heart that his father never had. If anybody could ever open your husband's eyes, it would be his son. We don't yet know if he will. What's missing for your son is that you haven't told him yet that you are proud of him. Your son is everything his father was meant to be, and you saw it in his father, but it was locked up. You were hoping that you could unlock it.

"Your husband feels rejected by the fact that you left him. In his mind, people are always turning their backs and leaving him. You did what you could; then you had to leave him. What would change his perception is if he could learn to be there for himself, and love himself."

Gina's Transformation:

After the Reading, Gina was able to finally end the relationship with Don. What follows is her description of that process:

"In my Reading, it was a matter of ending a long-term relationship with my husband. The Reading was an enormous confirmation for me, and it was an extraordinary help to me in completely ending this relationship; it was good for me. Indeed, it was final in the sense that it was so good. These weren't wasted years, even though it was a very difficult marriage. Before, I could get into a downward spiral and think that I had wasted the best years of my life, but the Reading revealed to me that I could now breathe a sigh of relief, and say to myself, 'Indeed, it's good the way it is.' I knew that I had—as it were—accepted this karma and I could finish it by letting go of him, consciously. It gave the whole thing a deeper meaning which was a great help to me. Although I know this, of course, or sense it, and think that life has meaning, each of us does have our own story. And then, when you gain so much clarity and meaning, it feels very freeing.

"Earlier, people around me would ask, 'Why are you staying with this man? You don't need to stay with him. You can of course leave him.' But this was never so simple. This relationship was difficult from the start, and I was never really in love with him. I did feel a deep connection to him. The only person who didn't talk like the others was my Buddhist teacher. She would often listen to me, and she was one of the people who didn't tell me to leave him. She said that I was on a good path. She knew me very well, and she supported me in a neutral way.

"This past life with my husband as my son led me to a very good and clear conclusion of my thirty-year relationship with this man. That was half my life. I can say today that it was a good life, even though it was difficult. If I can now come to terms with it and find peace, and feel it, then this is a wonderful gift.

"The danger is there: If one is together for such a long time with such a difficult person, one asks oneself, 'Why have I done this?' If you can't answer this question, then things don't feel good. Through the insights from this Reading, I understand the essence, the value of my time with him, and that helped me to sort out and transform the relationship.

"My son was involved in an incident in which he was stabbed by a man with a knife and almost lost his life. I wanted him to go into therapy at the time. The Reading told me that there was a karmic aspect to this stabbing and that my son always wanted to help and be the hero. That touched me. I will never forget that Maitra began to smile as soon as I said his name, and she told me that I had absolutely nothing to worry about because he was a very good young man. This relieved me so deeply, and so many worries dissolved. I had always felt he was good.

"This Reading took place several years ago, and things have turned out exactly as described to me. At that time, Maitra was already able to tell me that my son wouldn't listen to me if I recommended, for example, that he seek therapy. Perhaps he will someday. So far, he hasn't considered it important. But he has developed in a very good direction; this pleases me. I sense that we are getting closer. Earlier, his father, Don, my ex-husband, always viewed me as aloof. He considered my views to be somewhat 'weird.' At that time, I used to worry about which of his father's views he was going to adopt. But now I can feel that he can accept some things from me, and this has turned out to be the case.

"I find this healing work incredibly helpful. The Reading told me that if my ex-husband is going to listen to anybody, it will be to his son, and I can see that it's turning out that way. Of course, everything isn't perfect for my ex-husband, but the two of them have a good relationship, and he listens to our son. In the past life, my husband (then son) had to suffer so much from the fact that we lived so differently. From the outside, we were viewed as very strange people, and we lived somewhat closed off as members of a sect. As a result, spirituality is a sore point for him today. That was so clear to me when I received the insights from the past life.

"I was always very skeptical about going to a seer or clairvoyant. There are so many people who offer this kind of guidance. I've heard this and that about it. But I can immediately tell if I can trust someone or not, whether I can open myself up to them. Earlier, I didn't want to learn anything about past lives. This Reading and the kind of insights that I received, have given me a new understanding of my life."

Several months later, Gina and Maitra had another session. A second Reading with Gina found her even more receptive. The transcription of this Reading follows:

M: I see something interesting in your current life. I see a cycle within a cycle, within a cycle. In some way, you completed a cycle that began at your birth, and in another way, you completed a newer cycle that began when you were about twenty-eight or thirty years old. Was that when you became a Buddhist?

G: Yes, that's when I met my future Buddhist teacher. A bit later, I became a mother.

M: I see that the second cycle is also completing now. Then another one, a third cycle, is finishing that began maybe eight or ten years ago. So this is a big change. It's like a big ship that's been going on its own momentum. You decided to make some changes a few years ago. But there was a momentum, and this big ship has finally stopped, and you are now sitting in a calm ocean and you thought you knew what your next direction was going to be. But now that you are here, where is it?

You don't know. In the past, you were so immersed in what you were doing that you almost missed the end of a cycle. You wouldn't even notice when a shift or a change would happen. You just kept going because it's a cycle within a cycle within a cycle, and the momentum stopped, and now you are at a loss. You are not blocked, and there is nothing wrong with where you are. It is a time when you might find that you want to sleep more or be alone more. It's a time of re-establishing yourself at an even deeper level within.

You have been an extrovert, and now all of a sudden you are being asked to dive down deeper, to find out who is living behind the extrovert. I call it a plateau, where you come to a place where there is nothing there anymore. A plateau often comes with the end of a cycle, and you just have to wait until something wakes up inside of you. Sometimes the plateau will last a few months. Sometimes it could even be a year or two. In your case, I think you haven't been very conscious of a plateau before. Even when you ended a cycle, you were so absorbed in everything in the outer world, and busy, and you had projects. You didn't even notice the end of a cycle.

Now you need to find yourself more. You have found your path, and when you follow it, you become very involved with helping other people and cultivating friendships. I see how your involvement with other people can take you away from yourself.

Now you are trying to get established deeper inside, and that means you need to stop thinking that you need action or movement. Find out more about what's inside you. The interesting thing is that a lot of what you have been doing will come back again when you begin moving in your new cycle. For example, you might be teaching Buddhism. You don't know yet. You don't want to throw away what you've learned. It has value for you. Just wait and see what moves you from inside, not what you want to grab out here. It might be next spring, or it might be a year from next spring. You will be teaching somehow. But if your inner guidance puts you on a cruise ship, teaching dance, do it. Wherever it wants to take you, whatever moves you from inside, surrender to it.

G: When people asked me to teach, I always resisted. I didn't like being a teacher; I wanted to be a student.

M: The inner guidance or teacher hasn't moved you from inside yet. I don't know what it will be; the seed hasn't started to grow yet. Moving meditation is fine too. Right now, you need patience because you have been such an active person, and you have always been going after what you want. Now it's a waiting time. You are waiting for yourself to emerge, after birthing a clearer YOU from inside. Anything you want to do that takes you deeper inside is good. Have you ever done Holotropic Breathwork?

G: Yes.

M: That kind of thing takes you deeper inside. I keep seeing Thích Nhất Hạnh, a well- known Buddhist meditation teacher. If it takes you deeper inside, then do it. For you, right now, it's not about going out into the world. If you are going to do more retreats, do them without a goal. Of all the religions, I think Buddhism is the most likely to last into the next centuries. Many of the religions are going to disappear. People are becoming more spiritually aware and awake. Buddhism has so many practices that help people to wake up spiritually that some form of Buddhism will probably survive. The current Pope Francis is very aware of this. He's trying to create structures within the Catholic church that relate better to people: For example, blessing the Harley Davidson, and taking seriously Jesus' teaching about helping the poor. This Pope is a wise man, but I still don't think that Catholicism is going to last much longer.

G: I'd like to release myself from all religions.

M: Yes, it's fine to let it go.

G: It's not easy for me to just sit and wait.

M: That's what it is right now. That's your spiritual path right now—to open the space more and more inside. Habit is what keeps you from doing that, including your feeling that you are not patient enough. Your habit is to go in and go out, and be active, in action.

G: Yes, I agree.

M: Muktananda was my teacher, and I remember that he sat in a hut for twenty-five years before he finally felt his guidance moving him out. It's not so long. You have done bits and pieces all along, so you know the way inside, but staying there and making friends with your inner life, that's your challenge. You are OK. I don't see any big block in you.

G: Sometimes I just need this kind of confirmation.

M. Yes, we all do. Me too, we need other people, don't we?

G: Yes.

M: It is healing if we begin to forgive, at home in our own families. We can do our part to save the world. And every person learning to love unconditionally, especially learning to love themselves, is making a difference.

G: Yes, I understand. Fortunately, many people who aren't seen on the world stage, and Holy People in the Himalayas and other remote places, all over the world, are contributing to making the world better.

Microscopic

Ordinary life is illuminated
As consciousness expands
Doing the dishes
Playing with the kitten
The moment comes alight
As the microscopic level
Is revealed
The moment
The moment Is all
We swim in awareness
The past falls away
The future falls away
I welcome eternity
And in eternity
Beauty
Joy
Boundless love
The peace I have longed for
arrived with my birth
and was swallowed
by distraction
Come home
Come home to yourself
Let go
Let it all go
be here now
In this microscopic
precious moment.

- Maitra

For Your Toolkit: 1) Creating Balance

Another way of being gentle and loving with yourself is to create balance in your life.

Check to see how you are doing—is there balance in your life?

Can you spend a day at play without feeling guilty? Do you do enough of it? Do you take a vacation when you need it? Are you aware of being recharged when you come home, happy to be at work again? In your home, is there a balance in who's responsible for what, or does it all fall on you? If you live alone, have you managed things so that you don't feel overwhelmed, trying to get it all done, balancing the chores in an easily managed way?

Do you see how balance doesn't just happen? It must be consciously addressed. Balance is an expression of self-love in action. You care about yourself, you are kind to yourself, you are happy to meet your own needs.

These are some areas that challenge us to create balance—which brings harmony—which brings about a happy home—which leads to a happy life:

- Balancing work and play require constant attention;

- Balancing your inner and outer life—only you can know and create this;

- Balancing the needs of family members—this requires open communication;

- Balancing the Yin and Yang—knowing when to give/act (male) and when to receive (female) (we all have both);

- Balancing emotions by not denying them, not emoting them, being aware without judgment. Allowing.

These are just a few of the many challenges we face every day as we work to achieve Balance in our lives. Becoming more aware of it, and of our need for it, can bring opportunities for improvement, and move us in the direction of peace and harmony, moving us into the natural flow.

For Your Toolkit: 2) How We Learn

In her story, Gina had to learn patience, the behavior that was most challenging for her. This task of breaking lifetime patterns is one of the most difficult things we ever have to do; however, if we want to be free, we must overcome the limiting patterns that have imprisoned our families for generations. Here is a way to think about this that may enable you to keep going without beating yourself up:

Visualize a toddler in the process of potty training—(*Gina: Learning patience*):

1. I see a puddle on the floor—it's fun to play in—splashing away, unaware that it was me who made the puddle. This is called UNCONSCIOUS INCOMPETENCE.

2. Pee-pee running down my leg—oh, it's me! Mama said, "No"! Sometimes I can stop it, sometimes I can't. This is called CONSCIOUS INCOMPETENCE.

3. Oops, I have to go to the toilet. Run and catch it. Phew! This is called CONSCIOUS COMPETENCE.

4. Automatically heading for the bathroom; no thought process involved. This is called UNCONSCIOUS COMPETENCE.

Next time you catch yourself doing something you've been trying to change, say to yourself, "Oops, there it goes, running down my leg." Hopefully, you'll feel a little amusement!

Little by little, you will learn to lighten up. You can't jump from unconscious incompetence to unconscious competence—every step must be played out and acknowledged. And it's OK to have fun with it. Before you know it, you'll see yourself as a lifelong student of Life who enjoys every step of the process.

The more you know, the more you realize there is to learn. Endless Opportunity!

Chapter 17: My Schizophrenic Son

For Your Toolkit: Situation = Situation

(Lily, born 1954; Patrick, Lily's son, born 1982)

Lily, a kindergarten teacher, healer, and mother of four, came to Maitra for a Reading with a pressing question, "Why is my son ill?" He had been suffering from schizophrenia since 2001. Her concern about him was evident in her demeanor; she had been suffering from this. Maitra responded with compassion, as the relevant past life for both Lily and Patrick was immediately available to her. Here's what she described:

"In the Second World War, your son was an English pilot. He was shot down. His plane went down and he managed to get out of the plane and go down in a parachute. He landed somewhere in France in an orchard with plums and apples. It was spring and the trees were all in bloom. He landed in this beautiful place. He couldn't believe it. He was lying on the ground and there were all these blossoms all around him, and over him because he crashed down through the trees, and it smelled like heaven. He thinks for a little bit, 'Oh, maybe I am in heaven. Maybe I was killed and I am in heaven.' But no, a man comes from the house, maybe half a mile away, running through the trees, and speaks very fast in French, a language that the pilot doesn't understand.

"The pilot is not badly hurt. He twisted his ankle when he landed, but it wasn't broken. He also lost some skin off his elbow and arm. It needs a bandage, but it's not crippling. He has a big lump on his head where he hit the branch of the tree when he was falling through the trees, but it didn't knock him out. He is in fairly good shape.

"The man helps him out of his parachute and leads him to the house, and he thinks, 'Oh, I have landed in a friendly place, and these people are going to be kind to me.' And that's true, for a couple of days. They feed him. They make him a place to sleep; it's a glassed-in porch in the back of the house with a bed in it. He wakes up very early in the morning because there are no curtains over the windows, and the roof is also glass.

"The family includes the man who rescued him, his wife, and two teenage children, a boy and a girl. They ask him a lot of questions, such as where he's from. They don't know his language but they manage to communicate with him.

"On the third day, he was sitting at the breakfast table, drinking coffee, and everybody in the family had disappeared. Everybody had some reason for leaving, and he was sitting there by himself, thinking, 'What is this?' People have been so nice to him until now.

"All of a sudden, the kitchen door crashed open, and three German soldiers with guns crowded into the room. He didn't have a weapon or any way to defend himself, but they behaved like they were afraid of him. They threw him down on the floor and tied his hands behind his back; they were very rough with him. Of course, again, they didn't speak the same language, so he asked, 'Who are you? How did you find out I was here?' They didn't answer him, or try to communicate with him in any way; they took him first to the village police station where they locked him in a cell. A couple of days pass by. Again, the French were kind to him, feeding him well, and he was starting to relax and thinking, 'Maybe this is going to be OK.' Four more days passed by; then a man came in, in a black uniform from the SS.

"He had some soldiers with him. They put a bag over his head, put him in the back of a truck, on the floor, and it seemed like they went a long, long way, but he was not sure of this. They might be tricking him by driving him around and around because it feels to him that they are driving in circles. He couldn't tell because he had this black bag over his head. The next thing that happened was, that they took him out of the truck. He is out in the woods. They have him kneel, the three soldiers are all pointing their guns at him, and he was sure they were going to shoot him right then. That's what he was supposed to think.

"This SS officer, the man in the black uniform, got out of the truck, and he sat down on a stool, crossed his legs, lit a cigarette, and said in English, 'Are you ready to die today?' And your son said, 'NO!'

"The officer said, 'Then you are going to tell me everything you know about what you're doing here, how you got here, where you came from, and everything you know.'

"Patrick said, 'OK, I don't mind telling you everything I know, but I don't really know anything. I'm a pilot.' He told the officer where he came from, why he was with this family, and what his father did. He was talking, talking, talking.

"He was telling a lot of things that weren't important, hoping that this was going to satisfy this man. But no, the officer said, 'Stop.' And your son said, 'I am telling you everything I know.'

"The officer said, 'No, I want to know who you are, and who ordered you to come here, where your airplane came from, and what the plans for the war are.'

"And he answered, 'They don't tell me the plans, they just tell me where they want me to fly the plane.'

"The officer very casually got up, went over to the truck, got a gun, and shot him in the foot. He was immediately in shock. He was on his knees and the officer had to walk around behind him to shoot him in the foot. Your son said, 'What did you do that for? I'm telling you everything I know. (He's screaming now). I'm telling you everything you want to know.'

"The officer said, 'You know something. I know what happens between soldiers, things float around, rumors float around.'

"Patrick doesn't see the harm in it. He just said, 'We are winning in Africa. The German Army is retreating there.'

"The officer got upset, threw him on the ground, and went back to the truck. Then the other soldiers put the bag back over his head, picked him up, and put him in the back of the truck. (Aside to mother: I am telling you this so you know how they tortured him.) They kept doing cruel things to him. He never knew if he was going to be allowed to sleep through the night. He never knew if something he said would make the officer angry and he would be shot again. The officer shot him again in the right shoulder. He wasn't trying to kill him. He was determined to get him to tell everything he knew.

"Of course, he didn't know much. He was telling everything he knew. He was even making up some things to try to satisfy this officer, who was making it his project to try to get information out of this pilot. It went on, for nearly two months. Earlier, they had him in a cell with a window where sunlight came in. He could hear things. He could hear people in other cells. They could even talk to each other sometimes, and he was aware that there was activity. It felt like he knew a little bit about where he was.

"When the officer gave up on him, they put him in a cell, underground, without light, windows, or air circulation. It was just three walls, and the fourth wall was bars, including the door. The whole basement was dark, and as far as he could tell, there was nobody else down there. There was no mat to sleep on, or a toilet to use. There was a bucket in the corner, and once a day they would bring him some water and some mush; it wasn't enough to nourish him. He was locked down there for another two or three months. Then he was taken away with some other men. They were all put in the back of the truck and taken out into the countryside, where they had to dig a big ditch. Then, they were all shot and fell into the ditch.

"Backing up a bit, he managed to keep hold of himself until the time when they put him in this dark basement. He didn't hear anything, he couldn't see anything, he couldn't smell anything. Eventually, he went into a fantasy world. He was hungry all the time, getting thinner and thinner. He could never get warm—that was another problem—because it was underground. Even in the times of the year when it might be warm outside, it was numbingly cold in his cell, regardless of the weather outside. Finally, cold and starving, he began to hallucinate.

"What had happened was this: The war was over and the Germans were cleaning things up and leaving. Twelve prisoners were still locked up, and they just took them out and shot them without a real reason."

Because the unhealed, extreme trauma was clear in this past life, Maitra went on to describe, in more detail, the healing that could take place for Patrick in the present. The transcription of Maitra's commentary on this topic, and Lily's response follows:

M: Let's say this is karma. But it's not karma in the sense that he did something to deserve further suffering. He is not mentally ill today because he did something wrong. He is ill because he didn't have the chance in that lifetime to recuperate from these repeated traumas.

What constitutes healing for him is very simple. It's having people around who are very friendly and kind to him. It's being able to see sunshine and walk outside. Predictability is probably the most important thing for him. He needs to know he doesn't have to be afraid that somebody is going to change their mind and hurt him again. He needs a routine, like eating at a certain time or going for a walk at a certain time. Routine helps him to stay present in his body and begin to adjust himself to the world as it is. His reality was shattered; they broke him.

Sometimes when people get broken, they have a chance in the same lifetime to repair themselves, at least to some extent. But he never had the chance to do that. And there was no logic to any of it. He had nothing they wanted. He was a pilot, happy to follow orders and do his job well, but he had no real knowledge of the details behind the orders.

Here's a little background: When he was a teenager in his past life, his math teacher discovered that he had a brilliant mind for math. He came from a little factory town in northern England, where the most that would have been expected of him was to follow his father into a factory. But this math teacher discovered that he had a really good mind for mathematics, and he took your son under his wing and got him into a school for training pilots.

This boy came from a family that didn't have much, but they had enough to eat. He grew up in poverty, in the sense of not having any expectations for the future until this teacher found him. So, he went from ordinariness to being a shining star. He was the most successful person who had ever come from his village. When he would go home between flights, everybody wanted to buy him a beer, buy him dinner, or have him over to their house. He felt very lucky that someone had discovered that he had a good mind and that he could shine at something.

He went from that to this crazy situation in Germany as a prisoner, where he couldn't predict from one minute to the next, what they were going to do to him. And he had no power to change anything.

He's getting better now because he is in a situation where people are kind to him and he knows what to expect. He is slowly beginning to feel safe. I'm not going to predict that he will be cured. I don't see that. But I am seeing small improvements along the way.

So that was your question, 'Why is your son mentally ill?' It is because he was so damaged. That was a lifetime with the experience of being brutally knocked off balance, over and over again, and never being able to get his feet under him and find his equilibrium.

L: When his mind started to be ill, he would often lie on the sofa for hours, for days, listening to the same song, 'I'm in heaven …' And when I heard you saying in the past life, that he was lying in this orchard with the blooming trees after he fell from the airplane, and he was thinking that he may be in heaven, I was deeply moved.

M: Yes, that song was from that time.

Lily's Transformation

By the end of the Reading, Lily had begun to relax, the stress began to lift from her face, and by the time of her interview several months later, she looked like a mother with an ordinary concern:

"When I look back now, I see that I was asking myself, as a mother, 'What did I do wrong?' Whenever I would see my son and get a sense of how he was doing, I would feel hurt and get stirred up. When the Reading told me of his past life in the war, and showed me how it was connected, I gained a very different understanding. It touched me deeply.

"When I now see Patrick, I can encounter him differently because I perceive more connections. It's like combing the knots out of one's hair in the morning. It's like, 'Oh, I'm not guilty.' I can share this feeling with him. I can experience joy through the love that binds us. This brought me to a very different place, to the knowledge that, as souls, we are connected through the beautiful memories, and also the painful ones. There is another perspective; I have learned to say 'Yes' to this. Since then, things have gotten easier. The pain hasn't lessened, but by being able to look at things differently, something in my son has also changed.

"The last time he visited me, he was very clear. He could talk with us, and he could eat with us. Patrick initiated this visit; he had asked if he could come home again. This is what was so good for me about the Reading—it went so deep, to the roots, and gave me access to different approaches. I felt the sadness once again when I listened to the CD, his terrible experience, and what was done to him in his past life during World War II. Then there were the parallels, how I perceived him in school, at home, and his beingness. So much old sadness came to the surface in me once again, and I often didn't know what to do with it. I felt that Maitra really 'saw' and understood me and that everything was the way it should be; I could begin to talk about how I was feeling throughout all of this. It was good for me to hear that my son now needs clear and loving structures in this life. He needs people he can trust, and consistency in his relationships that will give him a sense of security. He needs to know that he will have this as long as he needs it so that he can live without feeling threatened.

"I was excited to listen to the Reading once more because Patrick reacts very strongly to two German friends of mine. I couldn't understand this. He felt extraordinarily threatened by them as if he were in great danger. He was in puberty at the time and he also had a very strong reaction to my German partner.

"The Reading gave me an entirely new perspective, and also a new line of inquiry. I have a part to play in this situation. I am trying to figure out what's next. This is my path, and I don't want to be judgmental. Somehow the paths of my son and I have crossed again. Trust is an issue that appears to me in all aspects of my life. It hits a central nerve. So much is now clear to me about these issues; I was able to clarify the question of my guilt. Many pictures come to me in this web of insights. I now see my childhood with my parents as a perfect situation for my personal growth. If I feel my way into myself today, I see that it couldn't have been better, and I can see how I have developed. Even though there have been painful experiences, I feel very thankful. Patrick is my greatest motivator for breaking out of limiting patterns and freeing myself from old beliefs that have been handed down for generations.

"In the process, I caught myself thinking that Patrick had to first be OK before I could look at myself. That was about four years ago. At that time, I learned that what concerns me, also concerns him, and vice versa. I realized that I am allowed to look after myself.

"The Reading also indicated that my son took birth again too soon. He had had so many traumatic experiences that he never had time to find himself. He would barely become a little oriented in one place or another, and the next incident occurred. He had hardly any time to understand anything that happened to him. The statement that it was too early for him to come back to his current life, refers to the fact that it was difficult for him to process the events. Yet my child is here, and he is a gift to me.

"Sometimes I have beautiful encounters with Patrick. When he came here about a year and a half ago, I had made tea for him. He looked at me, and it was a very intimate encounter, in which we met with a feeling of 'I see you,

you see me.' I then gave him my hand and I told him that I loved him. He could take it in and feel it. This memory goes very deep, and when I think of it, it continues to nourish me. It has stayed with me. If you have had this kind of connection with another person, regardless of what happens later, it remains with you. For him, it was a moment when he wasn't ashamed of anything, when he wasn't hearing strange voices in his head, and he wasn't feeling ill; he was completely present.

"The Reading didn't only talk about the difficult issues, but also about his background, where he was born, that he had been a mathematical genius, that his teacher had mentored him, and then got him into a school where they train pilots. Everyone in his village admired him. He had achieved something special. These kinds of statements gave me even more insights into all aspects of his being."

Light will someday split you open,
Even if your life is now a cage.
Little by little, you will turn into stars.
Little by little, you will turn into
The whole sweet, amorous universe.

—Hafiz

For Your Toolkit: Situation = Situation

For this toolkit, let's take the Reading above as an example: The situation at the beginning was "My son is a schizophrenic," abbreviated as MSIAS. If we stop with that

—MSIAS = MSIAS—

we can deal with the problems that arise with objectivity, clarity and compassion.

But what we do, unfortunately, is change the equation MSIAS = "Oh, my God, what did I do wrong? I must be a bad mother." Or "Maybe it's his father's fault" or __________ fill in the blank as you wish, on and on. So the equation becomes

MSIAS = OMGWDIDWIMBABMOMIHFF

In this process, our minds have made up endless explanations that may have nothing to do with the original situation. We probably all know people who have done this for years and are trapped in an endless loop of self-blame and blaming others, when in fact no one is to blame. This situation is, simply put: The son's lesson for this lifetime is to do the best he can as a schizophrenic and realize that he is not to blame.

Do you begin to see how we create our suffering and cripple our ability to deal with the original problem? We can become so lost in our emotional reactions to our thoughts that we are then unable to deal effectively with the problem.

The solution? Resist the endless attempts to assign blame and focus on the fact of the son's illness. My son is a schizophrenic = My son is a schizophrenic. Then the best, most effective ways of dealing with it can emerge. Then there is no pressure on the son or the mother to be different than they are. Acceptance of "what is" can bring peace.

The challenge here is to master your mind; if you are successful, little by little, you will enjoy your life much more. Situation=Situation. Period.

Kudos to Ken Keyes, the author of his *Handbook to Higher Consciousness*, where you'll find this and other helpful new ways of thinking!

Chapter 18: Reconciliation with My Father

For Your Toolkit: Personalizing

(Randy, born 1970)

Randy, until recently a government social worker, had worked with young people and is now self-employed; he considers himself an unconventional thinker, a traveler through life, who lives in close touch with nature. He is a father to four children. After attending one of Maitra's talks, he came for a Reading because he wanted to better understand his relationship to money. After a brief discussion of his problems with money, most of which centered around his relationship with his father, Maitra began to relate what she was seeing:

"I see a Roman general. He's your father, and it is a lifetime where you were his son. You wanted to have his approval, and show him that you were worthy of his love. You were the model soldier. The problem was that you didn't believe in what you were doing. You were living his reality, trying to get him to acknowledge you.

"Your father thought that if he praised you, he would be showing favoritism to his son. He would acknowledge another person for doing the same thing you did, but he wouldn't do the same for you. When he finally gave you a promotion, it was long overdue.

"As a result of the promotion, you were given an important assignment: You were sent behind enemy lines with a small group of seven men. This was your big chance to finally get him to recognize you. You not only did what he assigned to you, you decided to go further so that you could impress him.

"I can't see exactly what you did to go further, but half of your men were killed. You couldn't bear to go back to your father and say, 'I lost half of my men.' Instead, you just pushed even further, to do more and put everyone at risk again. Once again, half of your group was wiped out.

"By now you had lost confidence in yourself. Your leg was badly injured; the two remaining men managed to get you through the enemy lines, and back to your people. You had completed the job that you were given to do in the beginning, and you had even been successful in making more progress. But your father only wanted to know how you lost all those men. He said, 'I trusted you with my best people and you got them all killed. I want you to go home to your mother and I don't want to see you again.'

"You had no choice about going home because you were unable to walk. But later, when your father came home, he acted as if you weren't there. You were devastated. Today, you are carrying not only guilt for the death of these men, but you are also carrying this rejection from your father. Deep within, you feel hopeless about your worth. In this lifetime, instead of trying to prove yourself to him, you are trying to prove that you don't need him. But this is the same thing: it is your need to have your father's acceptance and love. More than that, you want his acknowledgment as an equal, and you want to be seen."

As the dynamic with his father, and the karmic patterns began to be clear, there quickly emerged another lifetime with his father:

"This time the lifetime goes far back, to Athens. At that time, you were brothers. You were very competitive with each other. You were always competing athletically. You were in a race together and your brother was ahead of you. He turned around, to see where you were, and he fell. Instead of racing past him, you stopped and picked him up, and helped him to get back into the race again.

"Somewhere toward the finish line, you were racing pretty much side by side, when a dog suddenly came out onto the track. When you tried to avoid him, you fell. Your brother paused, just a beat, and looked at you, and then he just took off and won the race. He never, ever acknowledged to you or anyone else what you had done for him.

"This was such a deep hurt in you that you haven't gotten past it, the unfairness of it, and the fact that he had the opportunity to make it right. And, ironically, your pride kept you from saying anything. You thought it was up to him to tell people that you would have won the race if you hadn't stopped to help him. Your brother never told anyone; you didn't either.

"The feeling of betrayal by your brother/father and that you can't trust him has remained with you into this incarnation; you remain determined not to forgive him. There was this thing between the two of you; he knew, and you knew, that in that situation, you were the better man, but he wouldn't tell anyone what had happened.

"So you got stuck feeling superior, and you can't connect with him. He owes you from a long, long time ago. But it hurts your pride to go to him. Today, you think the money he gives you is tainted. The money is just energy, neither positive nor negative, but because it comes from him, in your mind, it is tainted.

"Unfortunately, you closed the door to forgiving him and healing the relationship; if you were open to healing it, you wouldn't have to fight."

Randy has begun to see how he is perpetuating the distrust between him and his father and is ready to reconsider it. Below you will find a transcript of his discussion with Maitra:

R: I am happy that some doors are beginning to open.

M: You have come to equate money with love, and you are pushing it away. You have a lot to forgive your father for. If you want to be free, you must forgive him. Otherwise, you remain bound to him for as many lifetimes as it takes. You do love him, so you already know that you are capable of moving beyond the competitiveness and the difficulties.

R: I am free of the competition.

M: No, not yet. When you are free from it, there won't be an issue. You will be like brothers. Regarding the money, you must take it and accept it symbolically, because that would mean that the places where you have closed off your receptivity can begin to open again.

You think you're alone, and nobody can help you, but it's not true. I am very happy that you came here, to clear this up.

Randy's Transformation

After several months of thought and experimentation with the ideas from the Reading, Randy is beginning to change his perspective on his relationship with his father, as revealed in his observations:

"The insights and information from the past lives moved a lot inside of me. Both positions are familiar to me: Being a participant playing a role, as well as being in the position of the observer. So I went home with these stories and had a long conversation with my mother because she is sensitive and open to these kinds of insights. I also wanted to discuss it with my father, although I noticed this wasn't as important after my conversation with my mother. Processing the insights was most important. I thought it over: If I don't tell him about it, am I then the person who doesn't say anything, as I was in the past life, even though I now have access to it, and I'm keeping it to myself? Yet I felt that it was important for me to first look into myself.

"I find it difficult to say 'No,' if someone needs or wants something from me. What's happened to me regarding money since the Reading, is that I'm having an easier time setting an appropriate price for my work when somebody wants something from me.

"I now see that when I lost my job due to an argument with my boss, it was my responsibility. I was pushed to a limit because my previous way of living with a regular income ended abruptly. Then I decided to no longer work just for money, but rather to do some work that I liked to do. It was a matter of finding my confidence. In this phase, I also learned how to budget and determine what I can afford, and to have fewer expectations when I'm helping people.

"Through the Reading, I could understand why I am generally so active and why I am involved in so many projects today. This is a good illustration of my wanting to 'be seen.' Something has now shifted in me. I am aware that I didn't want to do things the way my father did. I didn't aspire to a military career, or to go into politics. I very consciously took a different path. I could have studied medicine. Nevertheless, I emphatically said 'No' to this. My parents would have also liked me to become a lawyer because I'm very articulate. Again, 'No.'

"After my brother emigrated to North America, and my parents became grandparents to our children, many things changed. Today, my parents say that they have been able to learn a lot from how we raise our children. They also value our involvement in the community and how we live. My relationship with my father is heading toward peace. After having been a rebel, I'm learning how to hold my own.

"When the Reading told me about the race in Athens, I had, and still have, very strong, images. I can draw them; I see all the details, the buildings in the background, the racetrack, etc. I can relate to the images described in the Reading that illustrate the subtle feelings still operating between my father and me. I can't judge whether I'm a better person because my father didn't help me in the same way as I helped him at that time, and we have never talked about it. Nevertheless, I was deeply moved, especially because I looked up to him as the successful one. I have always had a longing, up until today, that he sees and accepts me.

"I'm learning, from this experience, to heal from childhood injuries and to open myself to being reconciled with my father, and accepting him, as well as others, without conditions. Even if our relationship is still occasionally put to the test, I am making less of an effort to be viewed as different. Now I can accept myself, for the most part. I understand the meaning of the things that I create and I trust my visions.

"Am I still rebellious? Today it's no longer about revolution for me; I'm learning to be able to stand up for what I believe, without having to fight. I was once traveling in India when an old man asked me what I was doing there. I answered him, saying that I was writing about the world and hope. He looked at me and responded, smiling, with an old proverb: 'Hope is the first doubt of life.' I was irritated at first. It turned my ideas upside-down. When I began to think about this more deeply, it took me to the moment when reality is experienced as magical—pure and without judgment. The rebel in me is fading through my readiness to accept everything as it is."

Your task is not to seek for love, but merely to seek and find all the barriers within yourself that you have built against it.

—Rumi

For Your Toolkit: Personalizing

This teaching comes from Patricia Sun, a spiritual teacher and host of a radio show in California. This is Maitra's version of her teaching on how to take things less personally:

Imagine that you are in your living room and you see the moon through the window. When you see it, you say to it, 'Moon, so good to see you! Where have you been?' The moon doesn't respond; you go about your business, and several minutes later you notice that the moon has traveled to the other side of the window.

'Moon!' you say, 'What are you doing? You never said one word to me and now you're going away again.' The moon says nothing. You leave the room for a few minutes, and when you return, the moon is gone. You immediately throw yourself down on the floor, sobbing and beating your fist on the floor. Continuing to cry, you say loudly, 'You never cared about me. You just go your own way and never think of anybody else! Why didn't you tell me you don't love me anymore?' (This lament can stretch for months or even years.)

What was the moon doing?

Just being the moon, following its path. None of its behavior has anything to do with you. If you could begin to see everyone as the moon and understand that their behavior has nothing to do with you (even when they and you think it does), much of your pain and suffering regarding relationships will begin to dissipate.

Did you really expect the moon to consider your feelings before it rotated around us? We keep on thinking, 'If that person loved me, they would __________ (fill in the blank).' These kinds of expectations are an aspect of personalizing that keeps you from the happiness that we all long for. You will have to let go of some (or all!) of the expectations that were programmed into you since childhood.

Freedom and happiness are attainable, if you want them enough to let go of your expectations.

Chapter 19: My Relationship with My Mother

For Your Toolkit: Owning Your Power

(Laura, born 1955)

Laura, a mother of four, a kindergarten teacher, and later an artist and art teacher, came for a Reading after hearing one of Maitra's talks. She came with the question: "Is there a connection between my breast cancer and my relationship with my mother?" She was dealing well with her cancer, and it was in remission when she came for the Reading. Laura was familiar with the idea of karma and suspected there might be something there to uncover.

Maitra moved into a previous incarnation with Laura and her mother immediately:

"I see a sandy, ochre-colored landscape, with mountain ranges in the distance. I see you in a community of women who live together. The housing is relatively simple; it's a warm climate, and the women aren't wearing much clothing. I see your mother, an imposing woman leader of this community; she holds a strong position of power. She is the authoritarian head of this community. You are her daughter, like today, when you are again in these roles.

"The women in this community had children; everybody looked after them together because the assignments among everyone were fluid. Several were already mothers, others weren't yet. There was a hierarchical relationship between you and your mother; there was a certain tension between the two of you.

"This tension arose because you had different opinions; your mother's leadership was very authoritarian, and the women were kept down. There were strict rules and regulations within the community that everyone had to follow. As the daughter of the ruler, you were expected to be her successor and to accept her style of leadership. It was assumed that things would continue in the same way because leaders, traditionally, would pass the rules on to their successors.

"When you were growing up, you had already developed different views; you were in favor of more unity and equality among the women. Your ideas and concepts were more inclusive for those living together in the community: For example, one should build community together, it should be less hierarchical, and less authoritative. One could say, it should be more compassionate and tolerant. You simply had a different view, an underlying concept, that was different from what had been customary. This led to a conflict between you and your mother; she placed many expectations on you.

"You began to have more and more doubts about how your mother ruled, and you began, in your own way, to cut the umbilical cord. You already had a different consciousness than your mother and other ideas, and you didn't want to play by her rules. It was against your principles, and against your intuitive feel for life, to treat the women as if they were inferior, or even humiliate them, as she did, to keep your position.

"As a result, there was a split; you removed yourself from her authority and built up your own way of living in a community. This wasn't easy for your mother. She couldn't understand you; she was disappointed because she had to let you go. And you took with you the people who agreed with your kind of leadership and way of life.

"Today, we call the women who lived in these communities 'Amazons.' They were strong, independent women who created their own way of life, meeting ritually with men once a year in spring to procreate."

Laura's Transformation

Laura's interview was some months later, and she was eager to share her insights:

"Because I perceive things primarily visually, I experienced the Reading with Maitra as a film. I saw many inner pictures, with strong colors of a hilly, light brown, ochre-colored landscape. There weren't many bright colors. There is a feeling of strength, accompanied by the wind. This is not a strength that anchors a person; this power pulls at you. This is a feminine characteristic, a female power. But there are no maternal images. There is lots of movement, and it feels intense. I see these pictures clearly, and I feel them. They come to me, and I remember them.

"These images from the past life made it clear to me that community is very important to me, and that I like to share my visions and ideas with others. I'm clear when it comes to my mother's attitude: 'I am the queen. I am the ruler, and things are the way I want them.' This is how I've always experienced her, and I still disagree with her.

"The Reading brought up many images, and they explained a lot of things to me. They have helped me, again and again, to better understand my relationship with my mother, and why I have kept a healthy distance from her. I see myself today at a different point in life. As a mother, one always has a certain amount of power, for example, when the children are small. But I wasn't interested in power. I was interested in justice, community, and social behavior within these power relations.

"My mother tried to give us confidence in our individuality. This was very important to her. It's important to me that my own children become happy human beings, and that they can be happy with other people.

"I can identify strongly with the militarism of the Amazons. I recognize my fighting spirit, and I view it positively. The negative side of it is my extreme drive to fight to the point of vindictiveness. These aggressive parts of me offer a clear relationship to this past life, and this helps me to better manage my strong feelings and reactions. I'm becoming aware that I still have this protective instinct; it has been stored in my cells from an earlier time when it perhaps made more sense within another cultural context. In conflicts, I often feel that I would like most of all to be able to protect myself with a sword or a knife. I now understand much better why this is so deeply imprinted in me. It helps me to manage my feelings better.

"I am aware that my husband doesn't show this kind of behavior at all. It amazes me, and I'm beginning to notice how powerful this tendency is in me. I don't speak with many people about these emotions and impulses. I wouldn't have a problem thrusting a knife into someone's ribs, for example, if it were necessary to defend myself or someone else.

"I was often in a position where I had to defend others. Now I've reached a point where I recognize that I have to defend myself. I think this relates to my relationship with my mother; she frequently crosses boundaries. Until recently, I never had the feeling that I had to defend myself from her. But now, when I try to understand this more clearly, I realize that I didn't have any safe space as a child, except for my dream world. Up until now, I didn't need to protect myself, and I didn't feel any anger toward my mother.

"Yet the question arises, more and more frequently—I think also because of the breast cancer diagnosis: 'How can I better protect myself and set my boundaries?' There is a conflict in me about setting clear boundaries with my mother because I do like her. 'How can I be loving to her, without her taking advantage of me? What am I to do with my feeling that I am responsible for all of her issues and grievances?' That's the issue that is beginning to get resolved. Because I'm very good at sensing how other people are doing, I sometimes tend to get overly invested in their problems. I am gradually learning to better define my limits. I couldn't learn to do this as a child because my mother didn't recognize my boundaries. It could be related to the power that she wielded in her past life as the leader. The Reading, with its insights into the karmic connections, helped me become more aware of her temperament and my own.

"Today, I know that I can create the distance that I need from my mother. I create a protective shield and keep an inner distance. I am getting better and better at this, because I understand her better, due to the insights that I got from my past life. I see her in a position of power; she demands it and wields it on everyone around her.

"I have become conscious of injuries from my mother ever since I've had breast cancer. When I was in the hospital for the breast surgery, there were unbelievable moments, when even the doctors would have to come to terms with the power that she wielded over me and others. They even noticed how she elevates herself and puts others down. She wants to be the queen and the ruler.

"The story from my past life explained a lot of things to me. Everything is not yet resolved, but I can now deal with it better. I can feel my claims to power, but I have an exaggerated defensive and protective mindset that is not always appropriate. I want to look at this dynamic within me, and as I become more conscious of it, I will be able to better integrate it. I feel strongly that my motivation and goals were always different from those of my mother.

"The Reading didn't suddenly change everything, but it did have an impact over weeks and months. It pointed out changes I have made and the many opportunities I have to develop further. My mother is the way she is, but I can continue to grow. I can decide how to live my life, and who I would like to be. It feels as if my mother is stuck, living in some old patterns. I now recognize these patterns from the past life, and that we still have very different goals.

"For me, the Reading is like a simple instructional manual, a kind of translation, and that is very helpful to me. Over and over again, I feel my aggressiveness in relationships; today I ask myself what my goal is and how I can use my energy in a more meaningful way. I'd like to be able to channel my strong emotions better, so I can reach positive goals. I'd like to be focused in such a way that, if I aim an arrow, it will reach the target—and enable me to move forward. I can also forgive. I would like to see myself as a person who fosters harmony and unity.

"I can't understand when someone shows their desire for harmony half-heartedly. Harmony is very important to me. As I've already mentioned, my protective instinct is strong, and sometimes I don't know where it comes from. Today I can use this story as a tool, in times when conflicts need to be resolved and I can feel the warrior in me.

"I'm quite amazed by my strong, primitive impulses. I feel an entire range of defense mechanisms becoming activated. I feel very comfortable in the role of defender or even aggressor. Sometimes, things have to be taken care of and then it's done. Even during chemotherapy, I didn't feel as if I were in the role of a victim. I could do whatever was necessary to take care of myself while I was there, and then move on. I have dignity when I have some control."

People say walking on water is a miracle, but to me walking peacefully on earth is the real miracle.

—Thích Nhất Hạnh

For Your Toolkit: Owning Your Power

At times, Laura's mother was so controlling that her behavior verged on abusing her power. Sometimes, her behavior crossed the line into real abuse. Her daughter was in revolt and trying to find her power, without becoming like her mother.

Our task, to own our power, is well defined by the dilemma of these two women: How do we take ownership of our power and exercise it, without being abusive or controlling?

Let's look at two public figures who exemplify "Right Use" of power versus those who have caused so much suffering by abusing their power. As you consider these powerful figures, bear in mind what you know, or think to be their intention, when they use their power.

The Dalai Lama is an excellent example of Right Use of power because he is the head of a government—although in exile—as well as a spiritual teacher respected by all the world. Notice that his power is NOT over anybody; rather, his intention, or use of power, is to educate and enlighten others. He is the embodiment of Compassion. His Holiness says, "Love and compassion are necessities, not luxuries. Without them, humanity cannot survive."

And then there is Nelson Mandela: After thirty years in prison, he emerged to become the head of the government in South Africa. How did this happen? Because the power that he had accrued, by refusing to hate his oppressors, was acknowledged and trusted by those same people, the white government. His intention with his power was to heal the wounds of apartheid. As he said, "It is in your hands to create a better world for all who live in it."

Cedar Barstow writes about a compassionate use of power. In her book, *Right Use of Power: The Heart of Ethics*, she defines power as the capacity or potential to bring change. Right use of power, then, would be the capacity or potential to bring about change for the "greatest good for all concerned." When you contemplate exercising your power, ask yourself, "What is my intent? Is it for the greatest good for all concerned?"

If your intentions are clear and good, you need not fear to use your power.

Chapter 20: Feeling and Releasing: Letting Go of My Rage

For Your Toolkit: Healing Your Inner Child

(John, born 1953)

John, an office manager for a non-profit that advocates for people's rights, reluctantly attended Maitra's talk with a friend but was surprised that so much of what he heard rang true for him. Then he surprised himself again by signing up for a Reading. Here is a transcript of his initial conversation with Maitra:

J: Maitra, I was deeply moved by your talk. I feel trapped in a cage, exactly as you described in your lecture. I just want to change something. I've been working at the same place for eleven years, and I have so many ideas. The thought of working there until I retire doesn't feel good.

I know how to bring harmony into homes and other environments. But I don't yet fully trust myself to pursue it. I have 2,000 brochures at home and would like to distribute them, but I have a barrier that prevents me from going through with this. It feels as if there is a wall, a basic fear, that keeps me locked in. I have so many ideas one day, and then, the next day, I think to myself, 'Oh, no, that won't work. I can't do that.' My friends have also noticed my ambivalence, and it affects my relationships. My wife has accepted the situation; she has come to terms with it, but there has been conflict in recent years. I can explain this; I had a big conflict with my father.

M: Is your father still alive?

J: No, my parents are dead. My father was very authoritarian and beat us a lot, and he drank. I rejected him as a father. Perhaps this is the origin of the conflict.

M: How old were you when you pushed your father away?

J: Throughout my childhood, as long as I can remember.

M: When you were three or four years old, was he too strict or too harsh?

J: I think, when I was five or six years old, I had an affectionate relationship with my mother. My father was simply too strict for me.

M: Would you be willing to try something that might throw light on your relationship with your father?

J: Yes.

M: Imagine him sitting at the end of your bed, and visualize that you have plopped down behind him. You put your hands on his shoulders and feel: What do you feel from him?

J: I sense that he wanted to do his best for us.

M: What are your feelings for him?

J: I feel a certain distance from him. At the moment, I don't perceive him as an authoritarian person, but more as a small, shy man.

M: Yes, yes. Do you feel love for him?

J: Yes, I can feel it.

M: And do you want to understand him?

J: Yes.

M: Imagine yourself going inside of him so that you are now inside his head, and when you look through his eyes, you are looking at yourself, his small son. When you look at John, what do you see?

J: I see a little Johnny in front of me.

M: Yes. What was your father's name?

J: Ralph.

M: What do you see when you look at little Johnny? What do you feel? Ralph, do you love this little boy?

J: Yes, I do.

M: What do you think of him?

J: Somehow, I can't access this feeling.

M: Do you know what I hear him saying when he looks at you?

J: What?

M: (speaking for Ralph) I see my heart.

J: Hmm.

M: What I feel from your father is that he was very afraid for you and worried about you. He thought you were too soft, and that it was his responsibility to make you strong for this world. He could see your light, and he believed that you wouldn't be able to make it in this world. You were too soft. He tried to strengthen you by being so strict with you. Can you feel how much he loved you?

J: Yes.

M: He was a man who lacked the tools to express himself, and he was unable to feel safe and comfortable in this world. He saw your innocence, and your sensitivity, and thought this wouldn't work for you. This explains why you built this wall around yourself, to please him, and because you loved him. You accepted the restrictions that he placed on you. And when you think about going out into the world, with your big heart and your sensitivity toward others, you're convinced that you won't be able to manage in this world because you have allowed your father's fear to define you.

The truth is, your father's version of reality killed him. His harshness separated him from other people; it isolated him. He was very lonely. And he could never see another way.

You have already broken many of these childhood patterns, haven't you?

J: Yes, I think so.

M: When you break free, and realize who you are, you become your father's teacher, whether he is in the body or not. Your father is present with us right now (in spirit), and he is hoping that you can liberate yourself. Tell me your full name and your date of birth.

J: I have a problem with my name. I always have the feeling that I should have another name.

M: What's the problem with your name?

J: I simply don't like the sound of my name; it doesn't feel like me.

M: Really? I agree, another name would be better, but you must discover it for yourself and use it. Your name is indeed too small for you. But first, you need to accept this little boy, your inner child, with his name. John is his name.

There's a story about Ram Dass, a world-famous spiritual teacher. Do you know him?

J: No.

M: His birth name was Richard Alpert. One evening, Ram Dass was on-stage speaking to a large audience, when he glimpsed something out of the corner of his eye. He turned his head and saw little Richard Alpert sitting on a stool, in the corner, sucking his thumb. When he had become Ram Dass (his spiritual name), he let this part of himself go, this little sensitive boy, Richard. When he saw the boy that day, he realized he had abandoned little Richard and that it was important to embrace, love, and heal his inner child.

This is the issue: You must resolve your confusion about your identity. Your challenge is to accept and love this little Johnny. When he is integrated, you can come into more of your potential.

What might your name be then?

J: I don't know. Otherwise, I would have given myself a different name, already a long time ago. I couldn't find another one until now.

M: (reading, surprised) Oh my goodness! OK, this is what I'm receiving. My guide says, "Richard the Lionheart." I asked, "You mean John was Richard the Lionheart?" And my guide said, "Yes."

I know very little about Richard the Lionheart—he was English, a warrior, and became a King. I don't know exactly what this means for you, but it would be good to follow up on it. Learn about him. Perhaps there is a better name for you, but Richard is a name that means courage.

Your inner prison is not very strong. It will restrict you, as long as you allow it, but the moment you decide that you don't need it anymore, it will fall away. A new name will help make that possible.

I have the feeling that you are ready to make this change. You have been constricted for a long time, and you have some good, creative ideas for when you are free to be yourself. You already have brochures and you've done all the preparations to make a new beginning.

At this point, Maitra suggested to John that a past life looking at the karma between him and his father might help to clarify things so that he could be free to be himself. This is the karma that she saw with his father:

"Your father, who is also your father today, was in the Roman army. He was your superior, an officer. You served as his assistant, his indispensable right hand. He relied on you for everything. I see a battle; both armies retreated and they all went their separate ways. The wounded were carried away. There was a cease-fire. Everything was destroyed, your father couldn't be found, and you realized that he had been captured. If he had been killed, his body would have been found on the battleground. This enraged you and everyone else because this wasn't the agreement. It hadn't been agreed that anyone would take prisoners. The agreement was a cease-fire, a retreat, and a time for negotiations.

"Your rank didn't allow you to take part in the negotiations. During the night, you had decided to go, taking with you a few soldiers, to find the place where he was being held captive and bring him back. You went into the enemy camp with five other men. You killed the guard, and you made your way, very quietly and carefully, to the tent where you thought he was being held captive.

"You opened the tent, ready to fight, but he wasn't there. There were a few other prisoners, whom no one had yet noticed were missing. You could free these people, but they had no idea where to find your father.

"The negotiations broke off the next day, and they dragged your father out, and put him on display. They threatened to execute him if your army didn't voluntarily surrender. He was a general in the field, but others ranked above him. They were all furious about this. They didn't want to surrender. And above all, they didn't want to be blackmailed. So they said, 'NO!' And you had to watch your father, the General, be beheaded. The result was a renewal of the battle.

"This traumatic experience stayed with you for a long time. You became an extremely angry and single-minded person. You moved through many lifetimes with this energy of pain and rage. Fairness and keeping agreements continued to be important to you. The memory of your father's beheading was excruciating for you because you had failed to rescue him. Before the next phase of that war was over, you had, in your rage at the broken agreements, killed many people. You hated the enemy, and you hated yourself for hating the enemy."

John was shaken by this information—he had never viewed himself as an angry man, but rather more of a victim. Maitra was able to help him put this into perspective. A transcription of their discussion follows:

M: After many lives in which you suffered from debilitating inner conflict, something finally began to change inside. You awakened spiritually, and you made a vow to never kill anyone again.

If anger arises in you today, the memory, though vague, reminds you of where the rage led you in the past. If this rage took over, you would kill again. Your vow stops you not only from losing control but from feeling any kind of rage. We're looking at a very long span of time, approximately from the Roman Empire, 2000 years ago, until today, and you no longer have the automatic impulse in you to lose control and kill someone. You know yourself well enough to know that you would no longer do this, with or without the vow. You have anger in you, that arises and can be expressed, but it can no longer get out of control in this way. I don't think you fully understand how much you have evolved from those events. You are still afraid that your rage could get out of control. I don't know if you are ready to put aside this vow or promise; perhaps you still don't trust yourself enough.

It will help you to do some release work with the anger. One way to do that is to get a cardboard box, tape the top shut, and kick it to pieces, the next time the rage threatens to get out of control. Of course, it may feel risky to know how much anger you have. But when you do this in a safe environment, it will lead you to a place where you can free yourself, and resolve the pain and anger in you. This explains why you have kept yourself in a cage: You have restricted yourself because you don't want to hurt anybody.

Your creative potential, the scope of your mind, doesn't have enough space, as long as you keep yourself locked in this cage. Richard the Lionheart represents the courageous mind, but he is also a warrior. He has proven himself in battle. If you accept and integrate the warrior in you, this fighting spirit can help you heal.

Do you know Dan Millman's book, *The Way of the Peaceful Warrior*? This is an aspect of your challenge. For me, this is *you*. You can't reach your potential without feeling the warrior inside and taking it into account.

How are you? How are you doing?

J: Yes, this makes sense. My wife has said that she is afraid of my rage.

M: Yes, she can feel it. Can you also feel it? It is time to face it and deal with it so that it is channeled and emerges in safe ways. Another way to release anger is by beating a bed with a tennis racquet. Then you'll be sure that nothing gets broken. That will help because your fear of being destructive is still there.

I knew a man who wanted to raise money for a charity. He bought an old, beat-up car and charged people ten dollars a strike to smash the car with a sledge hammer. He made a lot of money for his charity in this way. Whatever method or methods you choose, it will be freeing. When you are free, if you still want to, you can take your brochures and distribute them.

Regarding your work, do you understand what you are doing? It is clear enough in one way, but I think you move people more than you realize. You help people when they need support. You tend to think about this in a way that makes you feel that you don't do enough. I hope you can begin to see the value of your work because you are helping lots of people. It is the energy that you give, the fact that you care. Learn to be satisfied with yourself.

You get to the point where you see that you can proceed on the spiritual path only so fast, because of your own karmic limitations. Here you begin to recognize the timing of spiritual work. You cannot get ahead of yourself, or be phony-holy, because it comes back and hits you in the head.

—Ram Dass

For Your Toolkit: Healing Your Inner Child

There is an "inner child" within each of us who carries the traumas that we suffered as a child. The resulting long-term fears, anger, and sadness may be buried deep in our unconscious, but they stay with us, and have an effect on us until we heal them. A person, who is spiritually awake—conscious of the interconnectedness of all life—soon becomes aware of reactions that are out of proportion to the current events that may have seemed to cause them.

You can begin this healing process on your own, by setting aside five minutes or so in the morning when you wake up, and another five minutes or so, as you're getting ready for bed. Use those few minutes to visualize (imagine) yourself at about four years old, and have a conversation, focused on establishing trust, with this child, who has been a part of you, though you've not been conscious of it, for all these years. Find out what your inner child needs and provide it for this little one. When I started this work with the inner child, my little one wanted to ride the merry-go-round, and it took twelve times around before she said it was enough. Imagine me, age thirty-five, amongst all the children riding over and over again by myself, while the parents watched us from the sidelines!

If your childhood was a difficult one, you may want to consider doing healing work with your inner child. I suggest you first educate yourself about the inner child; there are many books and workbooks available to help you understand this concept. Here are two books I especially like: For beginners, John Bradshaw's *Homecoming: Reclaiming and Healing Your Inner Child*, and for a more all-encompassing spiritual view, read Thích Nhất Hạnh's *Reconciliation: Healing the Inner Child*. There are also workshops to help you heal.

Like past lives, this re-parenting process, as it is also called, will change your past by changing your programming. It will help you to be more 'free to be' you—the spontaneous, loving, authentic You that got lost somewhere along the way.

CHAPTER 21: MY PROFESSION AND MY SKIN

FOR YOUR TOOLKIT: GETTING OFF THE WHEEL OF KARMA

Dreams and Readings with Jim (born 1989) and Jim's mother, Susanne (born 1963)

Susanne, an artist and healer, came to Maitra, still reeling from the effects of a powerful series of dreams about her son, Jim, who was, at that time, a dedicated and serious pre-med student. The fear that the dreams had roused in her was palpable. A transcript of Susanne's description of her dream follows:

"I see a Parthenon on a hill, like the Acropolis in Athens. It is a holy mountain, and I am in a spacious room and fully engaged with the people around me. I see a large picture with a figure on it. There were many students in the room and the picture was to be unveiled. I'm called out of the room at some point and I am now near the Parthenon, which I had seen high up on a hill in front of me. I met Jim, my son, there and we knew each other well in the dream. He tells me that he wants to leave, that he wants to go to Marduk. I was surprised by his plans and his determination. On the one hand, I thought this was good and I recognized his desire to experience and discover the world; on the other hand, it frightened me. A difficult farewell lay ahead; he would travel far away, and who knows when, or whether he would return.

"I didn't feel like his mother in the dream, as I do today, but rather like a girlfriend or sister about the same age, who knew him well and felt close to him. We were both students.

"A bit later, I had another dream about Jim, my son, who suffers from neurodermatitis. In the dream, he arrives home with a skin rash above his right eye. He is sad, and says to me, 'Look, I have a rash again, it's here again.' I am perplexed because I know that as soon as the rash is healed, it shows up again somewhere else. I know he suffers, and I try to help him to calm down. In the dream, I can feel the despair he's fighting.

"The same night, toward morning, I had another dream. I was with Jim in a strange, bare room. He seemed to be sick and lay on his side on the floor. There were other people in the room with dark skin, North Africans or Asians. They were young and weren't that concerned about the sick person on the floor.

"He was lying in pain and I bent over him. It was horrible for me to see him like this, and I couldn't help him. He writhed in pain, but he was already too weak to stand up; I saw that he was vomiting. A thick, light-colored fluid flowed from his mouth that looked like pus; it was horrifying. What could I do? Then I saw how the area around his mouth had dissolved, the gums had quickly disintegrated, and this part of his face had transformed into a skull. Everything dissolved and the teeth moved forward. He let out an unendingly agonized, despairing scream, deep and long, and filled with every imaginable emotion. This long, excruciating scream woke me up; I continued to hear his screaming.

"I was overwhelmed by these images, and his screaming echoed in my ears. The dream felt so real; I had the feeling that I had heard it here in my bedroom. I asked myself, 'What is it that has made me dream something so disturbing?' Fear arose in me, and I wondered if it was a premonition of death. But I also had the feeling that it might have played out in another dimension or a different life. I was teary the entire day; my emotional response was so strong. As soon as I was alone, I cried over the horrible images and the helplessness I had felt in this dream. It was terrifying.

"At that time, I knew Maitra's work and her access to the Akashic Records. I decided to do a Reading with her because I was having difficulties dealing with this dream and its implications. I also asked Jim—I had told him about the dream—whether he wanted to have a Reading. He agreed to it. So it happened that we had our Readings on the same day, Jim first, and then me.

"When I began to relate my traumatic dream, Maitra listened very carefully. When I was finished, she said that I had seen a part of a past life in the dream, and this had also been revealed to Jim in his Reading. She thought that I had understood the traumatic part of the dream and that I had seen how his life at that time was painfully coming to an end. Jim was already on his way elsewhere after his Reading. Maitra encouraged me to call him and get his permission for us to talk about the past life that he had just experienced in his Reading. I reached him by phone and he agreed."

When Susanne and Jim compared notes, it became apparent that Susanne was tuned in to her son and aware of the difficult karma with which he was dealing. Although the details were quite different, energetically there was a lot of similarity. This offers a beautiful lesson in the awareness that connects us to the people with whom we are close.

Jim came to his Reading primarily with the question as to whether medical school is the right path for him. Sometimes he has doubts. He considers the very strong, rational way of teaching in medicine to be one-sided and he gets the feeling that his intuitive approach is unacceptable to the powers that be; he has to hide this part of himself.

Since he'd been suffering from neurodermatitis for several years, he'd also like to know what advice Maitra can give him about this, and whether there could be karmic reasons for it. The following is Jim's Reading with a particularly challenging past life:

M: Tell me your full name, the one you use.

J: Jim ...

M: Your name tells me you have many opportunities and exciting choices ahead of you.

After hearing his name, Maitra found it was an easy transition to the following past life:

M: "You were a Greek man captured and enslaved when you were involved in a battle at sea. You were an officer on the ship, an aide to the captain. You were training to become a captain yourself. But that didn't make any difference when you became a slave; you were then simply a body, a laborer. At the time, there were many battles and raids by pirates on the Mediterranean Sea. Ships were plundered, and people were enslaved and sold.

"I see a very clear picture of the pyramids in Egypt. You and many others were brought here as slaves. You are helping to carry and move these big stones. Many of your life circumstances were connected to this. You were a worker slave, and you also had a talent for working with animals. Many people and animals were needed to move these huge stones. The foreman noticed that you were good at dealing with the animals so he took you away from your previous heavy labor."

Jim, excited, was moved to say something: "Last summer I became absorbed with the pyramids and Egyptian culture. I read a lot about it, and I grappled with it, and with the theme of slavery."

Maitra responded:

"Yes, this fits perfectly. You were carrying something heavy on your shoulders with ropes. The foreman freed you from this work and sent you to work with the animals because not many people understood how to convince the animals to work so hard. This was a mixed blessing for you. On the one hand, you no longer had to do this very hard physical labor. You could now do something that wasn't as demanding on your body, but at the same time, you hated being forced to work these animals to death; they couldn't live for very long under such harsh conditions. Nor could the people.

"Nobody was concerned about the conditions of the slaves. No workers, human or animal, got enough time to rest, or enough to eat. There were simply so many slaves that you could work them to death. They were replaceable, expendable.

"Time went by and then something happened to one of the mules. One animal bit an animal next to it, and this caused the entire line of them to come to a halt. People were injured, and time was lost. You were next to the animal who did the biting at the time, and you were found guilty of being negligent. You were sent back to your previous work, hauling stones.

"The same overseer, who had returned you to the line of haulers, had killed the two animals; he continued to watch you the entire time. He was brutal, he beat you for no reason, screamed at you, and you became more and more enraged. You understood the mule very well, the one that had become aggressive and bit its neighbor.

"There was a young boy next to you in the workers' line, about seventeen years old. He was small for his age and very anxious. Because he was so small, everybody—the other slaves and the foremen—would pick on him. He could never do anything right. You thought he was courageous and doing his best. You tried to protect him, by working even harder so that people wouldn't notice how exhausted he already was.

"The foreman came over to the two of you during a mealtime, while everyone stopped for a few minutes to have some bread and water. You were sitting on a stone, and the young boy was sitting on the ground and was leaning against the same stone. The two of you were talking to each other very softly so that nobody could hear you, and he said to you, 'I can't do this after today.' And you answered, 'Don't lose your courage, just act as if you are working, and I'll try to take over as much of the work as I can. Rest from time to time, and just act as if you were pulling.' He tried not to cry, but tears ran down his face, and he repeated, 'I can't do this anymore, I can't go on.'

"Suddenly somebody was standing over the two of you. It was the overseer with his whip. He went over to the young man and kicked him: 'If you think that you can get away with not doing your work, you're wrong. I have been watching you.' Then he turned to you and also kicked you in the leg, and said, 'You think you can trick me by what you're doing?!'

"Then he began to whip the boy on his head and shoulders. He beat him to the ground and didn't stop kicking and beating him. Now you lost control. You could no longer bear it; you lost your temper—you stood up, took the whip out of his hand and began to hit him on the head. Then a small rebellion began in the rows of other men.

"Everyone hated this foreman because he was so brutal, and the other slaves also began to hit him. They shoved you aside and began to beat him with stones, and when they stopped, he was lying on the ground, bloody; he was dead.

"Other supervisors came over to you and asked, 'Who started this?' They realized that if they were to execute all of you, there would be too many of you, and it would be detrimental to the work that had to get done, so they couldn't do that. But they wanted to know who had instigated it and everyone said, 'He started it, himself,' and pointed to the dead foreman.

"The supervisor asked again, 'But who was the one who resisted him?' Nobody said a word and they all stood together, silent. Then the supervisor said, 'Then all of you will be punished.'

"The punishment was many whippings. The first one they grabbed was the small boy whom you had earlier defended when he was whipped by this foreman. He looked the most afraid and guilty. They gave him many lashes with the whip and it killed him. He didn't want to live any longer; the lashes hit his body in such a way that he immediately died. Then you said, 'Don't beat any others, I was the one.'

"This is what they had been waiting for. Your punishment was something like 100 lashes. That was enough to kill you and was also their intent. They wanted to punish you so much that you wouldn't be able to survive, and they wanted everyone to see this so that they would obey later. They had no use for slaves who rebelled or resisted.

"But you said to yourself, 'That was the only thing I could do because I was so helpless and they were so strong.' You knew that they intended to kill you. The only thing you could do was refuse to acquiesce. Even if you knew that it was hopeless, you could choose to say something to show them that you were still a man. That's why you decided to resist.

"The punishment was carried out the next day; they rounded up all the slaves and workers to watch it. The workers were excused from work during this time to show them what happens if you rebel against a supervisor.

"Every time they whipped you, you would say something defiant that would provoke them: 'You can hurt my body, but you can't hurt my spirit.' You would curse and swear at them: 'May your entire family die from the same punishments. May all of you lose everything you own.' Three men would take turns beating you because it was too exhausting for just one person. As long as you were still able to speak, you managed to hold onto your self-respect and not feel like a victim by cursing them: 'May you lose your eyesight.' And when it was your skin that was hurt, defiled, and bleeding: 'May what you are doing to me, be done to you.'

"You died; in fact, you bled to death. The whip injured you terribly; it tore your skin open so deeply in crucial spots. Today, you would understand this because you are now studying medicine. You didn't remain alive as long as they wanted you to, because you lost so much blood. And you lost so much energy during all of this, that you could no longer speak, but you nevertheless screamed your outrage with all your remaining strength.

"Every time you said something, you could feel a surge of hope in the slaves. You felt their identification with you, their pride in you until the last moment, and that somebody dared to rebel, even if he would be executed for it.

"In the end, you were happy to die. It was a great relief to leave your body and to no longer have to bear so much pain. You met with two spiritual guides who immediately communicated the following to you: 'You need to see that you let yourself be pulled into the slaveholder's reality. Sadly, you did to them what they did to you. Internally, you are more mature. Before you became a slave, you were a leader, a person who was on his way to becoming a captain of a ship; you were in a position of great responsibility and respect. If you hadn't been so intelligent and mature, you wouldn't have been tested in this way.'

"The guides explained to you about the testing, and that you let yourself fall to a lower level. You responded to them, saying, 'Look at all these people, who also watched this; it gave them hope for the first time.'

"And the spiritual guides, who spoke to you, said, 'You're right, it gave them hope, but this hope was also accompanied by the feeling of wanting to destroy an enemy. There was this energy of war, the energy of fighting back, and retaliation.'

"They continued to say, 'You therefore have to pay attention. You have to straighten this out. You know what Jesus said, that you have to turn the other cheek. He didn't mean by this that you shouldn't stand up for yourself. He meant that you shouldn't sink to the same low level, that you shouldn't do the same to others as what is done to you, and that you should be a thinking and conscious person. Don't injure another person who has injured you, which means, 'Don't do what they do.' When Jesus was in agony on the cross, he didn't curse those who put him there. Instead, he said, 'Father, forgive them, for they know not what they do.'

"Let's remember here the exact words of the Golden Rule: 'Do unto others as you would have them do unto you.' When you admitted that you were the one who started the conflict, you followed this commandment, the Golden Rule. That confession spared others from punishment, from suffering."

Maitra continued to explain the karmic implications, giving examples. She knew it was vital for Jim to understand:

"In today's world, we can say that the Dalai Lama is a person who knows how to do this. Nelson Mandela is another; he suffered in prison, came out and forgave everybody, including all those who hurt him, locked him up, and kept him in prison over all these years. Mandela reminds us: 'As I walked out the door toward the gate that would lead to my freedom, I knew if I didn't leave my bitterness and hatred behind, I'd still be in prison.' Later, he was recognized as a bringer of peace between the races in South Africa. These are some examples of people who did what your soul wants you to do.

"I think you have already tested yourself in many lives, and you are not a warrior who intends to kill people. You are not seeking revenge. You had lives—I could count them—at least three lifetimes, in which you tried to resolve conflicts that led you into similar situations. What remains in this life, is what you feel in your body. It is the effect of the curses that you sent out into the universe in that previous life. They're coming back to you, even though you haven't said such a thing to anyone in your present life. If you had understood how the universe works, you would have known that it comes back to you. Whatever you send out, comes back, good or bad. Today we say, 'What goes around, comes around.' This is the universal Law of Karma.

"What is coming back to you is the feeling of revenge and the curses that you had wished on others. Your body is somehow or other in conflict with this energy. I don't know how you handle rage these days. Do you find that you are sometimes very temperamental or become angry very quickly? But you never go so far as to want to hurt somebody nor would you kill them. (Pause) Yes! I can see it—through martial arts, you have found a way to channel this energy so that you don't harm others.

"What you must do next is find the compassion for yourself, that you so easily find for others.

"The man who you were at that time—we can call him Adrian—when I look at him, I can't condemn him for what he did. I can't say that he did something terrible, although he cursed these people. It was all that was left for him, he was so helpless. He fought back in the only way that he could think of. But he cursed those people without understanding the consequences of his behavior. He didn't know anything about karma, that it would come back to him.

"Your task for today is to forgive Adrian for being, understandably, full of hatred and having a thirst for revenge. We can understand it today, but from the perspective of the soul, it is now necessary for you to stop punishing yourself. The stress that you have today is a kind of mirroring of how your soul viewed this event in the past life.

"Today, you expect yourself to be the best, to be perfect, to be flawless. But the current stress that you are feeling from that attitude affects your body; it's what you are doing to yourself. To forgive yourself, to find compassion for yourself, means that you desire to end your suffering, from deep in your heart. That will transform the curses into blessings, do you understand? The curses come back to you and this is what is now affecting you—these terrible irritations in your body, in your skin. These curses need to be transformed into blessings. It could be that talking about it today will be sufficient for you to understand this so that when another opportunity comes to you, you will recognize that you have released yourself from that pattern.

"You can make up for this in the moment, and correct it. But if you don't improve as much as you would like, there is a technique to heal it. You can imagine yourself in that past life situation and remember those curses that you hurled at the perpetrators. Also remember, you didn't only curse those men who killed you, and those who ordered them to kill you, but also their families. To punish your torturers for what they did to you, you even wanted their innocent families to suffer.

"Just visualize everything you said to them, and write it out on paper, and then take another piece of paper and change these curses into blessings. For example, if you said, 'It is my wish that your family would die out, that your children would die, that your grandchildren would die, and your name will die out,' then you should write on the other piece of paper, 'It is my wish that your family would learn something from this, about what happened, and that your family will flourish, and may a happy and healthy family be your legacy, a family that has learned not to mistreat other people.'

"You mustn't ignore what you experienced and what they did to you. You can still point to the fact that a lesson has to be learned from this, but without punishment and hatred. You can now wish that they will have a new consciousness that makes them happy by changing, erasing, and rewriting these curses as blessings. And when you are finished doing this, burn the paper with the curses, so that this energy will come to an end and you can free yourself from it and leave it behind you.

"You won't be the only one who experiences this healing; all the souls who were affected by the curses will be affected by the blessings. You will then gain a better understanding of why you are studying medicine today. You have chosen this course of study as your profession because you have felt intuitively that healing needs to happen for you and everyone else affected by these curses. I think you are already on the right track. I can't tell you if you should continue your medical studies. You'll be able to feel what is right for you.

"If you go through this process, it will become evident, and you will know if you would like to continue this course of study. I want to acknowledge that your intuition is good, and your inner guidance is strong. You have already felt it, you have already been moved by this energy. You feel the need to heal yourself and others. This wasn't so clear until now because you didn't consciously know about the curses, although you did know it inside of you, intuitively.

"If you continue your studies, it will also be a healing of this past life; if you don't continue them, it will be because you have the feeling that you have already done enough to heal. Maybe you would like to do something else. I don't know how things will turn out for you. I think that the fear of doing something wrong or losing control, comes from this experience. You surely understand why you acted in this way that led to your death. I hope you will be able to forgive yourself. There is a part of you that hopes that you will never have to repeat anything like that or be in a situation again with so much responsibility. Currently, you are responsible for the negativity that you have placed in the world. But I don't think it's still that strong and overwhelming. You have already done a lot of work to heal. Now that you are more conscious, you can recapture some of the painful images and heal them."

At this point, Maitra checked in with Jim to see how he was processing all of this. She asked, "When I told you the story, were you able to see the pictures along with it?

J: Yes.

M: Now you know what you need to do with these images. I suspect that you have very strong feelings about the topic of slavery. Have you ever thought about it? Do you know that it still exists in this world?

J: Yes, I feel ashamed and it hurts me when I read about it.

M: We have to change our consciousness. I think your shame comes from this memory. It was just below the level of consciousness, and now you are beginning to become aware of it. I hope that this has already begun to shift a lot of things, but you may need to do more to heal it. You will have to come to terms with this; nobody else can make this decision for you. The judge is inside of you and will tell you when you've done enough. When you release yourself, you will be free.

I'm remembering a man named Jack Schwarz. His is your story, too, in your way. It's a matter of replacing hate with an open heart, with love. Hate cannot stand up to an open heart. This is part of your story because Jack was also tortured. He can be your inspiration. His story is an amazing one.

Jack was a Jewish author and teacher from the Netherlands who landed in a concentration camp during World War II. He was tortured daily because they believed he had information that he did not have. He tried reasoning, then fighting them to no avail. He tried screaming, he tried being silent, everything he could think of as the torture went on and on. Finally, he said to himself, 'The only thing I haven't tried is love.' So the next time they were cutting him, he opened his heart and as they cut, his wound healed before their eyes. When it happened several times, the men doing the torture became terrified at what they could not understand, and he was never tortured again. Jack survived the war and went on to demonstrate this healing in presentations all over the world. In San Francisco, I saw him put a railroad spike through his arm and then pull it out, bleeding profusely, and heal it before our eyes. He walked around the audience and showed us; that there was not a mark on his arm.

Jim's Transformation

The following interview with Jim took place a few years after the Reading:

"Throughout the entire Reading, I had a very strong, emotionally-charged response. I continuously got goose bumps; something in me resonated strongly with this story. Through the Reading, and the insights into this tragic past life, I gained a new level of understanding, and some relief from my painful skin condition. My troubles with my skin didn't simply disappear.

"The cause of my tragic ending in the past life was that I lost control over my feelings and resisted the brutality of the foreman. This opened up a whole flood of further consequences, resulting in our two deaths from the whippings. In some way, in the present, I became aware that deep down, inside of me, I was still afraid of losing control over myself. Underneath this fear, is a feeling that it could end badly, that I could be punished, or even lose my life. Over many years, I have been able to channel and work off some of this energy and also some of my fears through martial arts.

"It occurred to me afterward that, throughout my entire life, I have often been involved with hot-tempered people, as if I attract this type of person. I would get into situations where these people would have emotional outbursts, and this recurred in many different circumstances. I asked myself what this had to do with me. I can see now that it had something to do with these deep, old past life experiences, and that something in me was being mirrored. If I have people around me who are somewhat explosive or easily upset, I tend to withdraw. Because I continue to attract these kinds of situations, I ask myself if I can learn to allow feelings, above all, strong and uncomfortable ones like rage, give up some control, and even make mistakes. I'd like to be less of a perfectionist.

"I lived for a year in an apartment with housemates, and one time I had a memory, just a glimpse like a lightning flash, of this past life from the Reading. I was working together with my three housemates in the common garden. One of them was especially impulsive and volatile. I was carrying weeds in a wheelbarrow. It was a hot day and I had taken off my shirt. He came toward me, with a branch in his hand and whipped me with it as a joke, across my back, to push me forward. All the images and feelings of this past life flashed through my mind. It was so unexpected; I was completely shocked by this graphic memory.

"It was such an amazing surprise to have this vivid memory. It was already a few years since the Reading. For a time, I felt that I was in an altered state; this memory caught up with me, and became real to me. The feeling was of an 'Aha experience,' a deeper insight, and some connections began to align in me.

"I felt that these three housemates were always a bit against me. They would sometimes attack me for rather insignificant things as if I had done something wrong to them. They often demanded that I respond exactly as they wanted; their demands frequently seemed pretty extreme. Of course, some of this was justified, but sometimes I felt that what they wanted from me was simply too demanding and excessive. In that moment, when my roommate whipped me, 'for the fun of it,' these old memories flared up again. I made all these connections, and it felt as if these three housemates at that time were the overseers in my past life, carrying out my death sentence by whipping me to death. I realized that they were still dealing with it unconsciously, on a subtle level, but for me, everything became clear, although I didn't share my memories or my perspective with them.

"When I became aware of this, I felt myself forgive them for everything. I tried to express this reconciliation, silently, at that moment in the garden so that they would somehow be able to perceive it. Sometimes it felt like I was waiting for the right moment to tell them that I forgave them, without them having to understand all the connections. I simply felt this need to forgive, and a wish that they would also be able to forgive me because I felt weighed down by my having cursed them. I think that something deep inside of me was also resolved. My time living with these housemates had come to an end.

"The neurodermatitis has gradually lessened over the past few years. I feel much better in my whole body."

Susanne's Transformation

Now we return to Susanne, Jim's mother, and her dream about Jim. Several years later, she has gained a lot of insight into the dream and can articulate her discoveries:

"This time with the dreams about my son that started on the Acropolis was very intense for me. Everything that the Readings revealed to my son and and me on that day moved me deeply, and in a way relieved me. I understood, on a deeper level, that images and messages from dreams and also from external images such as films or information from books can evoke events or memories from past lives, although at that time I wasn't yet able to understand them clearly.

"I began to realize that we, as creatures with souls, are all on a path and that we have more complex connections among ourselves than our given roles, such as mother and son. Through these experiences, it was as if I reached an overarching higher level of all our connections, and I began to view myself and my surroundings from a completely new perspective. I was therefore very grateful to the Readings for pulling aside the veil and helping me see a new level of reality. This led to an enormous expansion of my consciousness.

"In the dream, I was amazed when I said goodbye to my friend or brother, and he said that he wanted to go to Marduk. Once I learned that Marduk was a God (Mesopotamian), I took this to mean that the young man was going on a spiritual journey, that this was an awakening, and that nothing was going to stop him. Spirituality remains very important to my son and me today, and we have intimate exchanges about it. We have a deep feeling that this spiritual orientation has connected us over many lives.

"Yet, the leave-taking in the dream from my friend on the Acropolis was very difficult. The fact remained that I never saw him again, that he didn't come back. When Jim was a child and was going on a longer trip, whenever I had to say goodbye to him, I was always overly concerned for him. I was often very sad if he was gone for a long time. I was afraid that he would never return. It was one of those phases of separation anxiety that all parents, and especially mothers, go through, but, with him, it was so intense and connected with the fear of separation.

"After the Reading about my son, those fears ended. Today, when he leaves, it is easier and more natural than earlier. I've also become aware that, as souls, we have known each other for many lifetimes, and today, this love and connectedness continue to unfold. It's a wonderful gift that I can feel and express this closeness and trust with him. It is also wonderful that Jim had the openness to accept help. It was an incredible, healing encounter; I am eternally grateful."

We cannot dodge the fact that every single action we do has its effect on the whole. A new type of thinking is essential if mankind is to survive.

—Albert Einstein

For Your Toolkit: Getting off the Wheel of Karma

Most people think of karma as payback; it isn't, even if it looks that way. The Law of Karma is a natural law; it automatically provides the lessons we need to ultimately come to understand that we are all One. Think of karma as an accurate reflection, on all levels, of what we are. Karma is not who we think we are, but who we show ourselves to be, through our actions, thoughts, and intentions.

On the way to this enlightened realization of Oneness, we may, for example, come to see that we are connected (connection is not the same as Oneness). We may see that we are all One family, or that we are powerless to behave in a way that harms others, without it coming back to bite us. This is the ongoing gift of the Law of Karma. It allows us to open our eyes and directs us to come to know that we are nothing other than One; we are One with the nature of the whole beneficent universe, known as Love, known as Light, known as God, also known as Emptiness.

What can you do to get "off the wheel"? Find the courage to face your pain. Seek help when you need it. Give up blaming others for *anything*, and take full responsibility for what you have created in your life—good, bad, and indifferent. Learn to love yourself unconditionally. Speak the truth. Take risks in personal relationships: Be genuine. Take care of yourself. Treat everyone, including yourself, with loving-kindness. Find creative ways to express your heart. If you do all that, Grace will descend upon you and the wheel will fall away.

Someone asked the Saint Ramana Maharshi, "Baba, what should we do to help others?" Ramana Maharshi replied, "There are no others." When you realize that, you are said to be 'off the wheel of karma.' That is Liberation. Karma always leads us toward liberation.

Chapter 22: Inability to Trust: ADHD (Attention Deficit Hyperactivity Disorder)

For Your Toolkit: Not Knowing

(Andrew, born 1956)

Andrew, a librarian, came for his first Reading. He had been referred to Maitra by a friend, who was studying with her. He had tried many times to get help with his problems, but he had often been disappointed. He came to his session with the hope that he would receive some insight that would help him understand himself better. Andrew's deep sadness, a kind of all-encompassing melancholy, made it impossible for him to relax, either his body or his mind. This is his description of his problems:

A: I have so many questions about my life, and sometimes I repress them. I don't believe there are any answers, and this makes me sad. I am hyperactive, and therefore often nervous and scattered. My ADHD problems have given me difficulties my entire life. I've never felt comfortable in my body. I've also been suffering for a long time with my sexual identity. Because I am convinced that I incarnate from one life to the next, being sexually confused is almost logical. As human beings, we have taken on both female and male bodies in many past lives.

In the present, it is difficult for me to love and accept myself. I realize that I put pressure on myself to conform to social norms and gender roles, and

I have often felt discriminated against. I have difficulties in my relationships with both men and women. If I could have accepted my unusual nature, I would have been able to live more authentically as an artist. Somehow or other, I have lacked the courage.

M: I'm getting a conflicting message. Is it OK with you if I tell you something very difficult?

A: Yes, I'm ready for this.

Andrew's response was an immediate trigger for revealing a past life of great suffering:

"You were a prisoner in Vietnam during the war. You were not a soldier; you were attached to the embassy in South Vietnam. One day, wanting a new experience, you went out with a group of soldiers. There was an attack by the North Vietnamese and many of the men around you were killed; you were shot in the leg, so you couldn't escape, and you were taken to a prison. You were tortured because they thought that you had information that would help them. You would have told them anything they wanted to know. But the worst thing, the thing that had such a devastating effect on you, is that they put you in a cage.

"The cage is down in a hole; when it rains, the water gets in it, and you can't get dry. It's lowered down into the ground. When they wanted to bring you up again, they could bring you up with the chain. The cage is made of bamboo, with no walls around it to keep you warm because it's down in the ground. And when it's hot, there is no breeze to cool you either. You have only one pair of shorts on, and you can't stand up or even stretch your legs out or lie down. You were always in a crouched position.

"The thing I hesitated to tell you, is that you went out of your mind to protect yourself, to get away from the pain in your body and the pain in your mind; you couldn't understand why they were doing this to you. You hadn't done anything to them. You were not a soldier. You weren't a threat to them. This is what you kept saying to them, when they would question you from time to time, trying again and again to get information.

"You died in that cage, after more than two years. Because they fed you just enough to keep you alive, you looked like a skeleton covered with skin. You lost all desire for food; you just gave up. Your death was peaceful.

"You went to sleep and left your body, but you were lost for quite a long time after your death. It was a relief to be out of your body, which was so full of pain because you couldn't straighten up. The bullet wound in your leg was never treated or even cleaned; it was infected, so you also had a lot of pain in the leg that was shot. Often, they would 'forget' to give you food or water for several days. The time leading up to your death was extremely traumatic and full of unrelenting pain. After your death, you wandered for a long time, looking for help. But, when a Being, a guide, would approach you to offer help, you were too afraid to accept it. Finally, a guide approached who had the face of your father. He spoke to you in a very stern way. He said, 'You must let someone help you. The people, who are coming to help, are not your enemies. They are not going to hurt you. So, you need someone to help you; otherwise, you will continue to be lost and alone, and I know you don't like that.'

"You started to cry, and you said: 'Papa ...' Then you saw that he wasn't your Papa. He was an angel. And he smiled at you and he put his hand on your head and said: 'I give you a blessing. You wouldn't listen to anybody, but I thought if I showed you your father, maybe you would listen, and you would be able to accept help.' Then, because you finally understood that they were not the enemy, you could receive assistance.

"When you came into your body in this life, you still carried these feelings of disorientation, of not being able to get comfortable in your body, of being fearful of people even as a child, and not knowing whom to trust, and taking a long time to feel as if you could trust anybody. Even today, this is still an issue."

Andrew was silent during and after the Reading of the past life. It awakened in him a deeper sense of himself as if knowing about his past life had opened a door within him. A transcript of his exchange with Maitra follows:

A: Yes, as a child, I was timid and inhibited. It was almost unimaginable for me to allow physical contact.

M: Are you doing yoga?

A: My father gave me a book more than forty years ago. And I opened that book and started to practice, from time to time, the *asanas* (postures), as they seemed familiar to me. But today it's hard for me to practice yoga, even though I know that it would be good for me. I can't do it regularly. I'm too unsteady.

M: Your familiarity with yoga comes from many lifetimes ago. Yoga will heal the last lifetime if you let it. The stretching, the freedom in the body is an antidote to the memory of Vietnam. When you start to do it today, you don't want to come back into your body, because your memory of being in that cage, and being so confined, is still so painful, and you want to avoid it. So you push away the very thing that would heal you. Yoga will slowly bring you back into your body, more and more. You will begin to feel your power again. Your father somehow saw what you needed. Was he usually very sensitive?

A: I think he just got this book from someone and passed it on to me.

M: He must have sensed that you needed to get into your body and feel its boundaries because the way that you managed to handle being in that cage was to leave your body. And you were in that cage for several years. It was painful. Everything in your body hurt, everything. You just didn't want to be in your body during that experience.

A: My father tried to help me for thirty years; it's so difficult for me to accept his help because I don't have trust in myself.

M: It's all the karma from the previous life. It's not karma in the sense that you did something wrong. It's karma, meaning you suffered so much that you are still trying to release yourself from it. To heal, you need to forgive your captors and yourself.

Now I want to know why you don't want your father to help you. What is it?

A: My parents judged me because I was more interested in the Eastern Indian religions and philosophies, rather than in the Christian or Catholic church. My sisters and the whole family also judged me for this. As a consequence, I decided that I couldn't accept anything from them. But we try to be friends today, my father, my mother, and I; I try to let them know what I'm thinking, and that I believe in past lives which are real for me. They are reluctant to listen to these ideas, or to people they consider to be unsuccessful in life.

M: Your parents honestly don't understand such things. It's like asking somebody who is blind to see. You must accept them where they are. They are doing their best. Your father needs to help you. If you want to help your father, let him help you. He feels that he did something wrong. Let him know that he is OK the way he is. It's a good step toward your thinking that you are OK the way you are. Listen: Your father judges you because you don't think the way he does. And you judge your father because he doesn't think the way you do. Who is going to break this pattern? Only you. He can't.

Andrew's Transformation:

Andrew was receptive to the story about his excruciating experiences in his past life. He came slowly to understand the effect of that suffering on his present life. His interview, eighteen months later, describes his process:

"At first, I was shocked. I have been involved with the laws of karma and reincarnation for over thirty years and I do not doubt that these laws exist. Karma is a universal law—action and reaction—but it isn't that easy to understand when one has experienced karma in action. Of course, I ask myself the question, 'Why would one want to experience something so gruesome?' But maybe I need to look at it differently. Perhaps it's like this: Something got stuck many lifetimes ago, and through remembering this past life experience, I was able to release the karma. Nevertheless, I was very shocked. I tried to listen very carefully. Afterward, I listened to the CD again. It affected me deeply again. I was somewhat depressed for the following two to three weeks.

"The experience of the past life, of being locked up in that small cage, was very traumatic. Today, I can understand that I have brought some of the emotions connected with it into this life. I still feel a lot of mistrust, and unfortunately, I don't even trust myself. In the beginning, it felt awful that I had ended up in such a desperate situation. Now, I have decided to recreate my life and use this information in a lasting and positive way from a karmic perspective.

"The Reading described my process of dying in the past life like the angel offering my father's face so that I would be able to engage with him. This message made a deep impression on me. I did historical research on the Vietnam War afterward and it all fit together. Before the Americans arrived, the Vietnam War was already underway. This was in about 1965 when the Americans got involved. A terrible war.

"Now, a bit later, I feel better and I think that it shifted something inside of me. I'm much better at being myself and remaining myself. I had the task to forgive myself and to forgive others. That's a part of my life plan. Often there is difficulty when we encounter others. Because I'm very perceptive, I notice when people behave in problematic ways, and this makes me wonder why they are doing this, and why they relate to others in this way. There are some behaviors that I have a hard time accepting. These are real challenges for me. If I had more trust in the universe, I would think, 'Oh well, it went well, it's not so bad.' Something has changed in me; I am calmer and I am continuing to practice accepting people more and I'm sticking with it.

"The four letters ADHD are an attempt to describe somebody's temperament. After several years of psychotherapy and various tests, my therapist told me that my symptoms could be attributed to ADHD. At the time, I was forty-four years old. This ADHD is part of me, and due to my various personality traits, one can get the feeling that I have a handicap. I'm not talking about an illness. ADHD is a curse and a blessing. I have a gift; I can empathize better with women than most men I know. On the other hand, I am unable to play a man's role well. So, it isn't a question of good or bad. It always depends on what I do with it. In comparison to when I was young, and how society is changing on this issue today, patterns of behavior between the sexes are no longer as rigid and there is room for much more individuality.

"Due to my difficulties and my hyperactivity, I had often been a burden to my parents. Maybe I used them as educators or psychologists because I wasn't able to express everything that was on my mind. When something difficult happens to me, I ask myself: 'Why is this happening to me? Why wasn't I better able to handle things in this or that situation? Why can't I stay calmer?' As a hyperactive person, I already have answers to these questions about my condition because I often feel unstable. There are situations in which I feel well, and I have good days, and then somebody says or does something, and my good mood is gone. Today, I'm learning more and more how to let go of difficulties that I encounter with others. Many years of therapy were also helpful.

"In the past life, I had to come to terms with all the pain that I have endured. I realized that I had needed to distance myself from my own body, to bear the pain. Perhaps I come across to people as peculiar or crazy. This doesn't describe me correctly. On the contrary, in my mind, it makes me unique. It confirms to me that I am allowed to be myself. I understand myself better today. For a long time, I didn't dare to be myself. I still have fears related to being locked up in a cage again. For example, I've noticed that I have great difficulties being in small, tight spaces. It was always difficult for me to be open to relationships, as I feared constraint, a result of my traumatic experiences in my past life. I don't want to feel restricted. I need to have freedom of movement."

Some months later, Andrew had another session with Maitra, in which they addressed a different subject. This session was about a woman, Shirley, who was very dear to Andrew; however, there were difficulties when they were together, and he wanted to resolve them. For a short time, they lived together as a family, with her two sons. At the time, her sons were five and eight years old and became very dear to him. Their love is reciprocal, but they have frequent misunderstandings. He would like to know if there are connections to past lives, that they have been unable to let go of. Despite their difficulties, Andrew finds the intimacy that they have very beautiful. It's a loving, spiritual relationship. They sense that they have something to give one another.

Maitra quickly recognized the signs of a karmic relationship and opened the door to some of those memories:

M: Let's have a look at the relationship with Shirley.

The minute I feel my way into her, I have difficulty breathing. I feel like I have a weight on my chest. I'm not sure if it's fear. Sometimes I feel fear and anxiety this way, and I do think there is some of that, but there also seems to be something else; she feels so responsible for everything. Life feels like a burden to her. The burden takes many different faces: The faces of her children, and the faces of her parents. If this applies to both of her parents, or perhaps to one that is still living, or to you, or to anyone that she is in a relationship with, she is very conflicted about it.

It feels like she takes on responsibility for your happiness and well-being. There is a push-pull: 'Come close, I love you, stay away, it's too much.' When you two are together, I see from her perspective that if things start to be too intimate, she has to push you away. For you, it's so hard to get to the point of intimacy, of trusting someone enough, and opening your heart to them, and then, when you get there, she pushes you away. You confront each other, each within your limits. The fear of intimacy, which you both have, manifests in different ways.

Do you want me to look for the karma?

A: Yes.

The door is open; Andrew has agreed to look at the karmic aspects of the relationship.

This is what Maitra saw:

"You are both working together on the production line in a factory in England. There are big machines; it's the late 1800s, maybe two or three lifetimes back. You were a supervisor. You had worked on the line as well, but you had been given more responsibility and had become the supervisor.

"At this point, you were living alone because your wife had died after a long illness. She died of consumption, which is the last stage of tuberculosis. She was ill for a long time and everything in your life was centered around her because you were worried about her all the time. You kept having dreams that you would come home one day, and she would be gone. Dead. But you had to keep working because it was the only way to eat. Your nightmare came true. You did come home one day to find her gone, and just a sweet, little note: She had written 'I love you' on a paper and laid it across her chest because she knew that you would find her that way. She knew that she was dying. When you were around, she would try to look better, but as soon as you would leave, she would know that she was going downhill every day. You were sensing it, even though she would put on a smile for you. You also knew that she was failing more every day.

"Your work gave you one day off when she died. Then you were back to work again and very sad for quite a long time. One day, there was a new woman there, Anna (Shirley from today), who was working on the line. You were keeping an eye on her, to make sure that she was doing things right. You weren't conscious of being attracted to her. You were still too depressed and sad.

"Then she was hurt; there was an accident and a machine came down on her hand. It was just one finger, and everyone was afraid she was going to lose it. It turned black. But you were instantly there, so you caught her before she passed out from the pain. You knew what to do, and so you carried her into your office where she could lie down. This is when you began to get to know her.

"When she regained consciousness, she started to hum. You said to her, 'Why are you humming?' And she said, 'It helps with the pain. It hurts so much. If I don't hum, I scream. But if I'm humming, that's what I think about.' This caught your attention. This young woman had a way of dealing with pain. You thought, 'Well, OK, that works for her.'

"Usually, going home was the saddest time for you because the house was empty; always before, no matter how sick your wife was, you would be happy to get home to see her. On this day, when you went home, you started to hum. Pretty soon you were singing a song that you used to sing with your wife, and you were singing the songs of your childhood.

"Then you went back to work. But the young woman didn't come back to work for a few days because of her injury. When she did come back, you waited for her to have a break, and then you told her that you thought you were beginning to recover from your wife's death because she had shown you how to focus your mind differently, and this, the humming and singing, was helping you.

"The two of you became better acquainted. She was working to take care of her mother, who was a widow and had no way of supporting herself. Anyway, to make a long story short: You ended up moving in with her and her mother, and it was a win for everybody. It was a win for you because you weren't alone anymore. It was a win for her because the burden of caring for her mother was lightened with your help. It was a win for the mother because it relieved her guilt about being a burden to her daughter. I'm not saying it was all 'happy, happy, happy.' Of course, there were challenges, but you all felt that it was an improvement in your lives to be together. You found your heart again; your capacity for love was bigger than you thought."

This previous life with his lady-friend Shirley illuminated the attraction between them in the present, but it helped delineate the problems as well. Maitra went on to explain to Andrew:

"The problem between you is more that each of you has a strong limitation on how close you can be with other people. You challenge that in each other. When she comes close, and you need to be able to be more open and increase the amount of trust, that's when she pushes you away. She feels too vulnerable when she gets close. It will be helpful to find some ways to acknowledge each other's needs, such as her asking for distance when she needs it. And you need to learn not to take that personally."

Andrew's Transformation:

A year later, Andrew commented on how the Reading had affected his attitude toward relationships:

"I was very pleased by the positive experience that I had with a long-time girlfriend that was also shown to me in the Reading. That comforted me. I could also tell my girlfriend about it, and she could accept it. Sometimes we have difficulties. She's like the opposite of me. She's full of energy for new relationships, and I'm still afraid of being hurt. Because I haven't yet fully accepted myself, I am afraid of being accepted. Today, I experience life, with all its responsibilities and challenges, more and more as a possibility, and not as a difficulty. I continue to grow, and I am thankful for all the experiences that life has given me."

Enough-ness

Alone, I walk
Daring belief
in my fullness

All my questions
answered
As soon as asked

Resistance
Like an ancient friend
Gone but not forgotten

She might
drop in again
at any time

My cup is full
My heart is open
My roots are deep

The past is gone
In its proper place
Filed away

The future
Vibrates in the NOW
Enough-ness fills me

Thank God I am empty
enough for
this joy.

—Maitra

For Your Toolkit: Not Knowing

One of the keys to a happy life is getting comfortable with 'not knowing.'

It is one of the tests we all have to face as we evolve and grow in wisdom. Can we trust the Universe, or God, enough to proceed on our way without knowing? Can we be at peace with ourselves, accepting that there are things we will never understand?

Our desire to understand, sometimes to the point of compulsion, keeps us focused on what is around us in the outer world; it can often turn into an exercise in who to blame. What would serve us better would be to learn to stay Present. We can learn to find that infinite, peaceful place in the immediate NOW, and stay centered there. With practice and intention, we can be there and do our work, walk our walk, and communicate our truth centered in the NOW. With this deeper sense of trust, we can be 'in the world but not of it'; this is a necessary step on the path to self-realization.

I believe in this so deeply that my preparation for a Reading is to empty my mind—to let go of everything that I think I know about that person and just be present and open myself to guidance from the Universe. This often brings insight far beyond my ability to perceive or understand.

When you become aware that you are going in circles trying to figure something out, try this: Without putting pressure on yourself, take note of the conflict that has a grip on you, and how unproductive it has become to think about it, and remind yourself to let it go (See p.163, Situation = Situation).

Then visualize putting your problem in the "lap of the Infinite"—or the Buddha, or Mother Mary, or whatever your word is for the Infinite.

Acceptance of 'not knowing' opens the way to your innate wisdom.

Chapter 23: Healing an Old Wound

For Your Toolkit: Cleaning the Energy

(Lisa, born 1959)

Lisa, a mother and grandmother, teaches at a massage school and is also a sculptor. She had met with Maitra several times. She told the story of how her former husband withdrew from her, signaling a significant change in their relationship. She often dreamt at this time that he was focused on her sister, and had very strong feelings for her. She felt this intuitively; it disturbed her, and she couldn't make sense of it. When she spoke to him about it, his response was, "Don't worry about it, it's nothing, calm down, just a bit of jealousy." She told him that she would leave if nothing changed.

Lisa's story came flooding out of her:

"Suddenly, everything was on the table. He had been in love with my sister for a long time, and he wanted a love affair with her. I had had enough. He complained, 'Now everything is ruined.' He said he assumed they wouldn't take things further, out of consideration for the families. I realized then, it was time to end the marriage, which I did.

"I wanted to understand why I had such a strong reaction and why these events had happened. I also wanted to examine and clarify my relationship with my sister."

Over several sessions, the Readings gave her deep insights and an understanding of the karmic entanglements. Here is one of her past lives:

"It was in northern England or Ireland. The people, descendants of the Celts, were worshipping nature. There was a women's circle, and you were competing with a woman named Elizabeth for the High Priestess position. Elizabeth, in that lifetime, is today your sister. The elderly leader was ill, but she had retained control. You were still going to her for guidance and instruction, but when there would be a meeting, she would tell you or Elizabeth to lead part of the meeting. You would each take part of it, or sometimes one of you might take the whole thing. You went to the teacher before and after the meetings, and reported everything that had happened. She was slowly withdrawing her energy and she was the one who was going to decide who was to be the new leader.

"However, it wasn't just up to her. There was a man; the man is your husband in this life. He was the High Priest and he had the final say. In other words, the women could decide who would be the new leader among themselves, but then it would go to him for final approval. For nearly a year, your teacher had been bedridden and unable to participate in the meetings—but she had remained in charge.

"The time for the full moon ceremony came, on the spring equinox, when the men and women came together for the yearly fertility rites. Everybody came together for the ceremony; the celebration went on all night, and men and women had ritual sex. The children that were born of those unions were destined to be priests and priestesses. Children were born from marriages as well, but this was special; this was something different.

"Your teacher had decided who was to be the next High Priestess; she chose you. She had decided that you were the better one for this position. She had told you her choice, but she had to wait for the approval of the High Priest. It's not clear why she did not tell Elizabeth, but she told you because she wanted you to prepare yourself for this position.

"There was a large gathering, much larger than usual, where people came from quite far away to meet together for this very important spring equinox gathering. The High Priest knew both of you and he knew the High Priestess had chosen you. He knew what you were going through, and your capabilities. But he astonished everybody at the beginning of the ceremony. He called forward Elizabeth (today your sister) to be initiated as the new High Priestess.

"You were so shocked, so devastated. Elizabeth was also surprised because she had guessed that you were the one, although she hadn't been told anything. She knew there were preparations to be made, and she hadn't been notified to do them. She was as surprised as you. During the rest of the ceremony that night, sometimes you were cold, sometimes you were hot, sometimes your mind was racing, sometimes you couldn't think at all.

"You were experiencing a series of explosive, overwhelming emotions. The High Priest was tuned in to you. Every once in a while, he stretched out his hand; sometimes you were close enough that he could touch you, but sometimes you could just feel his energy helping to steady you, to ground yourself, and stay in control. He could see how close you were to losing control. You nearly passed out three or four times during the evening. You would just, by force of will, hold yourself in your body because everything in you had been prepared for the next level of leadership. And without stepping into the new position, you felt you didn't know who you were, whether you wanted to live, or how you could deal with Elizabeth being the High Priestess. You were lost.

"After a month or two, you saw how Elizabeth was struggling. You were spending time with your teacher, who was dying, and you realized that if you had been given the new responsibility, you would have been unable to have this time with your teacher. You were very grateful and happy that you could be with her as she was dying. She was conscious and giving her final teachings.

"Once you were over the initial shock of not being chosen, you accepted his decision, but it remained a painful wound. For a long time, every time you would see the High Priest or hear about him, you wanted to run to him and say, 'Why? Why? Why? My teacher thought I was the better-prepared one. Why didn't you think so?' You could never bring yourself to ask him.

"When he was dying, he called both you and your sister to him, and he spoke to her first. He told her that she had shown that she was worthy of the responsibility and that she had done a good job. He knew that you both wondered why she was chosen and not you, and he said, 'I can give no reason that would satisfy you. It was what I felt guided to do.' He said he felt vindicated in that decision because of the way that you had taken hold of other responsibilities and had been such a good support for Elizabeth, and also for the whole group.

"You forced yourself to get over the shock and your disappointment. You were generous in the way that you resolved it in yourself, and you were there for her. You often thought to yourself, 'I wonder if she would have been able to do this for me if the shoe had been on the other foot.' When the High Priest (now your husband) was dying, he said to you, 'You showed the strength and flexibility of your character, in the way that you handled the situation; when it is your turn, you will be one of the truly great teachers. You don't have to worry about being passed over again. Your turn will come, because it's your destiny to be in that position.'

"Ten years went by, and your sister had a stroke, or possibly a brain tumor. Her mind broke down, and after a short time of her handling things in a disjointed way, a vote was taken among all the women, and you were raised to the position of High Priestess. But she had loyal followers. They were loyal to her even though she had done some things that showed that her faculties were not all there. They also thought that, if everyone was patient, she would come back because she had the right to the position. So they began to plot against you and eventually poisoned you.

"Some herbal things were put in your food. For about two or three months, you just got weaker and weaker, and sicker and sicker, and then it was clear that you couldn't handle your responsibilities anymore. It was a time of great change for these women. It was around that same time that the Romans were coming in and trying to break up these groups. Your time in that position was short-lived. Her followers didn't want you to take over. Interestingly, I don't think it was her idea, and she wasn't involved in poisoning you; it was her followers. If they had asked her, she would have said 'Leave it alone,' because she was aware that she couldn't handle everything.

"If we examine the triangle then and now, the High Priest chose her in that lifetime over you, without fully understanding what he was doing. He didn't have a reason; he just followed what he felt. But you felt betrayed and you had a very strong reaction. Yet, in the end, you acquitted yourself well. You learned that you could take a deep disappointment and come back from it, and do a wonderful job that everyone would recognize.

"You weren't prepared for what happened later in that life. The minute you first felt sick, you suspected poison, and you were very careful with your food, but they were very clever too. Elizabeth had come into her position in the spring, and by the time fall came around and you replaced her, it was harvest time and they were harvesting apples and making a lot of apple juice and cider. Fresh apple juice was served with the meals almost every day.

"There was an old tent with a cider press, out in the open where everyone could see it. They used this press to squeeze the juice out of the apples. There were public containers. You never figured out that it was the juice because everyone could see what was done with it. You never thought to look into the cups that were used to serve the cider. They would coat the inside of your cup, which was marked with your name, with this herbal concoction—it was quite tasteless and very toxic. It poisoned the apple juice you were drinking, which made you very thirsty. You were drinking a lot of apple juice; no one thought to look into the cups. If anybody looked into it, they wouldn't see anything; it was invisible. The people who were cleaning the dishes poisoned you."

Maitra continued, elaborating on the meaning of the past life and its relevance for the present: "When the events in this life today began to happen, it felt like, 'It's just too much, please, not again.' Underneath it all was fear. In the past life, you never really knew for sure what was making you ill. Perhaps, in this present time, you never felt like someone was trying to kill you, but underneath your feelings were these fears: 'What is next? Is it dangerous? Am I in danger?' It's much more than 'my husband is just playing around with my sister and me, in a contemptuous way.' He was contemptuous because you told him how it was affecting you. And he went ahead and continued with what he was doing; it didn't matter to him how you felt. That's contempt. You were powerless; he had the power.

"You had a reaction to him choosing her over you again and again, even though he didn't leave you to be with her. They were playing with your feelings. I don't think he was doing that in the past life. The way he distanced himself from you this time was devastating for you. He thought you were preparing to leave him, and he tried to pull you back into the old relationship, the way your marriage was earlier, by making you jealous.

"He wasn't planning on going anywhere with your sister. It was only about you in all of this. He wanted you to come to him and beg him not to mess around with your sister. Then he would show you that he still loves you. He continued to try to repair things. However, through the separation, you reached another level of clarity. He lost your trust. He had done something that had deeply hurt you, but he's telling himself, and you, that he hadn't done anything wrong. He still doesn't fully understand how dependent he was on you. If one person in a relationship changes significantly, the habitual emotional exchange is different. Indeed, you didn't need your husband in the same way as you did early in the relationship. He sensed that, and it felt to him as if you no longer needed him, and that meant that you no longer cared for him. You left him emotionally when you changed. If he had been able to meet you in this more independent space, it would have been possible for a new partnership to have developed; this is what you hoped for. He wasn't able to meet you there, so he tried to bring you back to his level.

"You had several lifetimes with your husband and your confidence in him was shaken many times. The fact that he wanted your sister shook your confidence, and your self-worth. You began to question whether you were lovable. You have worked your way through most of this, and now the self-doubt that is left in the cells of your body, is becoming clear; it's there to be healed.

"Also, your time for mothering is essentially over. Your children are both finding themselves, and you want to celebrate that. But you miss their need for you. It was part of your identity. Now you are realizing that that part is over. You are asking yourself: 'Who am I now? Do I have a role as a mother? What's next for me?' They call this the empty nest syndrome when a woman comes back to herself again when her children are grown, and, even though there may be times when you can still help them, it's not the same. Their dependence on you is finished. It's time to let go.

"This past life shook your confidence. But you are springing back more quickly every time. It took less than a year, and you have more confidence now than you had before. You were giving him too much power, and now you're learning to stay with yourself."

Lisa's Transformation

Lisa describes the effect that the past life Reading had on her and the resulting changes in her life:

"When it became clear that a relationship was developing between my husband and my sister, I was devastated. This situation shattered something inside of me that I hadn't been aware of until then. From this moment forward, I could feel that everything was different, and I reached a decision. From the depth of my soul, I heard an outcry, 'No, not again!' I was done with this.

"I was in survival mode. I no longer felt secure within my own home, so I was staying with friends during this time. I wanted to avoid my husband who was still living in our home. I didn't have much more to say to him, and I had to function since I was working a lot at that time. At night, I would often suddenly wake up out of my restless sleep and would feel dehydrated, as if I were dying of thirst.

"After the Reading, I re-experienced so many earlier events with great intensity. The memory of poisoning through apple cider brought about the feeling of being dehydrated. It's amazing how these traumatic cell memories are awakened under stress, and re-experienced on another level. I also had paranoid thoughts: 'I can no longer trust anyone! I have to be on guard.' The old trauma felt real again. It wasn't a straightforward feeling of being physically killed, yet I felt defenseless.

"Earlier, there was a point in my marriage when I had hoped to be able to move forward with my husband. The children were out of the house, and a different phase in our relationship was beginning. I wanted our relationship to grow, with more intimacy and better communication, so that it would be possible for us to continue together. However, his relationship with my sister shattered my hope at this point; my dream to continue with him was gone. It was a very deep awakening and freed up an incredible amount of energy. I was able to release myself from old patterns of behavior. I found a new clarity, and with it, the ability to make decisions and the strength to act on them. I have grown into a more authentic, independent way of life. My health has stabilized. I have energy for work and creativity again. I am so grateful for the insight into this karmic memory, into connecting more deeply with my soul. This experience has awakened and enriched me with powerful realizations. An ancient wound is healing. On a spiritual level, I am prepared for the next phase of my life."

Lisa, with new insight, describes her karmic relationship with her sister as follows:

"When I met my future husband, I was working at a company, together with my sister. She and her family were renting an apartment in the house that my husband and I owned. We lived together for ten years as a community.

"When I look back today, I know that this close bond with my sister was very special and unusual. During the long period in which we lived together, there weren't any big conflicts or differences of opinion. It was as if there was an unspoken agreement between us.

We always helped each other with the housework and with caring for the children.

"Many years earlier, I had consulted a therapist, who asked me the question, 'Do you have a sister? In your relationship with your sister, do you stay aware of your own needs?' She had seen a past life in which my sister and I were Siamese twins and felt that this bond continued to have a strong effect today. It was now a matter of fully detaching from this co-dependence so that each of us could lead an autonomous life. These energies were then released, through a ritual, with the help of the therapist.

"When I arrived home, I began to feel in my body the effect of what I had just learned. I could feel something being released. It felt as if I was slowly beginning to feel myself. I was separating from an energy that had been a part of my self-image until then; it had prevented me from feeling my own needs for a long time. Then I ran through memories of reports and films with Siamese twins; they moved and engaged me very deeply each time. I didn't know why until I heard about that past life. One of the images went through me like a lightning bolt. In 1987, I painted a large picture with my sister, approximately 6 feet by 30 feet, during an art workshop. We painted together on the floor of a large art studio for two weeks. Various figures emerged from this, and strangely, a double creature. At the very end—we painted from left to right— Siamese twins appeared. I got the picture out and unrolled the entire length of it in front of the house. I could hardly believe it. We had painted something together without knowing what we were depicting. Yet these intuitive images appeared that were clearly operating deep in her and my unconscious and had mysteriously emerged. My counselor hadn't known anything about this picture.

"My sister was no longer living in the house at the time. She had moved out. A few days after I discovered the painting, she came to my house early one morning; this hadn't happened since she had moved out. She said that she had just had the urge to stop by.

"I could feel that she had come by so I could tell her about my experience regarding the painting. I told her about the past life and our karma as Siamese twins, and about why we had lived together for so long. I said that this strong connection had resolved so that each of us could now live on our own and be independent of each other, and that this was why it had been necessary for her to move out and establish her own home. I don't think my sister was involved in reincarnation at this time; she just listened to me, without saying much. She seemed to accept what I said.

"After a relationship began between my sister and my husband, and I had separated from him, I had another Reading with Maitra and asked for insight into my life with my sister as Siamese twins. I wanted to understand everything better."

Upon hearing Lisa's request, clear images immediately began to unfold for Maitra, and she described the past life with the two sisters as Siamese twins:

"I see a picture of your sister with one of her legs hidden. It's folded up as if she is going into the lotus position, but then her leg is pulled inside of her. When you were Siamese twins, a leg was missing, or rather, one of her legs was crippled, and inside her.

"She feels crippled without you. You don't have the same feeling because the two of you had three legs, and the fourth leg was hers, but it was pulled inside. You were joined together at the torso. If they had cut you apart, you would have been whole and she would have been crippled.

"Today, you could walk away, and be independent, but she doesn't feel like she can. Even now. If she could be with her husband, he would be propping her up, helping her to walk, helping her to feel whole.

"If we can just enlarge this image a bit, it's like she is hopping around on one leg. She can't get the other leg to unfold. She has never really felt in balance since she left you. You brought balance to her. It wasn't the same for you. You didn't have the same dependence on her that she had on you. You could separate and walk your path, and while you liked to have her in your life, it wasn't a necessity. With her, it's a necessity, and that is why she is angry at you. You took away what made her feel whole; she tried to substitute your husband for you."

Allowing the graphic images of the past life to sink in a bit, Lisa was open to hearing more about its meaning or significance:

"What your husband likes very much is for someone to depend on him. As you got more and more independent, he felt more and more like he was of no use. He could fix things around the house, but you didn't need him anymore. Your husband and your sister, too, were more dependent on you than you were on them. And you never really knew this because you were sailing along, singing your song, and being yourself.

"This is the dilemma of the woman who begins to take her power. She doesn't need others to the extent that they need you. She just wants them to be happy, so she will be happier. She wants to be sharing with those she cares about because she loves them, but she doesn't need them. Notice the difference.

"In that lifetime, her leg was folded up inside, and very small, and she still feels that way, as if she doesn't have two feet to stand on. She can't find her balance. She needs somebody else to hold onto so that she can feel whole. If I were working with her, I would work to get that leg to come out and get it to grow and provide her with the balance she needs. That may be why she is doing yoga. It's a way of trying to find her balance.

"Your husband is of two minds. He is controlling his impulses while being aware of how destructive he feels. He even sometimes thinks about destroying the house as a way to get back at you. It's good for you to have somebody else in the house. Your roommate will say something to him if he gets too far out of line. She is pretty fearless. You attracted a kind of 'guardian' energy in her. When your husband is in his right mind, he is pretty fair. But right now, he's not in his right mind a lot of the time. He is clinging to yoga, trying to hold himself together, trying to avoid being destructive, and not wanting to hurt you.

"When he takes the next step and moves into another apartment, which he could do at any time, then you will know that the crisis is over. Right now, it's a crisis. The best thing, from his point of view, is not to be there. That is what he is doing. He goes and sits in a bar or sees friends. So far, he is in control of himself and thinking more positively about giving yoga classes. When he finds another woman, he will have another focus, and you will be safer. Right now, you need to keep some good protection around you.

"If your sister entered into a fuller relationship with him, it would disrupt her whole life because it isn't really what she wants. She wants to go back to being dependent on you, but she can't. He is a substitute for you. She feels crippled.

"You can help with that. You can't go against her wishes, but if she will accept your help, then you can help her release and heal the leg that is inside. There is an effective healing technique that you can use while you are sleeping when a waking exchange is not possible (See p.130, The Hypnagogic State).

"Before you go to sleep at night, give yourself directions about what to do in the sleep-state. Say to yourself, 'I want to take my guides to go and work with her guides, to help her unfurl and grow that leg; let it come down to the ground if that is what she wishes so that she can become balanced and independent.' Let that be your gift to her."

**Do not let the behavior of others
Destroy your Inner Peace.**

—Dalai Lama

**As I identify more with my soul,
I feel more detached from the drama of my incarnation.
As I become more aware as a soul,
I am less an actor in the drama.
The soul is awareness.
The shift from the ego to the soul
happens through love.**

—Ram Dass

For Your Toolkit: Cleaning the Energy

We all want to live in a home that is a peaceful sanctuary; we can achieve this by making sure that the energy feels clean and clear. It should feel like an ocean breeze, fresh and pure.

In Lisa's home, there was a prolonged period of extreme stress, as the marriage was ending. Whenever there has been a major emotional event in your home, such as a death in the family, a fight between partners, or even just a few very stressful days, it's a good idea to clean the energy in your living space. This will help you re-establish a fresh, peaceful space where you can leave those events in the past.

Here are some ways to clean the energy:

1. Do a deep housecleaning. This includes cleaning the carpets and upholstery and vacuuming or washing the floors and walls. This will get rid of any negative energy that clings to those surfaces.

2. Light a sage wand or a Palo Santo wood stick, blow out the flames, and walk through your house with the smoking stick; this will erase all the negative energies that are still hanging around. These sticks are readily available, with instructions, at your favorite health-food stores.

3. This is my favorite method: Get a lightweight, long-handled frying pan at your local second-hand store. Put two handfuls of Epsom salts in it; then cover the salts with rubbing alcohol, leaving a thin layer of liquid on the top. Light the alcohol and salts, and, holding it away from you, walk carefully around your house, letting it burn all the negative energy. Put it down on a towel on the floor to let it completely burn out. Your home will feel as fresh and pure as if you were in a forest, or by a lake.

4. When we go to the seaside or for a walk in the woods, we feel refreshed and renewed because running water and growing plants give off negative ions, which are beneficial to the human body. Negative ions neutralize free radicals, that can damage cells. They revitalize cell metabolism, enhance immune function, purify the blood, and balance the autonomic nervous system, promoting deep sleep and healthy digestion. Positive ions, on the other hand, come from machines of all kinds, such as cars, and computers, and they have the opposite effect. Plants in your home, small fountains, or a negative ionizer will provide the fresh, healthy atmosphere you want in your sanctuary.

5. To fully establish a peaceful uplifting energy or higher vibration, after you finish cleaning, light some candles—and incense if you like—and put out some fresh flowers. Your favorite meditation music or some light classical music would be a great addition. Enjoy!

Chapter 24: Resolving Conflict in My Family

For Your Toolkit: The New Paradigm

(Carol, born 1963)

Carol is a social worker, assisting clients in vocational training. She is married, with two adult children. When Carol came to Maitra, she was in a lot of pain; she felt imprisoned by her family history. She didn't understand why she suddenly burst into tears during the Reading. At that point, she didn't even know if she was really sad. She wanted so much to be free of her family history. She thought she was the classic ugly duckling, and she didn't feel wanted.

Maitra was quick to remind her, "Don't forget who the ugly duckling was! The ugly duckling transformed into a beautiful swan."

Carol responded, "I have all this pain that I would like to heal and let go of. I can't continue doing what I'm doing. I'm struggling with family issues: My father is dead, my mother is ill, and my sisters and I inherited a beautiful vacation home with several apartments in an idyllic setting. I am the only one who has a real desire to spend time there or perhaps live there at some point. I would like to purchase an apartment for myself. But my two sisters don't want this. This situation hurts me a lot, and there's nothing I can do about it. I just want to be freed of this pain, and have inner peace. And I am plagued by the fear that this will never be possible.

Maitra asked if the sisters wanted to sell the property.

Carol explained, "They want to keep things like they are. They don't want to sell me an apartment. It's always been like this: The two of them against me."

Here is a further transcript of their conversation:

M: Do you think that you are the ugly one in the family? Or is it more that you think your sisters see you this way?

C: It was like this when we were children.

M: Didn't they think you were pretty?

C: It felt like I had more than one mother. Like I had three mothers, given the way they

behaved. I'm just different from everybody else in the family. What do you see in this regard?

M: I see a person who has suffered a lot. You couldn't find your place in this family. Did your sisters often fight with each other?

C: No, they didn't fight with each other. They fought with me. I want this pain to go away.

M: Old patterns are coming back to you now, and they are being played out in the property dispute. What kinds of fights did you have?

C: I would like to have an apartment in this house so much. They just said 'No.' They say I was the one who was always nit-picking in our family, and they may be right about that.

M: They were jealous of you! Because you were the baby, the one who got the attention. This is how they saw it. It's the opposite of what you thought. They thought you were the cutest one, who always got what you wanted. You were spoiled. They are the older sisters, who always had to take what was left. They put you down to make themselves feel better. I don't know where your mother was. She could have protected you; she should have stopped them.

C: My mother always suffered; she always cried when I came home from school. She cried all the time. I was much younger than my big sisters and was often alone or with my suffering mother.

M: So, you had a mother who was depressed. Having a depressed mother is in some ways worse than not having a mother at all. It's so confusing, because in your case you also have the older sisters who are jealous of you, and always telling you what to do. You were alone so you didn't have the power to fight them.

Is the house in your mother's name?

C: It belongs to all three of us. I would like to find a peaceful solution to this situation with the inheritance.

M: The thing to remember is that you felt abused as a child. That is what made you feel that you were the ugly duckling. Now all this pain has come up for a reason, because it's time to heal. It's been interfering with your ability to have the power you need so that you can create your life the way you want it. I want to ask you a strange question, so get ready: 'Did you love your sisters?'

C: I would like to.

M: When you were a child, did you love your sisters?

C: No. I liked the older one the most. She was twelve years older, and she was like a mother. I hated the other one. Sometimes, I can't stand her.

M: However, I did hear you say that you felt some connection and some love for your older sister. Still today?

C: Right now, it's very difficult. They are so close and I have no contact with them. Ever since I asked them if I could buy an apartment in that house, I have called them and talked to them very politely. I wrote them a very kind letter, and they wrote me a nasty letter back.

M: This issue with the house brings back the pain of your childhood. It throws you back into feeling like a victim. You were a victim of your sisters. Perhaps you already know this: Your mother didn't want another baby; she didn't want you.

C: Yes, I know this.

M: She told the other girls. You were born with six strikes against you right from the start. I'm going to ask you now to make a big leap. If this last baby had been somebody else, for example, your older sister, would your mother have still felt the same way, that she didn't want it?

C: Yes, yes.

M: All this was pushed down your throat. Nobody was happy. Everyone felt unloved by their mother. You became the scapegoat, the one who took in the negativity. Now imagine for one minute that, previous to your birth, you knew the situation you were born into. How could that situation benefit you? Why were you born into such a difficult family?

C: Either because of a past life, or so that I will learn a lot, and I will grow from it, perhaps so that I can help somebody in a similar situation.

M: Can you find some peace in that?

C: Yes, but I'm still in pain. It makes me so sad that I have so much pain, and I can't make any progress.

M: I think you have made some progress. Even though you have sad feelings, you have an objective view when I talk to you about it. You can have a little distance. I want to tell you the two words that came to me when I asked, 'Why did you choose this family?' You came into this very painful situation where you were a victim of your older sisters, and in many ways of your mother too. The two words I heard were 'develop compassion,' starting with compassion for yourself. That's why you chose this family.

C: I can't do that, yet. I have to learn how.

M: It will develop over time when you uncover these issues and heal them. Compassion is one result of healing. I want to look at the karma here. Your sisters heard your mother say, even before you were born, that she didn't want this baby. She said things like, 'I am going to give this baby away,' and so on. At the same time, because your mother felt guilty about having these feelings, she gave you a certain kind of attention that the other girls didn't get. Both of your sisters are jealous of you. Don't be so hard on yourself. Every time you cry, something is moving.

C: I cried so much for a long time.

M: It's OK, you needed to. It's how you release the sadness, the pain, and the confusion that you grew up with.

Here is the past life that Maitra was able to see:

"I am looking at an orphanage. This is around the time of World War I, and these are children whose parents either abandoned them, were killed, or died in some other way. These were children who were found living in the streets of European cities after the war was over— homeless, starving children. This orphanage is in a village in Belgium. It's at the foot of a mountain, and it's a huge mansion, like a big castle, and there are probably three or four hundred children in there, from very young ones to teenagers.

"When you were found, you were trying to take care of three or four other children. They were not related to you. You were on the street, and you found a little place where you could have some shelter. You were helping these younger children; your heart went out to them and you did your best to feed them.

"You were teaching them how to share. If somebody stole a loaf of bread, for example, they had to bring it back to the group, and everybody would then get some of the bread. This was a big thing because these children were in survival mode. If they got the loaf of bread, they just wanted to stuff it in their mouths. In a way, what I'm saying is that you were trying to civilize these children and give them a sense of belonging in a family.

"This was important for you, too, because you had also lost everything. Perhaps it was different for you because you were a little older, and you had had more time in a family that cared for you and made sure that you had enough to eat. Then, during the war, you lost everything. In your case, what I see is that you were coming home from school and your house and your parents were gone. A bomb had hit your home. For a little while, you went to neighbors, who helped you out for a bit, but then you were on your own.

"I see trucks coming through the city, very slowly, calling for children, saying, 'We can give you a place to live.' You were very suspicious of them. You followed a truck around and watched it pick up children, and you still didn't trust what you were seeing. On another day, you saw this truck again, and one of the children you knew was in the truck, in the front, helping with the children who were being picked up. You asked this child, 'Where do they take you?' And she described this place out in the country, and said, 'We have enough to eat, they give everybody new clothes, and a bed, a real bed with a pillow.'

"So, you decided, 'OK, I can trust them,' and you took the other children you had been caring for, and you all got on the truck. You went to the orphanage. You were probably thirteen, maybe fourteen. The four children that you had (kind of) 'adopted' were a lot younger than you. The people at the orphanage were sensitive and experienced, and they asked you a lot of questions. When they found out that there were five of you, they made a place for all of you to be together. They told you that it's temporary because the children are usually with others of the same age. But they let you stay together for a while because you had been a mother to these children.

"You were in this orphanage for a year, and you continued to look after the other children with whom you had made a connection in the street. They were all quite dependent on you. The people who were running the orphanage were concerned about this, so they separated you. Each child was placed with other children of their age, and you were with older teenagers. That went on for a while, but the children would come every day and find you, and they would cling to you, not wanting to let you go.

"People started coming to the orphanage; most of them came to adopt children, and there were also those who were coming to offer the older children a job, a place in the world. The people running the orphanage were not very happy about sending children out to work. They didn't want to support it, but the government was funding this orphanage. The government authorities thought that it was important for the children to move out of the orphanage, to live with a family or at a business, where they could earn their own money and take care of themselves. Also, every time a child left for a job, there was space for another child.

"You made a decision: You looked at the children you had been taking care of, and said to yourself, 'They are all going to be fine; yes, I think they can get along without me. There are lots of people who can take care of them, and I am going to take a job.' For you, this was freedom because ever since you had arrived at this orphanage, you had thought, 'What am I going to do?' For one thing, they did not give you any schooling. You already knew how to read and write, and it was very distressing to you that all these children were being brought up without any schooling. It wasn't something that you could fix.

"You took a job, although it didn't turn out very well. It was a factory job. The way that they presented it, was quite different from the way it was. You lived upstairs in the factory building, in a room with fifty other girls, one little bed just next to the other little bed, and you had to work every day from sunup to sundown. It was really hard, and you were there, maybe for a month or two, and then you said, 'No, this isn't going to work. There is no future in this.' You decided to run away. You found a better job with a family, taking care of their children. The children were going to school, and they included you in that. This was a much better situation.

"Two of the four children that you left in the orphanage are your sisters today. They are still angry at you for leaving them. You were afraid to tell them that you were leaving. You just left in the middle of the night.

"You talked to one of the workers there, and said, 'Please tell these four children I'm sorry, but I have to go. Tell them, I'll come back to see them.' You felt guilty about leaving them. A strong dependence had developed between you and these children when you were still in the streets, and nothing happened to change that when you were in the orphanage.

"From a karmic perspective, these two sisters of yours are still angry with you for just leaving and not saying anything to them. You never fixed that.

"You felt too guilty to go back and face them. You left them to try to figure everything out for themselves. These were children who lost their birth parents one way or another, and they were a lot younger than you so it was harder on them. They had formed this family feeling with you; you were caring for them and being responsible for them, and suddenly you just went away. You didn't abandon them in the street, you knew they would be cared for when you left. You knew they wouldn't go hungry or be abused. They would be OK.

"But still, you couldn't bring yourself to face them. You can see how some of that dynamic is still at work in your relationships with your sisters. In the past life, you felt you did everything you could for them. When you left them, they were in very good circumstances. But you felt guilty that you didn't say anything to them. You had promised that you were going to return and you never did. Here we are in the midst of that still painful situation. Some of your pain is also the guilt.

"This could have been two lifetimes ago because it was after World War I; that would have been 1920, or even earlier. The war ended in 1918. This fits with what I saw. You had so much guilt from not talking to them; you didn't dare to face them and say, 'I have to do this for myself now, and I have to leave you.' You loved them. That is why I asked you earlier, 'Do you feel love for them?' Somewhere in the mix, there is love and that's why it hurts so much.

"What you can do now is just let the past be, and work with it in the present. It brings more light into the situation and makes it clear that you are not the only victim. You are finally seeing that they also felt like victims.

"You were the oldest one in that lifetime, and because you were the oldest one, you had more choices. When you decided to leave, you chose to leave them behind. In this life, as the youngest, they saw you as the favored one, even though you didn't feel it. Even today they look at you that way. It seems to them like you get to have everything you want. They struggle a lot more. Now they are resisting your choice regarding the house."

Carol exclaimed, "Right now I feel much lighter. In the future, will I be able to move into the house of my parents?"

Maitra answered, "You are going to find a place in town. Eventually, you are going to be in the house that you want to be in. But be patient. Let it go for now, and trust that there will come a day when you will have what you want. The less pressure you put on it right now, the sooner it will come about."

Carol's Transformation

In the follow-up interview with Carol, she talks about how she came to seek Maitra's help and the patience she learned as a result of the Reading:

"I came to Maitra for a Reading because I believe in past lives. I see it like a coin: One side is the visible, and the other side is the world that we don't see. I believe that we develop spiritually. If one knows how to meditate and how to be aware of this invisible world, then we can experience it. When we see and understand more, we can learn to dissolve certain blockages. One can call this karma.

"At the time that I sought advice, I was in a great deal of pain. I wasn't doing well because I was involved in an inheritance dispute with my older sisters regarding my parents' vacation home. My sisters and I didn't agree on what should happen.

"I was curious as to how things would continue. I wanted to understand this better. I had a feeling that I had brought this conflict with my sisters from somewhere else, from a past life. I had this feeling throughout my entire childhood.

"I was extremely nervous when I went for the Reading. I wasn't doing well; I was crying a lot. I was nervous because I had never gone to a seer under such circumstances. I asked myself what she would probably say to me. Perhaps she would say, 'Forget what you want.' I was afraid I would feel even worse afterward. I imagined I would hear frightful stories, with horrible scenes like torture and traumatic death experiences. These images were already connected to my fears.

"Compared to the stories and pictures of past lives that I had had in my head, I experienced the past life in the Reading as almost comforting. Despite everything, I felt the events in it made for a good story. The fact that I had abandoned my sisters at that time, released a deep understanding and acceptance within me regarding my current relationship with my sisters. It revealed to me a lot about why I'm the way I am today.

"My sisters have never forgiven me for having abandoned them. At that time, the explanations in the Reading helped me to understand why my sisters behaved so vehemently against me. If one doesn't know exactly why people act in a certain way, it increases one's stress. I noticed that the information from the Reading helped me a lot, and I could integrate it. I could be reconciled with my family.

"I feel fulfilled and blessed in my current life with my family, my work, and my friends. Yet life, in and of itself, is frequently demanding and very challenging. I find it valuable to seek advice from a person like Maitra, who can help me overcome my difficulties. It was perfect timing because I was able to be open with her.

"I will never forget what was said in the Reading, that things will work out with my family, and I will get the apartment. At that time, the fulfillment of this wish was still very far away. And the apartment does belong to me today."

**There are only two ways to live your life.
One is as though nothing is a miracle.
The other is as though everything is a miracle.**

—Albert Einstein

For Your Toolkit: The New Paradigm

Let's look first at the Old Paradigm, which was "If I am right, you are wrong. If you are right, I am wrong." This is the kind of thinking that causes war, whether it's between nations, political parties, husband and wife, or, as in this story, sisters. With this attitude, conflict is inevitable. There can be no meeting place, no meeting of the minds, no discussion. There can be a winner, yes, but there will always be a loser.

The New Paradigm is based on a fundamental change in approach and/or underlying assumptions. It says that there is truth, or rightness in both of our positions, and our challenge is to find the common ground. The New Paradigm has given birth to a new approach to such diverse problems as peace negotiations and divorce settlements. It is called Mediation.

For mediation to work, everybody must set aside their ideas of right and wrong and open themselves to understanding the other person's point of view. We must look for the middle ground. In the Reading, the past life revealed what lay behind the attitudes of the different family members. The Reading made it possible for Carol to let go of her position and accept the situation; this allowed her to move to a new level of understanding. It allowed her to let go of the position of victim. There was healing in the family because one person was willing to look deeper and let go of her position.

In this model, a win-win is possible. Adopt this new assumption—the New Paradigm— which allows for the validity of differing points of view, asks us to define a middle ground and encourages us to let go of our judgment. With this way of looking at it, see what happens the next time you have a conflict with someone.

Chapter 25; I'm Losing my Face: Napalm Death in Vietnam

For Your Toolkit: Spiritual Awakening

(Alan, born 1992, the son; Regina, born 1964, his mother)

Alan, a high-school student, began to lose his hair when he was seventeen years old; previously he had a wonderful head of hair. He was getting more and more upset about it, and after discussing it at some length with his family, his parents suggested that he have a Reading. Alan went to Maitra, seeking help with the pain and despair he was feeling.

At this initial meeting, Alan confided his pain over losing his hair, the fact that he looked like an old man and that he didn't want to live. After hearing his story and its devastating effect, Maitra asked Alan if he believed in reincarnation. He was receptive. Then she told him what she was seeing:

"Your past life story begins in the 1960s when you were a university student in Chicago. You had a huge fight with your father, and, as a result, you dropped out of the university and enlisted in the army to go to the Vietnam War. Within a year, you were sent to Vietnam to fight. You had been there only a few months when you were sent 'up-country,' away from the more heavily populated areas.

"You were in an area with dense foliage, when an American plane, unable to see you, dropped napalm to clear the area. You were burned, over more than eighty percent of your body. Your hair and clothes were melted off, as was most of your skin. Your face, your whole head, was melted down to the bone in places. Yet you lived. There was excruciating pain, but only briefly, as the nerves were burned away.

"Then you were in the hospital, unable to move anything much, except your eyes. Your muscles contracted you into a fetal position. You could talk, a little, until that, too, became more and more difficult. When, finally, one of your friends relented and brought you a mirror, what you saw made you beg them to kill you.

"You felt you could never have a normal life in this condition, and you didn't want to live. After many days of this despair, at the insistence of the medics, you wrote a goodbye letter to your parents and told your father that you were sorry for enlisting out of anger. Finally, one of the medics, a friend, gave you an overdose of morphine, and strange as it may seem, you died happy."

Alan's Transformation

In a follow-up conversation with Alan, he described his reaction to his Reading and how it had affected him:

"I never took this story of a past life personally. I couldn't identify with it. I listened to it as a story that could happen to anybody. It was a war trauma that is repeated today, in various places in the world, all the time. Afterward, I couldn't feel any connection with the Vietnam War. It didn't stop my hair from falling out, but I did have a feeling of gratitude that I'm not in that situation today. I didn't think that much about it; my life just goes on. The effect it had on me is that I could see myself being happy now. I don't have to deal with going to war.

"I still vaguely remember lying on my stomach drawing and painting planes and helicopters when I was three years old. It was easy for me to express everything in that way. I just wanted to paint and everything had to be exactly right and fit together; I went into the details. My drawings couldn't be big enough; I had to draw bigger and bigger ones. I glued the pages of paper together so that I could paint bigger and bigger pictures, and I would add another page, and then another page.

"Our family used to travel a lot. Maybe those experiences at airports and in airplanes awakened karmic memories; that's possible.

"If I paint today, I'm more interested in looking, and I also copy paintings. In part, I also work with photos. In those days, I didn't copy things. When I was little, I would paint from my memories; I drew from inside. It's different now. When I paint, I need something to look at. Yet, there is a similarity: I stay with something until I'm satisfied with it, just like I did when I was little and went into so much detail. It all has to be exactly right for me to be able to just let it be.

"It's possible that I was able to decide to begin my studies because of what I learned from the Reading. To be sure, everybody around me was starting their studies at that time, so I did feel some pressure to focus my energy on it. Perhaps I could position myself better and have the feeling that I was moving forward professionally. I'm in a situation again where I have to decide whether I want to pursue further studies, but I'm in a very different place."

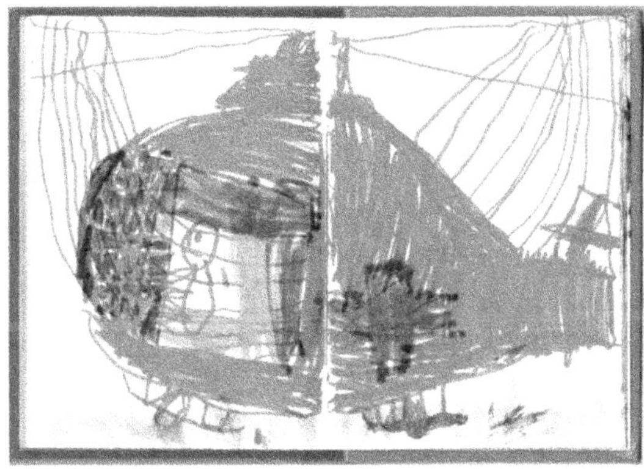

Alan, Age 4

Regina, Alan's mother, was a student of Maitra's for many years. She was able to put Alan's past life into better perspective for both of them by sharing some of his childhood experiences:

"As a child, Alan would often seem disoriented and chaotic; he hated restrictions such as requirements and rules. This pattern intensified when he began having a problem with his hair loss.

"At age seventeen, he was slowly losing some of his hair which visibly depressed him. He tried to affect it through nutrition and lifestyle, but when this didn't have any impact either, he felt noticeably worse. He came to me often in those days for help.

"I tried to help him resolve his obsession with his appearance, so that he could cope with daily life. I knew that he didn't have enough work to distract him at that time. He was often in his apartment, just sleeping; this was an indication to me of increasing depression.

"Alan told me that he wanted a new body, that this one was no longer of any use. He felt this, even though he was strong and healthy, and had grown tall and attractive. He told me that when he would wake up in the morning, it felt like his face was melting, that he was losing his face, and that he just looked shitty. In addition, he said that things didn't work out with women. He didn't think anybody would find him attractive like this. He thought that he wouldn't live past thirty. The idea of living the rest of his life without hair terrified him. He felt his whole youth was messed up, that in fact, he hadn't had one, and that everything was meaningless.

"I was concerned about him because I felt his despair; it robbed him of his energy and prevented him from moving forward. It had become an enormous weight on him and seemed to be increasingly taking over. He said that the skin on his scalp gave him a lot of pain; it felt like sharp stings, as if angry energies were attacking him from the outside. What could we do? He said he would accept any help if it would just give him some relief. So, we made an appointment for a Reading.

"As a child, Alan suffered many fears; if he had a fever, he would quickly slip into nightmares. He was full of anxiety. As a little boy, he was often unable to sleep. In early childhood, he had croup, and often bronchial congestion, so that he couldn't breathe well. At night, I would lie next to him, awake, and watch his breathing, afraid that he would suffocate. Later, he had trouble with wound healing. When he had small abrasions or scratches on his skin, they would become infected and full of pus; the wound would ooze for days. I saw the connection to the Reading; these wounds were similar to burns that didn't want to heal.

"After a family trip to the tropics by plane, Alan began to draw planes, and this went on for several months. When he witnessed the rescue operation of a paraglider who had crashed near the launch pad in the mountains, and a rescue helicopter took the injured woman away, he began to draw helicopters. All this was beyond the experience of a three-year-old boy. I understand today that these very early impressions brought back his traumatic memories from his past life. I have kept these drawings, and after the Reading, I spread them all out in front of him on the entire living room floor, and we looked at them together. It was overwhelming.

"He would draw and paint so intensively; he often didn't even want to go outside where the other children were playing because he was so immersed in his drawings. He would avoid groups and games. When he reached puberty, he had difficulties with authority and would resist anything that he felt was restrictive.

"In 2004, I took a trip with Alan to visit our relatives. We spent several days in Chicago. He particularly wanted to see this big city. After visiting our relatives, he directed me perfectly from the home of our relatives to O'Hare Airport, where we returned the rental car. I recall his clarity and calm; it now seems to me that he knew his way around and that this area was not foreign to him. Now that I have heard that he grew up in Chicago in the past life, it makes sense.

"Alan's depression eased after the Reading. One could feel an energetic change in him, and his earlier despair was gone. He was, and still is, sad about losing his hair, but he's no longer so fixated on it. He has become much calmer, and he has more confidence.

"Seeing my child in this kind of depression was frightening. Feelings of guilt and the nagging question of 'What did I do wrong?' came up for me as it would for any mother. However, Alan told me, when he was in this crisis, that it had nothing to do with us as parents, and that he had received everything that he needed from us.

"A few weeks after the Reading, Alan came home to visit. We were discussing it again, and he said 'I'm curious to find out what else will happen in my life.' This statement moved me deeply; it was meaningful to me because it meant that Alan could now anticipate a future for himself. Vietnam and his fear of an early death were behind him.

"The transformative powers at work here were like a miracle. This story and Alan's childhood, his being, and everything he was able to express preoccupied me, as his mother, for a long time afterward. It gave me deeper insight into karmic entanglements, and how they continue to affect you, even across lifetimes.

"Afterwards, Alan enrolled in an Art Academy for training in Scenography. Earlier, he thought that he would never pursue a course of studies and that academics were not for him. Later, he completed his Bachelor of Arts. He is a talented artist and musician, and he participates in many group art projects."

Nothing ever goes away until it teaches us what we need to know.

—Pema Chodron

For Your Toolkit: Spiritual Awakening

In this Reading, you can see the conflict that Alan is having between the obvious connections to the information in the Reading, i.e., childhood memories of war in the pictures he drew, and the panic when he began to lose his hair. It illustrates his inability to accept these as indications of a past life. This shows that his spiritual awakening was not yet complete; there was some resistance. Resistance is a part of the process of any significant change. Allow it.

A spiritual awakening can be illustrated by the moment a caterpillar leaves the cocoon and begins to realize he/she has wings, that he is not who he thought he was, and that life is about more than survival and seeking pleasure. It takes time to discover and stretch into your wings.

Some of the signs of a spiritual awakening are:

- Feeling disconnected, and alone;

- Synchronicities (seeming coincidences; connected events) are more apparent;

- A sudden reevaluation of beliefs;

- The falling away of old habits;

- The desire to learn such things as meditation or yoga;

- A clearer recognition of inauthentic behavior, and the ability to sense lies/deception;

- Wanting to help or contribute, and be of service;

- An attraction to spiritual teachers;

- Fatigue and other physical symptoms, sometimes painful;

- Curiosity about what's behind your behavior, yours and that of others;

- Compassion, without excusing inappropriate behavior in yourself and others.

If you recognize yourself here, perhaps it's time to find a teacher and/or others who, like you are waking up, and can accompany you on your spiritual journey. Then you will begin to connect with your soul family, your tribe, which may feel closer to you than your birth family.

Chapter 26: Healing Feelings of Guilt and Self-Reproach

For Your Toolkit: Trusting the Universe

(Alan, born 1992; Lana, Alan's girlfriend in his youth, 1987-2016)

Alan, of the previous Reading, returned three years later with another pressing problem. He had been informed of the death of a dear friend a few days earlier. The news came as a shock; he was traumatized. Lana, his childhood girlfriend, had been murdered by Matthew, her roommate. Alan was devastated. Two weeks later he reached out to Maitra. The following is a transcript of Maitra and Alan's exchange:

M: Lana is accepting that she is gone from her body and can't go back. She feels distressed that she couldn't say goodbye to anybody. She hasn't felt the trauma yet. I feel her sadness. She feels cut off from being able to communicate with the people she cares about.

She does have help from two Beings. One is a person, whom she knew, who had died some time ago; she is telling me, yes, it is a relative. The other one is probably one of her guides, not someone that she knew in a physical body, but someone whose energy she recognized. She feels like she has friends there with her, and they are helping her. She is going around to different people now to see if they are available, and if they can feel her. You've felt her presence, haven't you?

A: Yes.

M: You felt her, so she knows that her connection to you is one of the stronger ones because many people aren't open to being aware of her. They miss her and they grieve for her but they don't feel her when she comes close to them. She is in limbo right now. She can't think of anything in the future at all. She is just trying to get through each moment and make whatever contacts she can. Her two guides are accompanying her. She wants to check in with family back in Africa, and friends in many other countries. Some of them don't even know that she is gone yet. This is a strange thing to her because when she tries to make contact, they don't have any reason to be looking for her.

A: She was murdered on Tuesday, and I knew it on Friday. I got the message on Facebook. Her best friend from Paris wrote me a message.

M: Were you aware of her before you knew that she was dead?

A: Just after, I was so busy those days.

M. She is getting calmer now. She is sad because she has a lot of plans. She hasn't remembered, or she hasn't focused on, what her roommate did to her. I am not sure if she knew what happened; she was unconscious before she left her body. She knows something happened because she didn't want to die, but she hasn't felt the trauma yet.

She will probably have to go back and remember her death as a part of processing it. Right now, she is not remembering it. She doesn't realize that she was murdered. Her process right now is to get clear that she is what is called "dead"; she doesn't feel dead. She hasn't gone back to that moment of leaving her body. She passed out, unconscious for a while, before she left her body. Matthew continued to hold onto her neck and kept her from breathing.

Now I can tell you that she is OK. She has help. She is sad about it; she didn't feel finished. She has made contact with a few people. You don't have to worry about her. She doesn't feel lost or alone. In her way, she is saying goodbye to people. It is a mixed experience because so many of her friends don't realize that she is gone; they don't know that she is there to say goodbye. But it is her way of trying to reach closure with people.

Anytime she comes into your mind, and she is there a lot right now, you can say to her whatever you want to say. It would be helpful to her for you to say 'goodbye' because she is alone in doing that right now; people don't know that she is there.

A: The hardest part for me was that I knew about the problems with her roommate. He was attacking and chasing her around the apartment. She told me, but I didn't do anything about it.

M: The thing is, she didn't think that he would hurt her. She just thought that what she had already experienced was as far as he would go. Even now, like you, she is having a hard time realizing that this happened. If she had been really afraid of him, and she had said to you, "I need your help," then you would have helped her.

A: Sure. She didn't ask for help, but she told me some things.

M: How could you have known, when she didn't know, how far he would go?

A: Yes, that's true.

M: Matthew was in love with her.

A: She told me, that he tried to have sex with her and she had to push him away.

M: She didn't tell you the whole story. He was in love with her, and she didn't want him; he couldn't accept that. She wasn't attracted to him. She didn't want to have anything to do with him, and she didn't realize how unstable he was. These assaults happened several times. She felt that she was "managing" him OK. She didn't think he would go so far.

A: Yes, she was a tough woman.

M: You can't blame yourself, because if she had had any idea and had told you that she was afraid of him, you would have gone to help her, and you would have taken her home to your place.

A: I told her to keep a knife in her room, or call the police and inform the neighbors in the house.

M: So, you did try to help her as much as you could. It was one of those things; there probably isn't anybody who could have predicted it. He couldn't handle his feelings in the moment.

A: Terrible.

M: It is. He will spend the rest of his life in prison. He ruined his life and her life.

Send Lana your love; that will give her support. When people realize what happened, she will get more loving messages. You might have dreams where she will visit you and make contact that way. She also feels helpless like you, and she wants to comfort people.

For you, it is shocking to your whole system to know that someone had her life taken like that. It is traumatic. I hope you can get to the point where you don't blame yourself. I don't see anything else that you could have done.

A: But I can see a lot of things that I could have done.

M: If you had known. Even if you had known his family, none of them would have expected it. They knew that sometimes he acted crazy, but they wouldn't have guessed that he would kill someone. He wouldn't have guessed it either.

A: I still feel shocked and sad about the death of my friend ... I blame myself because I was her last contact as a friend, and she told me the problems about her murderer and I didn't do anything. I didn't even tell her she could stay with me. I just let her go back to her place, and then, two days later she was dead. I was the only one who could have done something. But I didn't do anything.

M: When she told you about the problems with this man, at that time he was not her murderer. At that time, he was her roommate, giving her problems.

A: Yes, but at that time, they already had fights and the police had come to the house once. I knew that, and she was a close friend of mine, and I didn't do anything. I feel so bad about it. I feel like I am not human. I can't believe that this is me.

M: Is it true that you didn't do anything?

A: I told her to move out. I told her to get pepper spray, but I didn't make her stay at another place or ask her if she felt OK about going back to her place.

M: At that time, did you have any feeling that she was in great danger?
A: No.

M: And if you had felt that she was in great danger, what would you have done?

A: I would have helped her of course.

M: Of course. You can only be where you are in the moment. We can always solve a problem in hindsight. But now, in this moment, you can have confidence in yourself, that if you had had any sense that she was in danger, you would have behaved differently. And, in truth, maybe the next time something similar happens, you will be more likely to be proactive.

Alan's Transformation

Some weeks later, Alan had his interview. He reflected on how his Reading with Maitra had affected him:

"Through this horrible loss of a loved one, I learned that small things that had bothered me earlier, are minor. In comparison, it doesn't matter if I have a full head of hair or just some hair, whether I pursued a course of study or not, what I'm doing now, and how I live my daily life. A friend, who was very important to me, died under tragic circumstances. This experience was so much bigger and more powerful than everything else. From this moment forward, I had so much more to think about and process than struggling with my minor concerns and outward appearance. The shock was so deep that it put all my other problems into perspective. There is a parallel between the traumatic experiences of burned soldiers in the Vietnam War and the shock from the loss of a girlfriend. Both are abrupt, traumatic, and catastrophic events.

"I hope that something like this will never happen again, but then some fear flares up: 'What if this were to happen again?' The shock gave me a feeling that death was lurking everywhere. I asked myself who the next person to die would be because a good friend of mine who had cancer also died at the same time. I am on guard that somebody else will die again.

"Life can be hell. It can be both, heaven and hell. I had to learn through this painful experience that both exist. Even here, in paradisiacal Switzerland, where we feel so safe, bad things happen. We have everything, and we live peaceful lives. We don't have to go to war, and even then, sad experiences can happen to us.

"As a contact person for the victim, I was heavily involved in this murder case. I was questioned and suspected of being the murderer because I was in contact with her two days before she was killed. Afterward, I had the feeling that maybe something I did or didn't do was why this had happened. Maybe I was somehow guilty. All of this had an unbelievable effect on me."

Two weeks later, Alan contacted Maitra again, and she described to Alan how she saw Lana's current state. A transcript of their conversation follows:

M: I see Lana floating. She is turned inward and very quiet. There are angelic beings around her, protecting her. She is getting over the shock of it. She is trying to adjust herself to the idea that she can't go back to her body. She was there at her memorial service when they talked about her.

You probably felt her presence, and she was listening, and to her, it felt like they were talking about somebody else. It was hard for her to connect. Intellectually, it made her happy that people came together and were saying the things that they did, but she was still in disbelief.

She is healing from the shock, and working on reconnecting with herself.

It's distressing for her that you are blaming yourself. She had a lot of trust in you and confidence that you would have helped her if she had asked. She thought it was just a matter of getting away from him. She knows that you would have responded in a minute. What she is working on right now is accepting what happened; she wants to be at peace with it. She recognizes that her physical body is gone, but she is not dead; that is a surprise to her because she doesn't have a strong belief in an afterlife. Now she is realizing that, yes, her body is gone, but her spirit is as strong as ever, and there is still so much to learn, and there are other ways to progress.

How will she be able to express her creativity? That frustration was weighing on her all the time, and she just couldn't find a way to let the creative energy move through her.

A: Yes, exactly!! She told me about that. She wanted to be creative, but she always had to do other things like working on her career.

M: She felt other things interfering, but she was also blocking herself. She is looking forward now to being able to move into her creativity from where she is now, before taking on another body. She is beginning to find some inner peace. Life isn't over for her; life continues differently. She can see possibilities that she could never see when she was in her body.

From time to time, you will continue to feel her presence because she is still feeling very connected to you and to other people here in the physical world; she has already asked her guides for permission: 'Can I check in with them? Can I know what is going on with my friends and my family?' She has already been told by her guides: 'Yes, you can check in with them to know what's going on. But your task is to be where you are now and meet the challenges that you have in the present.'

She is also showing me that she is beginning to see how she is blocking herself. She hadn't seen that before. She thought it was what other people wanted from her, what she was supposed to do, and that she had to make a living, all these kinds of things. She is beginning to understand that these were her decisions. She also decided to let this man come into her life even though she knew that his mind wasn't right. Did she tell you that?

A: Yes.

M: Surprisingly, she still wants to help him. She is showing me that he wants to die. He can't accept what he did either; he is telling the police what he thinks will result in the worst punishment for him. She is trying to give him some support so that he will realize that it is better to stay in the body and take advantage of it to learn. Lana is a truly generous spirit. Her trauma is already beginning to heal.

A: Yes, hopefully.

M: Amazingly, she is reaching out to him. She has already forgiven him. So, Alan, forgive yourself for whatever way you think you might have failed her. She is doing well.

A: Did she come to Switzerland because of me? Did she want to be closer to me again?

M: Partially. But she had other reasons to come too. And yes, there was an unusually strong connection between you. That she came to Switzerland was a half-conscious decision; she wasn't even aware of all the reasons. Don't take everything on yourself.

A: I didn't think that much about it. But just now I understand everything.

M: Yes. She is saying to you, 'Find your joy!' It is easy for you to find your sadness. Find your joy.

Your throat chakra is about halfway open. For you, it seems that going through traumas—whatever they might be—has the effect of pushing you into opening up more. For instance, you are opening your throat chakra, which has to do with your self-expression, your painting, and your music; it's all the ways you find to express yourself because that's your gift to the world. In a real way, it's your gift to yourself as well, because it makes you feel more alive. I feel this strongly with you right now. Even the sadness and the feelings of guilt, as they work through you, help you to open your chakra more.

A: Yes, that is possible. But I am still blaming myself. It is always there, and I ask myself, again and again, what I should or could have done.

M: Yes. It is alright to see other possibilities. But to blame and punish yourself shuts you down and is against life. Just learn from the things that you think you could have done better. See what they have to teach you. Your friend is not blaming you, and one month later, she is already moving out of regret. So, it is good for you to do that too. You're not here to live for other people. You are here to live your truth.

A: But in some ways, we are responsible to our close friends, and if they have problems, we try to help them. But I didn't help her. It feels like a big mistake in my life.

M: Don't make the mistake of thinking that you have to live for other people. You did try to help her at the same level as she was sharing her difficulties with you. If she had taken it to another level, you would have behaved differently. You are mad at yourself because you can't see the future. None of us can see that for ourselves.

A: But I missed a chance in my life to protect my friend from a dangerous person.

M: Alan, you had no idea, not an inkling, that death was anywhere near.

A: But I could have taken her away from this crazy man. I feel so bad, I was a bad friend.

M: If someone comes to you with a story like this in the future, you will probably take more action because you learned the hard way that things can get out of control very easily. But don't become paranoid by imagining something that isn't there. All I can tell you is that she doesn't see it that way. That is your disappointment in yourself. Nobody else judges you in this way.

A: Yes, I know. It is my problem.

M: It is your challenge to let it go. Nobody could have predicted it. When you saw her

last, she feared that there might be some trouble with him, but she didn't fear for her life.

By the time a second interview with Alan took place, some weeks later, Alan had had time to reflect and was beginning to accept what had happened and his place in it:

"I have felt some relief since the Reading because somehow or other it can't get worse. That was the worst thing I've ever gone through. To lose someone you love, through murder, is the worst. There will certainly be unexpected deaths in my life when somebody becomes ill or dies, but it won't happen again in this gruesome way. Nothing like this has ever happened to anybody I know. I hope it will never happen again. It's even worse if one's child dies in this way. It's hard for the whole family.

"I could manage losing my hair, if I could have my friend with me again. This loss brought me down to rock bottom. The only small, positive thing is to know that it can't get worse. What everyone fears has happened to me: Living with the fact that a loved one has been murdered. Previously my life had followed a familiar path; I lived a fairly untroubled life except for the crisis of my hair loss, until the moment when I heard this terrible news. The intensity of this experience was much more powerful than my fear and depression at losing my hair. I can live with this, and it no longer makes me question my value; I accept it the way it is. The Reading taught me to change my attitude and to see and accept life as it is.

"It sounds strange for me to say that things now feel lighter. Come what may, it won't shake me up as much. I now have more solid ground under my feet, and today I am amazed that I got myself back up on my feet after this difficult time. I have matured through it, and when I look around, everyone has something to conquer. That also teaches me to accept myself more, with or without a magnificent head of hair."

At this juncture, Maitra offered Alan a past life with Lana and Matthew, her roommate, who had killed her. She explained it could be helpful to know about the karma between them, to understand more. She clarified that their coming together again, and the resolution of those negative energies, didn't have anything to do with Alan:

"Lana created karma when she turned her back on him. It was a previous life, and I see Matthew in an impossible situation. Now I can see her; there was a crowd of people preparing to hang him. They had him on a horse, and they had put a rope around his neck when she arrived with a couple of other people who were also on horseback. When Matthew saw her, he thought that she was going to save him because she knew he wasn't guilty.

"This is in the western United States in the nineteenth century. He is accused of rustling cattle. She knew that he didn't do it because she was with him somewhere else when it happened. But she is afraid of all these people. They are both strangers in this place. They arrived together; they had been lovers, but not a couple. The sheriff caught him doing something that made him think that Matthew was the one who took the cattle, so when Lana came up and he saw her, he thought, 'Oh, thank God, I am saved because she is going to tell them that I was with her!' But she didn't. She turned her back on him. She rode away. She could have saved him and she didn't. She didn't like him in either lifetime. She was afraid they would think she was involved too, but also in the mix was the fact that she didn't like him very much. They weren't a couple, and they weren't getting along. She just didn't feel that she wanted to risk her life for him when it might be her life too, so she just closed her eyes, turned around, and rode away."

Maitra went on to explain the relationship between the past life and what had happened in the present: "When they met again in this life, there was a lot of tension between them, a real push-pull; he wanted something from her and she felt that she owed him something. She felt some guilt because, in the past life, she rode away and left him to his fate, and he was hanged. This time, because of her guilt, she let him into her life as much as she did. He was a really confused, mixed-up person, and she didn't care for him.

"In that past life, he wasn't guilty of stealing cattle; he was just a stranger there. Today, in killing Lana, he created more karma for himself. Turning her back on him in that previous lifetime doesn't excuse his killing her. It wasn't a balancing of karma. He did wrong. It was her guilt that left the door open for that. But she didn't deserve to die. She didn't kill him in the past life; she just refused to help him."

A few months later, Alan had gained some distance from these events. He explained how his view of these events had changed as he processed the Reading:

"I don't know much about reincarnation. I'm a very simple person. To be sure, I have seen other dimensions through experiences with drugs. But I don't give much importance to that, even though I have seen other realities in my dreams.

"When I'm painting or making music, the craft is important to me. When I paint, I have to concentrate fully to make something I'm satisfied with. I'm here and focused on the material. A painting or a piece of music should have a magical effect on me. If someone is looking at a picture, the eye should want to linger because it feels good to look at it; then it automatically opens up other dimensions.

"There are people whom I easily trust; I simply like to be with them. If I think about reincarnation, I can imagine that I have met people with whom I have been traveling for a long time. I have, of course, read about it, but I ask myself, 'Where will it lead? Are we caught in this eternal cycle? Do we have to go through man's total existence in millions of lives?' Then we would all have to do or experience everything once. That's how I imagine it, but there's a voice in me that tells me that I don't want this. I prefer to believe in life as I know it.

"Perhaps the past life makes Lana and Matthew's story more understandable, but it doesn't quite make sense to me. This murder was real to me. It doesn't matter to me if a past life affected it. It doesn't change things for me. This background doesn't help me process it any more easily.

"All this stuff about past lives, depending on the circumstances, could be everything, or it could be nothing. I don't think it's that important. I have to accept what happened to Lana and come to terms with it. I don't want to think about if this is a matter of karma. It is enough as it is. I don't need to look at other dimensions and process them in addition. What I'm experiencing in this life is already a lot.

"In the time that has passed, I have gotten some distance from this horrible event. If I think about what happened, I return to this sense of powerlessness and sorrow. Yet, some things have changed: I no longer think about it as much. It often comes to mind during the day, but no longer like in the beginning, when I thought about it from morning to night. I have some distance from what happened, and without some inner reconciliation, I couldn't go on living. It has made me more contemplative, and I'm no longer feeling as carefree and happy. I would like to become lighter and happier again."

Open your eyes of love,
And see Him who pervades the world!
Consider it well, and know
that this is your own country.

—Kabir

For Your Toolkit: Trusting the Universe

Trusting that there is a bigger plan at work in the Universe, trusting God or whatever term you use for God means that when tragedy happens, even though you may not understand it, you trust that there is purpose in it that, in the end, will be of benefit to everyone. A good example can be found in the New Testament: When Jesus was praying in the Garden before his arrest, he asked his Father to remove the cup of suffering. Then he surrendered, "Not my will, but yours be done." Here Jesus demonstrated the turning point in trusting the Universe for all of us.

In his surrender to the situation, he recognized that there was a bigger plan at work; he realized that God the Father was not punishing him, but using him to demonstrate a higher truth, even though he didn't fully understand it at that moment.

In the same way, in Alan's experience, there was an outworking of the Law of Karma, a lesson that both his friend and her killer needed to learn. Again, this was not a punishment, but a lesson that would ultimately benefit both of them. She needed to learn to have compassion for a fellow human, even at risk to herself, and he needed to learn the futility of revenge, which can trap us in an endless loop of hurting and being hurt, or, in this case, killing and being killed.

For all of us, it is crucial that we, through self-examination, define what we believe or know to be the nature of the Universe. If you believe the nature of the universe to be random, then of course you will be unable to trust it. In that case, it is time to discover and study Universal Law, such as the Law of Karma and the Law of Attraction. Learn about how the Universe works, and I am confident you will come to the same conclusion I did: The Universe works inexorably to benefit us. The true nature of the universe is universal or cosmic love, and it works over lifetimes. When we feel it, we call it God.

When we can quiet our doubts with trust in the beneficent nature of the Universe, we will have inner peace. We enter Paradise.

Chapter 27: The Tender Bond of Love

For Your Toolkit: Law of Attraction

(Gloria, born 1964)

Gloria, divorced, is an artist and teacher of art, and the mother of two adult children. She had had an affair with Pierre. Many years passed before he contacted her again, and they made love. She had been living alone for several years and she wanted to clarify why she had met this man and why they have this strong sexual attraction without commitment. She was reluctant to express all of her feelings for him and was not sure whether a committed relationship with him would be at all possible. She wanted to be able to clarify this for herself. She came to Maitra with this question: 'Is there a karmic connection with Pierre, a man for whom I have loving feelings?' Following is the exchange with Maitra regarding Gloria and Pierre:

M: Are you in love with Pierre?

G: Not really. When we are together, I feel love. I feel the inner connection.

M: I see. You don't let yourself fall in love with him. You feel love for him but you don't let yourself fall into it because he doesn't make himself available to you. He is here today and gone tomorrow. A commitment? Not likely. But you have such an appreciation for each other. There is something that makes him want to come back, again and again, and when he doesn't see you for a long time, you still come into his mind.

G: Why is it like this? I mean, I am older, and he's so young ...

M: No, you are not that old and he's not so young; you are both in your middle years.

What I see with him right now is, if you showed him that you wanted something more, he would be happy about it. He is always very careful not to overstep. Do you notice how tentative he is around your house? He is looking to see if things are OK with you. He doesn't necessarily say it all the time but he is sensitive to you. It's not his place. That's a description of him in the world. He is careful not to overstep his place. He understands that some people don't like him because of his color, because he is black. Pierre has accepted something about himself that is not true. He has accepted that he's not as good as white people; intellectually, he understands it's prejudice, but he can't quite shake it off.

And here's the thing: In the Caribbean, where he grew up, he was always looking for his place because he is part white. He didn't quite fit into the black culture either. He doesn't dwell on it or think about it very much. He believes that he's never going to fit in, so he keeps himself free to move on. Before anybody can hurt him, he is already ready to go so he can't be rejected. This has all happened to him before.

Underlying everything is his doubt, as to whether or not he can be loved. And you, with your sensitivity, can feel it, so you don't push him there. Did you ever tell him that you love him?

G: I show him that I love him but not with words. I never dare. I hold back because I don't know what he will do with it. Maybe he will hear it like a promise, and come back someday and make demands on me that I don't want to meet.

M: Here is what happens: You mirror what he does. If he tells you that he loves you, then you would have an advantage over him. If you tell him that you love him, then he has an advantage over you. You both have this belief. That's the basis of trust: Trusting someone enough to say what is true at the moment and knowing that it will be OK, and not used against you. You know there is a scared little guy in there, and he could just take off—poof, like that—if you say the wrong word. You can't count on him.

I think he is waiting for a signal to tell him that he can show his love. It's not just with you or with one person, but more generally. He is always a little guarded and you are well aware of this so you guard yourself too.

G: How do I affect the other person if I am so open and express my love? What's going on with the other person when I do that? How many expectations might I awaken in him?

M: That's not the bottom line. That's where you are guarding yourself; you guard by looking at him and seeing what he's going to do next before you decide what to do. What is going on underneath is that you are protecting yourself: Can you handle whatever comes as a result if he starts to have expectations?

G: This is my challenge. He appears and then he disappears. I could go there and see him. Would he disappear again, or would he be there for me? But I don't know much about his life. Would it be better for me just to end this relationship?

M: There is nothing in him that wants to hurt people. It is more about him being careful to protect himself. He's not very complicated. Protected, but not complex. He is careful with what he can assume. He tries not to assume anything.

Here is an interesting little piece of the puzzle of Pierre: In his last lifetime, he was an African Prince. You can see that in him; nobility is also there. But he doesn't know what to do with that; it confuses him a lot. Sometimes he feels like he is as good as anybody else, maybe even better, but he doesn't dare to let that come to the surface because, in his mind, nobody would understand it.

Look at the match between you. He looks to other people to see how to behave. And so do you. Before you decide to just be yourself, you are looking to see what effect it would have on him. You haven't decided to just be yourself yet, to let the chips fall where they may, because you don't yet trust that whatever has to be worked out, can be worked out in the moment. Ideally, you can be yourself without worrying about what anyone else is going to do with it.

Maybe you will start to see where you are still being careful to protect yourself. It's time to 'destroy your reputation,' as Rumi says. And don't worry if you feel like saying to Pierre, 'I love you!' Be yourself, whatever that means. It doesn't have to mean anything at all beyond what you just said. It might scare him; it might cause him to start to build a little dream, but so what? It's only an observation of what you are feeling.

That you love him and enjoy sex with him, that's lovely; it's a good exchange. You know sexual compatibility is actually pretty rare. It sometimes doesn't happen even when you have a strong feeling of being attracted to someone, or are in love with them.

In this Reading, it was inevitable that there would be a look at a past life; the energy demanded it:

"Oh, my goodness! It is in the South of what is now the United States. At that time, it was the Confederacy; it was in the early 1800s, before the Civil War. He was a slave owner. He was the son of a rich white man, a Frenchman in the South who owned a huge plantation with tobacco, cotton, and fruit orchards. This rich man, who was his father, had daughters but never a son with his white wife. But he had a son with his black mistress; their son was born looking white. Such things are unpredictable. This baby boy is the one who is Pierre, your lover today.

"His father convinced his wife, who was ill, to pretend that the baby boy was her son; she didn't fight this. His birth mother, the black woman, was the one who was taking care of him. So, he grew up thinking that his mother was the one in the bed, and the one who was lovingly caring for both of them was a servant. The two women liked each other.

"Gloria, you were black in that lifetime. You were a house slave. You came into the house when another servant died. At that point, the son didn't know yet that he was half-black. He fell in love with you and was sleeping with you right away, and it was clear to his father that he was more than a little interested in you. His father told him who his real mother was to warn him that, if the two of you had children, it would be difficult to predict what color they would be, and it would create a lot of problems. He said to his son, 'Better if you find a white woman to marry.' And he added, 'Or you could do what I did. You could keep her as a lover, a mistress, but be prepared for what might happen with the children. It's not going to be easy.'

"So, the son—Pierre in this life—came to you with this proposal: 'I will marry a white woman and will keep you as my mistress. You will no longer be a slave, and I will build you a little house.' And you said, 'Set me free. I don't want to be a slave.' He replied, 'If I set you free, then you don't have to stay here.' You answered him: 'Exactly. Maybe I don't want to stay here. I don't know.'

"This took place in what is now called the state of Georgia. You said to him, 'OK, but before you get married, I want you to take me to France. I want to see Paris; I want us to travel together.' He agreed. You couldn't travel together until you got to Europe because it was illegal in Georgia for you to be a couple. He took you to France; you fell in love with Paris, and you asked him, 'Are you going to set me free?' Pierre said, 'Yes, I will.' And you responded, 'Well then when I'm free, this is where I want to live. You can buy me a little apartment, and you can come and see me here, where we can be a couple, even if you are married to a wife at home.'

"At that time, it took a month to sail across the Atlantic and a month to get back. When you told him you wanted to live in Paris, you both knew what you were asking. He loved you and he said, 'Couldn't you come back and stay with me in America sometimes?' You replied to him: 'Here, in France, when we have children, they will be free from the beginning, and you can pay for them to go to the university, if they want to.' He hesitantly agreed. You had a son and then a daughter; they were beautiful children. You gratefully said to him, 'I'm happy to raise the children here where we can be free.' At that time, Paris was very open. You felt better there, you didn't have to watch everything you were doing, or be afraid that people were going to arrest you. In Georgia, even a very kind owner couldn't protect you from everything.

"You both accepted living apart. He was responsible for his father's plantation when his father got old. He had to stay there and take care of it, and he had a wife, and children with her. When he could get away, he would come and spend a month or two with you.

"You had a lovely apartment in Paris. He took good care of you. He would often beg you to come back to Georgia. He promised again to build you a house, but you said, 'I don't want my children to be brought up there.' At that time, in the South, you had to always carry your papers to prove that you were free.

"You loved each other throughout that life."

After the past life Reading, Maitra went on to explain how this is affecting the present:

M: Today, Pierre has become very good at being who people want him to be. It is rare for him to relax and just be himself. Perhaps he can let his guard down a bit more with you because of this history.

In the past life, he was always worried that you would find another man, living in Paris, but you said to him, 'I'm not interested in opening up that problem. I love you and I'm here, and whenever you come, you will find me here. I'm not looking for anybody else.' He was a wealthy man, with many responsibilities, but he managed to come at least once a year to be with you and his children.

G. With this background, I can understand our relationship better and live more freely. The love is still there but there is not much attachment.

M: You learned to live separately from each other and still be in love, but you didn't want to be back in Georgia. Your children would have been compromised. France was different then; there was more creativity. You were doing volunteer work in hospitals and with orphaned children. He was able to set things up so that you would never have to worry about money, even if something should happen to him.

Now he likes to keep things separate. That's who he is. You could imagine that he always had to hide who he was. What if somebody had found out that he was a Negro at that time? The only people who knew this were his biological mother, his father, and his father's wife. But there was always a chance that somebody would figure it out. Of course, the doctor of his father's wife knew it, but he was a crusty old guy who didn't follow the rules either. They could trust him not to say anything.

Gloria's Transformation

Some time went by, allowing Gloria to reflect on her relationship with Pierre. With her new understanding from the Reading, things between them did, in fact, become clearer to her.

"I find this story of the past life extraordinary, and it moves me deeply. Before I learned about this past life, I was in the process of planning a trip to Paris to visit friends. I wanted to ask Pierre if he would like to come with me and spend time in Paris. However, things didn't turn out this way. Other events intervened.

"The Reading described my emotional world and attitudes toward him very well. My reluctance to show him my feelings, and his way of distancing himself from his feelings are evident. We can still be close, even physically intimate, with each other in the moment.

"Because of his cultural background and his rootlessness in this current life—his mother is black and from the Caribbean, and his father is white and from France, and he looks African— he often distances himself a little. I can feel that it isn't easy for him to commit himself to anything. I can understand and accept much better the fact that he isn't always fully available, now that I know his background, and I continue to appreciate and like him so much when I see him.

"At that time, when I claimed my freedom for myself and our children, my need for independence was already apparent. I cherish my liberation as a woman; this still dominates my life. I have a longing for spiritual liberation, so that I can continue to grow and resolve karmic entanglements. By gaining new insights, I want to better understand myself in these relationships. I appreciate that he understood me at that time, and that he, as a free 'white' man, could make a life of freedom possible for me, a black woman. I can still feel today that he is open and supportive.

"The Reading clarified why it wouldn't work for me to live with him today. I feel better, and I can reflect on how I behave in relationships today. It's a matter of expressing authentic feelings, and being honest with myself and others.

"Through these few encounters with Pierre, there has arisen neither a dependency nor an emotional bond that is full of expectations. This has been a freeing experience for me. I view it as an opportunity for learning, and also as a gift. I have a completely new perspective.

"We repeatedly encounter familiar and trusted soulmates on our path through life; we are connected to them by the tender bond of love. The love is interwoven within the memories of our souls; we feel this bond of love again from the very first moment when we encounter each other.

"It helps me that I can feel our karmic connection. It brought us together again as lovers, and I can express my feelings without expectations. The Reading helped me to let go of some old conditioning, and I have more courage for spontaneous connections and feelings. I'm learning to make the most of the moment and just let things happen. I'm very grateful for the insights from the Reading that held up a mirror for me so that I could reflect and get to know myself better.

"When I reached puberty, I often dreamt of a dark-skinned boy who was lying beside me; sometimes I imagined him next to me in my waking hours. I was filled with a longing and there was something intimate in this. I think I was remembering Pierre at that time, my connection to him, and to his soul. Although we live independent lives today, and I can see that I can't live in a partnership with him, our encounters have awakened this longing, and a capacity for intimacy in me."

Run from what's comfortable
Forget safety.
Live where you fear to live.
Destroy your reputation.
Be notorious.

—Rumi

For Your Toolkit: Law of Attraction

This is a simplification, but think of it this way: Each of us has four bodies—a physical, an emotional, a mental, and a spiritual body. Each body vibrates at its own rate, depending on our level of development. The Law of Attraction says, "Like attracts Like"; this means that we attract people who vibrate at the same rate as we do, at each level of development. For example, in Gloria's case, the attraction is primarily in the physical body. A physical attraction alone, even if it is very strong, does not bode well for a lasting relationship. We need at least two bodies, vibrating at the same rate to have a workable relationship. For example, if Gloria and Pierre were also on the same spiritual path, their relationship might progress to something more. Or, if they also shared intellectual interests, and their mental bodies vibrated at the same rate, a relationship might be assured. It's rare, but if three bodies were vibrating at the same rate in the beginning of the relationship, then there would be lots of room for change. Today, when change is so rapid, this would give a good chance for a long-term relationship.

If you look at all your relationships through this lens, defining which bodies are engaged in each case, you will begin to understand why some relationships are so vibrant and last for many years, while others fade quickly away. Also, remember that, because the vibration of each body changes as we grow, it's literally true that we "grow apart" or "grow closer."

Understanding the Law of Attraction allows us to let go of blame and take these changes in relationships less personally. When relationships end, it's usually a case of people growing apart, rather than right or wrong. If children and parents don't understand each other, the cause may lie in their bodies vibrating at different rates, rather than either person being at fault. For example, when a child or a parent has a powerful learning experience, it will change the vibration of the mental body and possibly the emotional body.

Understanding this can help us accept each other and ourselves. Change in relationships is inevitable, and we don't always change at the same rate as the other guy.

Understanding this gives us a way out of the blame game! Freedom!

Chapter 28: Recognizing and Living One's Soul Plan

For Your Toolkit: Hanging out with the Enlightened Ones

(Alice, born 1966)

Alice, a mother of three grown children and a Shiatsu therapist with a successful career, was feeling restless and ready for some change. She described her state of mind in her initial conversation with Maitra:

A: I am in the process of trusting myself more and more, and finding answers from within. I would like to be better at feeling my inner path, the path of my soul. I can't yet feel that very well. I am a Shiatsu therapist. Fifteen years ago, I had the urge to follow this path. I began my massage training, and have moved forward step by step.

M: What are your doubts?

A: I no longer feel the energy that I had at the start. I don't have the same fire as earlier. I have a sense that things are moving in the direction of a spiritual transformation such as psychic work or even mediumship. On the one hand, I'm interested and have a good feeling about it. On the other hand, I have a lot of questions: Is this really something for me? Do I want to go in this direction? I feel this change, and this time it isn't a 'have to.'

M: Have you ever been to Japan? Do you feel drawn to Japan?

A: I've never been there, but I do feel an attraction to it.

M: Why haven't you gone there?

A: I booked a trip there two years ago, but then the tsunami came so I couldn't go, and I didn't book another trip. I didn't have another opportunity, or feel the same need to go there.

M: If you think about going there, what do you imagine will happen?

A: There's really nothing there that would be exciting. I'm sure there are beautiful places and cities to visit. I'm noticing now, at my age, that many of my friends are doing this or that with great enthusiasm, but things feel different to me, and then I think that I'm not like other people.

M: Why should you be like others?

A: Yes, I know.

There was a strong sense of a next step waiting to happen with Alice, prompting Maitra to say:

"When you told me that you are a Shiatsu therapist, the first thing I saw was that you were Japanese in a past life. You were one of the two people who initially developed Shiatsu. At that time it was called *anma*. You were involved in it from the start. In your current life, you wanted to reconnect with it and look around to see what is being done with it today. What has become of it? How has it further developed? How has it changed? How have the old structures been preserved?"

Alice was not expecting that but willingly accepted it. Here is the transcript of their conversation:

A: Does this explain why I have chosen it again in this life?

M: Yes, because it is your 'child.' And your 'child' can also continue to grow and develop.

A: If I enroll in further training, I'll be somewhat bored.

M: Look at what you've done: You have revolutionized 'healing.' Shiatsu was a revelation and a revolution. Something in you says, 'If I have done this once, then I can do it again. This is what motivates me: To discover something new, so that things really change for the better.'

A: The Shiatsu that I now practice is no longer the same Shiatsu as it once was. I have developed something that's my own form; it's unique.

M: One could look up the name of the founder; there were two people who worked together. Perhaps the name came from one of the people, but I see that two people were involved in it. You worked together, and inspired each other, and what you created and experienced together was rewarding and exciting.

A: When I attend continuing education classes and other classes for Shiatsu today, I often come back home afterwards and say to myself, 'Yes, it was all well and good, but I hold back because I don't want to show off and say, 'Hey, listen, I can also teach you all of this, I know all of this.'

M: But you would be pleased if they could teach you something, because you're always looking for something new and exciting, for both the known and the unknown.

Here's your next dilemma: You're always looking externally for answers, even for guidance. If you don't find it, you begin to be bored. You became a classic workaholic in the past life, in that you no longer had time for anything else. You sacrificed what you loved—your wife and your family—everything that was important to you, to your work, in order to develop this method of healing. You don't want to make this mistake again today. This makes you feel a bit insecure. You're thinking to yourself: 'Why don't I have the same values as other people? Why do I always look for something more?' But that's who you are. You have the energy of a pioneer: You love to be on the cusp, to cross boundaries, to move forward. If I were you, I would go to Japan and look at what they have done with Shiatsu. The people there are innovators; they continue to develop the familiar techniques even further. And you were one of the creators of this method.

A: I feel somewhat burned out and tired when I think about my work these days. And I'm not really up for new experiences. This way I can enjoy life. I have time now for other things, and I like that. I know work isn't everything.

M: You are in the process of learning that you want to give more attention to other things like your family and friends. You are finding a balance, a new harmoniousness, and learning to live your life so you don't miss the best things, as you did in the past life. You won't have to be alone at the end.

I hear you saying, "I have achieved something wonderful. Indeed, I left a legacy for the entire world, and people continue to benefit from it, but I lost my happiness in the process." This is your dilemma, your inner conflict. You are looking for the edge. We all encounter the upheaval and chaos in the world today. Our creativity burns in response to the suffering. We want to find ways to heal each other, to understand each other. We want to create methods for understanding how the body, mind, and spirit function. It is an amazing time to be living.

A: Does it make sense for me to go more toward psychic work and get more training? Or do you see some fear in me that would prevent me from doing this?

M: I don't see much fear in you. If you are afraid, it is of losing yourself in only one project, like you did before. You have begun to master this very well, remembering that it is painful if one no longer has family and friends. You need to have people around you, whom you care about. In this life, today, you don't want to lose any friends. The path of psychic healing is attracting you. Go in that direction until you become clear about what you want and where you stand. You already use your third eye in the work you're doing with Shiatsu. It is important for you to know that. If you develop your third eye further, you will be that much more powerful in your healing work. You will discover your own way of using it, as you did with Shiatsu. I am not a medium, I am a seer.

A: What is the difference?

M: I don't contact deceased people like your relatives, as a medium would. I shift my focus, alter my consciousness, look at the person I'm reading for, find and 'follow the energy' and tell you what I am "reading" from there.

What do you think of the words 'pioneer' or 'trailblazer'? That is how I see you. It isn't your way to follow what others have done. You can do it to be together with friends, but you aren't completely satisfied. You prefer to go to the outer limit, and then you want to cross that boundary too, and move into the unknown.

A: I don't fully trust myself there yet.

M: Yes, because in the past life, when you were one of the initiators of Shiatsu, you paid too high a price, and it cost you your personal happiness. You don't want to repeat this. Now you are looking for the path where you can have both. Your inner passion guides you and continues to carry you to the edge of what is known. You also want to be connected with the people you love and feel close to. It's important to you to keep these relationships happy and healthy. In this way, you will have achieved a balance between your life with people you love, and your urge to cross boundaries. It isn't always easy.

A: Sometimes, when I look at what everyone else is doing, my self-worth feels unstable.

M: You will have to give something up. You must stop, right now, comparing yourself with others. When you master that, you will begin to become more aware of your inner teacher. According to the Buddhist teachings, you earned merit, or good karma, when you invented Shiatsu. When you do work that will benefit others, such as creating a healing method, you collect merit. This credit will be to your benefit later, and you will have your heart's desire. You don't have negative karma. The fact that you sometimes feel unsure of yourself, is a reminder that you were so out of balance in the past life. Even if you often feel insecure, you have moments of absolute delight. Let all your doubts fall away; they are limiting you.

Now would be a good time for you to find a teacher. You probably won't find any teacher of Shiatsu who knows more than you. But a spiritual teacher will direct you more toward your inner self and will help you devote yourself to this inner guidance.

Have you visited saints and avatars like Mother Meera or Amma?

A: No.

M: Go to see Mother Meera; she's very humble. She is simply the universe; that's how I experienced her. She doesn't *do* anything with anybody except that, by her presence, she invites you to experience your Eternal Self more fully. It would be beneficial for you to meet her. She makes herself available, if one feels called to visit her, in order to have the experience of your own Divine Self.

A: I wish that someone would take me by the hand and lead me to something like this.

M: It is also possible to call her on the phone and ask her any questions that you have; her assistants will communicate her answers to you. She offers this kind of assistance to everybody who wants it. I think that these non-authoritarian teachers would be a revelation for you because they aren't seeking followers, and you can come and go as you please. They teach through their presence, not by asking you to change.

Amma is the "hugging" teacher, and she also gives one the feeling of no separation, the sense that you are One with the universe. These contacts will help you accept who you are and be at peace with yourself. Even when you are driven to cross boundaries, it's OK. You are who you are. It's a matter of you being able to trust yourself from moment to moment. It is simple, and it's difficult. In order to feel that we belong to the human species, we automatically look around us to see what others are doing and compare ourselves. It is revolutionary when we no longer do this, but I can assure you that this is evolution in action. When you drop the comparing, you will discover that you already have a deep connection with everyone else, and that you are One with everything. That is the edge you have been seeking.

At this point another past life made itself known to Maitra:

M: I see another past life, and I want to tell you that you had a life as a shaman. You were the pupil of a shaman in the Brazilian jungle. It was three or four lives back. You studied and worked with healing plants, and you helped people become free of suffering. You also worked as a healer and used natural substances, like the one we call Ayahuasca, to help people.

When you were in the jungle with all these people, you were in an altered state of consciousness and you created a very protective space for your students. They were under your protection when a wildfire broke out. The group was composed of about fifty people and half of them died in this fire; some died from the flames, and some from the smoke. You were so focused on your work and concentrating so much on the people and what happened to them there in the jungle, that you hadn't recognized the fire soon enough.

Are you interested in shamanism?

A: Yes, but if I don't have a strong, affirming 'Yes' about something, I prefer to wait.

Maitra began to see some connections between Alice's current lack of direction and occasional lack of confidence in what had happened in her past life:

M: You considered yourself responsible for the death of these people, and that's why this fear has remained in you. The ambivalence in you comes from this experience when it was a matter of being responsible for other people.

Alice's Transformation

Two years later, Alice was ready to talk about her journey with the information from the Reading: "I can say, from the depths of my heart, that the Reading has had a lasting effect, and I felt moved in my soul, accepted, and understood.

"My urge to achieve even more has calmed down and I became much quieter and calmer in the weeks afterwards. When I am with other people, I can let the healing flow without doing much. The gift that I have, the ability to guide people as they expand their consciousness, is beginning to flow more and more.

"I have learned from the Reading that it is my right to find balance so that I can take better care of myself and experience joy. In fact, I have more and more moments of joy. I have become brave enough to say 'No,' when my heart doesn't respond with a 'Yes' to something asked of me.

"I appreciate the suggestion to arrange a meeting with Mother Meera, and I look forward to this healing encounter."

Never hurt another's heart.
Even if a person hurts you, give him love.
I could not get angry with you, even in a dream.
If you cannot love each other, you cannot achieve your goal.

—Neem Karoli Baba (Maharaj-ji)

For Your Toolkit: Hanging out with the Enlightened Ones

I'm convinced that there are more living saints, or enlightened beings on the planet today than ever before. We need all the help we can get because we are on the edge of a huge evolutionary shift, and the resulting chaos is challenging.

When a person is going through the kind of profound shift that Alice was experiencing, visiting an enlightened being can help you to ground yourself in that higher vibration—Alice called it Harmony. It can also be called Divine Love or Peace.

When you are facing such compelling challenges, I urge you to go find one of these extraordinary people and attend one of their gatherings, or "sit" with them for a while. Some events cost money—the expenses can be huge—but basically nothing will be asked of you. You will be welcomed.

Most well-known teachers have a website listing the schedules of their appearances. There are the famous ones:

- The Dali Lhama

- Amma

- Mother Meera

- Guru Mai

- Mooji

- Gangaji

- Adyshanti

- Eckhart Tolle

Plus the ones who are not so famous, perhaps living down the street from you. (Some estimate that there are up to 10,000 enlightened people on the planet right now, although you'll find a lot of disagreement.)

Time spent sitting with the enlightened ones can only benefit you in countless ways.

Here are a few of the benefits that you will find in the presence of an enlightened being:

- You cannot deny your divine nature

- The possibility of self-realization becomes real

- Your interest in judging others begins to fade

- You feel Divine Love and Peace within yourself

- More hope for humanity seems obvious and natural

- You feel excited because there is so much more to learn; you have glimpsed your eternal nature which is unlimited, and unknowable.

Chapter 29: Accepting and Forgiving My Abusive Brother

For Your Toolkit: Forgiveness

(Isabel, born 1995)

Isabel is a masseuse and laying-on-of-hands healer. Isabel's family consisted of her mother and two other sisters. Her father died when she was six years old.

She continued to be plagued with memories of abuse in childhood by her brother, who is three years older. It began when she was about nine years old. She can't remember all of the events, but he repeatedly came into her room when everyone else was asleep. When everybody was in bed, Isabel knew that her brother would come into her room and what he would do. For Isabel, this was the bad time of day. She felt she was at his mercy. To be sure, they didn't have intercourse, but he wanted to be physically close and touch her all over her body. In the beginning, she strongly resisted, but over time she gave up. In a certain way, Isabel became numb because he went to her room so often.

At some point, it felt like Isabel came back to life, and she began to defend herself. During vacation, her mother once divided them up so that her two sisters were together in one room, and Isabel had to share a room with her brother. In this situation, when he approached her again, Isabel said to him,

"If you don't stop, I will jump out the window!" She was absolutely serious, and she would have taken her life. He approached her again and again and asked if he could join her, and she said 'No!' So, it gradually became clear that Isabel could say 'No,' and then it was over. There were some moments when Isabel almost felt sorry for him when she refused him, but by then she knew that she could stick with saying 'No!'

Isabel couldn't get help from her mother, and she wanted to protect her brother. She thought to herself, *If I get this ball rolling here, i.e. tell on him, everything in our family will be out of control and I will be the one who then has to bear responsibility.* Isabel feared that her mother would be totally overwhelmed and wouldn't be able to handle it. Isabel just didn't want to do this to her. She thought that she would be blamed for everything. She also couldn't tell her sisters anything about it. Isabel kept it a secret and tried to hold everything together herself.

Isabel's sisters were also furious at their brother from time to time, and they were very critical of his behavior. In these situations, Isabel was often tempted to tell the whole story and condemn him for what he was doing to her. But she held back because it would have turned the entire family on its head. Finally, Isabel decided to consult Maitra, after hearing one of her talks.

This is what Maitra discovered about Isabel's past life in their first meeting:

"You are a young woman on an island. You work for a living as a waitress in a restaurant. There's a cook, who would always try to get your attention, because he fell in love with you, and all he wants is for you to be his wife. It takes a while to persuade you to love him back.

"When the two of you finally get together and marry, you have a happy relationship, and after a short time, you become pregnant.

"One day, during your pregnancy, he had to leave you for a while to work on a ship. He didn't come back because the ship capsized, and he drowned.

"For the rest of that life, you worked and did your best to take care of your child, alone.

"And now in this life, the two of you become brother and sister, and he's very confused about his feelings for you. That would be the reason, but not an excuse for the sexual incidents. He never intended to hurt you. He feels guilty about what happened between the two of you. You must continue to hold the boundary that you courageously set when you were young; then you can relax with each other and redefine your relationship.

"And, of course, he loves you. As you do him."

Isabel's Transformation:

In a follow-up conversation with Isabel, some months later, she talks about the change in her way of thinking:

"After the Reading, there was a change in me. I began to consider the whole relationship with my brother from a different perspective. I no longer felt like a victim with all the thoughts of what had happened to me with him. My entire view of it changed. I understood it differently and could see that the whole thing was much more multi-layered than I had originally thought.

"At the beginning, I didn't know how to deal with this information. I understood why this had all happened and realized that this was connected to a past life. However, I didn't know how I should act toward him now. I was often still furious at him, and his behavior still irritated me. The Reading suggested that I begin to sow seeds of love, so to speak, on this pile of shit that had developed as a result of his behavior and his and my confusion.

"It was important for me to forgive him, and to be able to transform my anger at him into forgiveness and love. Now that I know this story, I can admit that there were more feelings in all of this. Through the connection from the past life, he felt attracted to me, and perhaps he wasn't able to act in any other way. I often thought about the saying 'Plant seeds of love.' Even if it's only by saying a nice word, having a positive thought, or being understanding, this is something that can grow.

"In the beginning, I found this quite difficult; however, this proverb guided me. It was powerful and gave me energy. I tried to stop understanding everything intellectually because my ethical-moral ideal said, 'One can't do that, that's impossible. A brother doesn't abuse his little sister!' But I can understand now that there were karmic connections, including mental, spiritual, and emotional connections, and I can look at it differently. After that, those feelings of being a victim began to dissolve. It gave me a new understanding of what had happened.

"In the past life, I was left a widow. Perhaps this rage, which I still often felt, was also connected to this experience because I was abandoned and left behind, alone with my child. He had left me alone, and I never knew why.

"Today, I know that, as a child in this difficult situation, I did feel empathy for my brother, and I couldn't refuse him. I can't explain this rationally. This played out on an entirely different level.

"Through the Reading, I'm learning to stop judging these actions. This makes it possible for me to have a better understanding and accept that there was a reason for all of these painful experiences. On the emotional level, I am less vulnerable today.

"Through the clarifications in the Reading, I now have some distance from this, and my role in the family system has changed. We are still living together today, and I encounter my brother more on an emotional level and can recognize his good qualities. He is a young man with a good heart, and I see his great need for love and affection. I can see that he is also a loving person. He loves all of us, and I can feel it.

"Although he sometimes still uses offensive language and acts macho, I nevertheless can see his authentic being. I can let go of troublesome situations with him relatively quickly, and I can set boundaries. Today, I am aware that my behavior has a strong effect on him. I can choose if I want to react to him with hate, rage, and rejection, or if I want to sow these seeds of love. My relationship with him has changed a lot. I wasn't able to do this earlier. He irritated me, and I constantly felt that his behavior was inappropriate because I had so much rage. This rage is transformed, and our relationship has become more loving and honest. I also see that he is becoming more sensitive.

"The Reading suggested that I tell him that I forgive him because he feels guilty and carries the memories of not only his hurtful behavior in this lifetime but also the past life abandonment. I don't want to address this directly, but I communicate it to him on a spiritual and emotional level. This Reading has helped me a lot, and I think that he feels better, too.

"When I had the Reading, I was overwhelmed in a way. I received all this information, and then the question came, 'What next?' But over time I could see that this knowledge was affecting my feelings. This has been so helpful. A lot of my perceptions shifted and I understand the karmic patterns that are now changing. I needed some time to process everything.

"The Reading also helped me take responsibility. I got valuable pointers on how to handle this. By going through this process, I am learning how to heal myself. This is very important to me because when I receive information, it doesn't yet mean that I have understood it completely in every cell.

I'm beginning a stage in which everything is transforming. Maitra doesn't promise to heal us. She hands over this responsibility to us in a very beautiful, understandable way.

"I had a long relationship—at least for me at my age—before I began my training as a healer. I ended this relationship because my partner wanted to have sex quite often and I could no longer take the pressure. It hurt me to refuse him—just like I felt sorry for my brother when I began to say 'No'—so I separated from my boyfriend even though I loved him. He didn't know anything about my family history and why I found it difficult to always be available to his needs. I loved him very much, and I found it difficult to let him go. But I felt so much pressure from him and this weighed me down.

"I have an easy time falling in love, but to have sex with someone with whom I have a deep emotional attachment can be difficult for me. It was always a battle between 'I'd like that,' and the deep rage that the pressure would awaken in me.

"Ever since I gained insight into these entanglements from the Reading, my general anger at men has lessened. I now know that I can always decide, at any time, what and how much I want to do. I no longer feel so powerless and victimized—in reality, I never was, it just felt that way. I can approach men now positively, be more relaxed, and enjoy them.

"Nevertheless, I haven't had a serious relationship since my last boyfriend. This could be a result of not finding the right person and because I have needed a lot of time to process my childhood and get some distance from it.

"I think that new obstacles may come up in me, as soon as I get involved in a serious relationship again. Everything that I am going through right now needs to be put into action. To open myself anew, to communicate clearly, and to be aware that I can decide when things will happen, are only some of the tasks that I have given myself. I think I'm now in a place to talk with my next partner honestly about this. I am very hopeful and full of excitement, and my view of these experiences in my childhood has changed for the better."

Out, beyond ideas of wrongdoing and rightdoing
There is a field ... I'll meet you there.
When the soul lies down in that grass
the world is too full to talk about.

—Rumi

For Your Toolkit: Forgiveness

We all know intuitively that holding on to past hurts quickly becomes an obstacle to our Freedom. Nelson Mandela once said: "When a deep injury is done to us, we never heal until we forgive." The theologian Lewis Smedes writes: "To forgive is to set a prisoner free and discover that the prisoner is you."

Keeping this advice in mind, recount to yourself the injury that hurt you so much. Then ask yourself: "Can I let go of all my feelings of blame, anger, and resentment toward the person, who hurt me?"

Ask yourself this question, as many times as necessary, and then practice answering 'Yes' until it feels genuine. You'll feel it when it lets go—your mind will say, "It's enough."

Forgiveness benefits the giver, whether or not it is known or received by the forgiven. This is good news because it means that we can forgive the other person—whether they are present or absent—without needing anything from them. Forgiveness does not imply any other result. You may still not wish to associate with that person. You don't need to forget what was done. Your letting go or forgiving will allow you to open your heart more. It opens the door to a future free of the fear of being hurt again.

You may want to take advantage of this bonus benefit: You now have the opportunity to examine what hurt you. Understanding this hurt will give you valuable self-knowledge. Additionally, you may have found a wound that needs healing, and you are now able to do that.

There can be a more radical result when you understand this fully. Then you may be moved to do the following: If someone hurts you, bow to them as your teacher, and say "Thank you!" (They don't have to be there.) You have now turned your hurt into something of value, a blessing. You have gained in wisdom and are strengthened by your painful experience.

Chapter 30: Solving a Seemingly Impossible Puzzle

For Your Toolkit: Expansion of Reality

(Linda, born 1958, her daughter Rose, born 1987)

Linda, a social worker and coach, was married and the mother of two daughters. She had come to Maitra because of her relationship with her older daughter, Rose. At that time, Rose was almost twenty-nine years old. Linda was worried that she was always too concerned and reactive about Rose's health and safety. She knew she was overreacting, but couldn't seem to change it. Here is a transcript of Maitra and Linda's initial conversation:

M: What is she doing that makes you worry about her?

L: Right now, she is going to the doctor because she feels burned out. She is very sensitive to noise and was, even as a child.

M: What is her profession?

L: She is a musician, an electric guitar player. She has a bachelor's degree and is now in a Master's Program in Interdisciplinary Arts.

M: That's quite an amazing thing to do! Why are you concerned? What is it that worries you? She is doing what she loves. That you worry too much tells me that you probably have some history or karma that's making you afraid for her.

L: Let me give you an example: Rose turned twenty-three in 2010. Around that time, something happened that made less and less sense to me. I had invited my daughter and her boyfriend to a concert. Other friends of ours were also there, about ten people. Everybody had taken their seats except for my daughter and her friend. I began to worry. We had just greeted each other at the coat check room, and everybody was looking forward to the concert. The concert hall was getting dark and the singer came on stage. But—where were my daughter and her friend?

I became very nervous and extremely worried. A panic attack gripped me. Images arose of my daughter collapsing, an ambulance being called and her being on the way to the hospital. I could only get through this panic state through deep breathing. From time to time, my mind would switch on. On the one hand, it wanted to calm me down, on the other, it was judging me, in the sense of "Now you're losing it!" I knew that I had to make it to intermission, somehow or other, and I did. During intermission, I left the auditorium. Soon I saw my daughter and her friend coming toward me, happy, and pleased with the performance. Literally, a burden fell from my heart when I saw them. They told me that they had found two better seats, further up front, and were sitting closer to the stage.

This is *one* example of many. I get myself into situations with her, again and again, in which I worry so much that it becomes intolerable. I realize that these reactions are not normal. I never had this feeling of uncontrollable fear toward my second daughter. I sense that these overwhelming fears don't have anything to do with letting go of one's children. But I don't know what to do about them. These fears put a strain on our relationship, even though I have never talked to her about them.

Maitra reassured Linda that what she considered to be overreactions had their basis in something from the past, from another life-time, and that once she understood this, she could relax and accept her daughter's behavior without overreacting. At the beginning of the Reading, Maitra sets the stage for the past life that follows:

M: When I go into Rose's energy field, I want to lean back. If I come forward, I don't know what will happen. I'm interpreting this funny position as her holding back. If anybody looks at this girl, they would never think that she's holding back. This girl is some level of genius. She is afraid of what will happen if she lets it be seen. It's so radical, so different. The amazing thing about her is that, even though she's holding back, people do think she is brilliant.

Whatever she decides to do, she does it well. Nobody has any idea of how much she is holding back. And you can feel this potential in her waiting, like a bomb. Like a bomb that dropped her on the earth and in your lap. And if it ever goes off, what is going to happen? I don't mean that it is in any way destructive. But I think that when she sets herself free, she is going to do something on this planet that is unique and amazing. And she'll do it when she finally feels safe, or when she decides to do it anyway, even if she doesn't feel safe. It's going to be so radical that it will cause people to question the nature of reality. It seems that she has a piece of the puzzle of human potential.

This little girl of yours came into the body in this lifetime and she knows something that nobody else has yet discovered. She is trying to create a platform to give what she intuitively knows. She wants to express it, but she looks around and says: 'It's too upsetting. People won't know what to do. It will cause conflict.' To her, it's like the ABCs, so basic, so fundamental. But she also understands what it will do. The image I keep seeing is of a grenade, which she carries within her.

Her contribution is going to revolutionize the way we see things, in some way.

As her mother, you can feel this potential in her. And you are fearful of what is going to happen. Two hundred years ago, even today in some parts of the planet, people like this would be killed. She is of the future. But look, she is not in Iran, not in China or Africa. She's not in a place where people have so much fear and superstition.

She will reveal this here in the West, where many people will be able to see and understand what she's saying. I don't know what she's going to do. Perhaps it will be a talk she gives, a book she writes, or a piece of music that she composes that turns everything upside down.

Other people have done this before; painters, who started new schools and everybody thinks it's dreadful to begin with because they haven't seen anything like it before. It's not that creating something new has never been done before, but they weren't your daughter! And music too, you know, every twenty or thirty years or whatever, can be just turned on its head. What people come up with musically can create fear and upset people. She has a gift that is like that, and it upsets what we have come to think of as the natural order. It's not going to kill her or anybody else. That's not what it is about. It's about the change in consciousness. Right now, she's gathering tools. She wants to have a good understanding of the whole creative process on all the different levels so that when she does step forward with this 'whatever it is,' there's a basis for it. She can defend it.

What I am saying is not surprising to you. It is more of a confirmation.

L: Yes, not surprising at all.

M: You don't have to be so afraid of it. She is going to do it in a part of the world where most people can accept radical new ideas.

L: Yes. That's good for her and me too. Can I show you a picture of her?

M: Yes, of course. Looking at the pictures ... You're right, she already lives in the future. She is waiting for something to fall into place around her, where there will be an opening for her. She's like Madonna—Madonna did that, and it turned our ideas upside down. Elvis did that. Obama did that.

L: I never could break the strength of her ideas; she always had her ideas.

M: She is channeling her potential right now in a safe way. And she is preparing herself for the time when she can let it come out. But there is also something else here. There is something so uncompromising about her. Her reality is her reality is her reality. And she can see that it's not the same as everybody else's. But that doesn't bother her. She doesn't feel that she has to change her view because it isn't the same as others. She knows things will be better when others can see what she sees. It will be a good thing.

With the last statement about Rose, it was time to bring the past life memory into the light:

"In that life, in World War II, you were her grandmother. This is the time of the Nazis moving into Belgium. You lived in a house with your daughter and your granddaughter, Anna, who is Rose in this life. Her mother Susan (your daughter), was the kind of person who didn't want to see things. She thought it's better if we don't see or think too much about what we hear. It's better if we don't pay attention to it. Just mind your own business and go to school. Do well in school, be a good girl and it will be OK.

"At that time, there was a list of all the Jewish families. And next door to you lived a woman that you have been friends with for most of your life, a Jewish woman and her family. Your granddaughter Anna loved this lady next door, who was more like a daughter to you. She was closer to the age of your daughter. But she and your daughter were not friends. It was you that was her friend. When the Nazis began to move against the Jews, you were so afraid for her and her family. And you said to her in front of your granddaughter: 'You should get your family together and leave. You should get out of here to a safe place. Go to England, go somewhere else.' And the neighbor would always say to you: 'They're not going to bother me. I've never been in trouble with anybody.' She didn't take the warning. She couldn't see it coming. And your granddaughter, through you, also began to feel that something bad was coming. She would go over there, almost every day. She was about nine. She would do things, such as going down to the cellar and getting the suitcases that belong to this family and bring them up, and say: 'Here are the suitcases. You should be packing, getting ready to go.' She would bring the train timetable, but the lady and her family just weren't listening. They had their home and their lives. He was a doctor, with a large practice.

"One night, in the middle of the night, there was a lot of noise. There was a big truck that pulled up in front of your house. People were yelling, and running back and forth. You and Anna looked out your windows and saw soldiers with guns. They were standing around by the truck. And then the door is open, and the lights are on in the house next door. And the next thing was that the two youngest children, teenagers, came flying out the door. And they're crying because they're so scared and calling for their parents. The father is trying to argue with the soldiers and saying, 'But I have a medical practice, I have people who count on me, I can't just leave work without giving notice.'

"The soldiers are not listening. They say, 'You can pack one bag and go get in the truck.' Anna was in the room next to yours, by the window. You could feel her getting upset and you began to dress, but you weren't so young and you were slow. By the time you got dressed, Anna was already down in the street. She was saying to them: 'You can't do this. You can't hurt these people. They are good people; they never hurt anybody. He is a doctor. He helps people.' They keep saying to her, 'Go home little girl, go home little girl.' And you put your slippers on, and your robe, and went down the stairs. You were out on the front stairs by the door, calling her and trying to help her realize she couldn't do this. She ran over to her friends.

"Anna is Rose, your daughter today. She figured out, if the truck wasn't running, they couldn't take people. So she ran over to the truck and opened the door. The soldiers are standing by the back of the truck. Nobody was in the cab. She takes the keys out of the truck. And then she runs toward your house with the keys—and they just shoot her in the back. It was logical to them. She's not allowed to take the keys from the truck. And you were standing there, screaming, and she was on the ground. And she is saying to you: 'Grandma, I just wanted to help. I just wanted to help,' and she's gone."

Maitra continued, helping Linda make more connections:

M: Rose, like Anna in her past life, is an independent thinker and quick to take action when she sees what to do. So, when you feel Rose's stubbornness, her conviction that she is right, it feels dangerous to you. It *was* dangerous in the past life, but she learned her lesson. She's going to do it a different way this time. And you notice, she didn't take those kinds of risks when she was nine years old in this life. She had her vision even then. She understood that she had to adjust to what was realistic, and she's done well. She went to school for something that gave her enough creative scope that she could continue moving toward her vision. Then she saw clearly what the next step would be, and she was in the middle of it now. She wants to live and she wants to do what she came here to do.

L: Before I came here, I was not sure if she was my mother in another life.

M: That could be, but in this particular lifetime you were the grandmother. And you were both on the side of the house where you could see what was happening next door. Her parents were on the other side of the house so they didn't even know. But you stood there and watched it and couldn't do anything. That's why it hits you so hard.

L: Yes, that's what I am feeling all the time. But my trust is getting bigger than the fear. It's getting better. For many years, it was always upside down. But I can more easily let her go now. She does the right thing. I know that I can trust her.

M: She's trying her best to prepare herself for what she came here to do. She knows some of it now. She knows that there is something big in store for her.

L: I'm always interested in what she's doing. But I can feel that it is hard for her to express it in words. This hurts sometimes. I would like to be more connected, but if I want to be more connected, I have to let her go.

M: I hope we've made this memory more accessible so that now you can understand it better and she will too. I think it will help.

L: Do you think it would help if I shared this Reading with her?

M: Yes, it would be good to share this Reading with her. She won't be surprised.

Linda's Transformation

A year later, Linda recalls her life after the Reading.

"After I received this Reading, my excessive concern for my daughter immediately let up. Amazingly, I can say that I haven't experienced any more panic attacks like that. A normal amount of joy and concern has set in; I also feel this way toward my other daughter.

"The story had a direct impact on me and I could understand it 100 percent. I didn't have to add anything to believe it. It felt sad and true. I was moved and had a strong feeling of solving a big puzzle. The suggestion that I don't have to understand my daughter also helped me a lot. To be sure this is a painful realization, yet it does help me."

> **Let yourself be silently drawn**
> **by the strange pull of what you really love.**
> **It will not lead you astray.**
>
> —Rumi

For Your Toolkit: Expansion of Reality

Einstein is often quoted as saying, "Everything is energy and that's all there is to it. Match the frequency of the reality you want and you cannot help but get that reality. It can be no other way. This is not philosophy. This is physics." When you understand this concept—that everything around us that appears to be solid is energy, too—you will begin to recognize this intrinsic truth that is inherent in everything. Then you will look deeper into the way things are, rather than judging and dismissing them out of hand.

Your trust in the Universe begins to deepen. You feel strengthened in your power to change things for the better by the way you think, act, and speak. You begin to understand the real power of blessing and prayer. Fear begins to dissipate. Your expanded understanding of the nature of Reality lets you relax and enjoy your life more, despite all your doubts. The challenges you face begin to seem more doable. You know that you are made of the same energy as the great, enlightened ones. This is the energy that pervades the Universe, and we call it God.

For a better understanding of these concepts, I offer you one of my favorite (well-worn) books: *Dr. Quantum's Little Book of Big Ideas* by Fred Wolf, Ph.D. It is fun and enlightening to read!

Chapter 31: Breaking Through the Wall Between My Son and Me

For Your Toolkit: Giving a Voice to Inner Conflict

(Rachel, born 1963)

Rachel was a nurse, who became a reflexologist and owned her own business. When she began to describe her problem with her son, he didn't show up immediately as the problem. Instead, Maitra saw a family pattern involving Rachel's mother that needed to be acknowledged first. Here is the initial exchange:

R. There is a wall between my oldest son, Ben, and me. I feel unsure of myself around him. He is a very loving person, but I can't get close to him.

M: How long have you been feeling this way?

R: I've felt this for many years. He is now thirty-three years old.

M: Over all these years, you've wanted love from your mother and you've also wanted her to change. You've done everything you could to get at least a bit of love from her. Can you describe what you want from her, what you want her to say? Something like, 'I'm so proud of you, especially how you interact with your children.'

What do you think Ben wants from you?

R: He wants recognition, and he wants to feel my love.

M: Exactly, but you only let him know the things that worry you. In the process, you forget to tell him and show him, how proud you are of him. He's a wonderful man.

Give your son some affection. Show him that you appreciate him. Tell him that you like him, that you love him. Express your love for him in a way he can feel it.

R: Yes, I understand. I just want to have a better sense of him, I want to experience being closer to him. Is there karma with my son?

Naturally, the karma with her son was easy to see; Rachel's deep longing to understand, her ongoing frustration had brought it to the fore.

"In that past life, you had three boys; your son today, Ben, was the youngest. The other boys were around eleven or twelve when he was born. This was a very recent lifetime, maybe your last one. He was trying so hard to be a big boy. He didn't care what anybody said; he had his business, doing whatever the older boys did. For example, if they were walking along on top of a fence, and he was too little to do it, he would try his best anyway.

"One Sunday, you all went down to a river for a picnic. It was a gathering of your large, extended family. The older children were getting into inner tubes and riding down the river on the tubes. Your youngest son was forbidden to do it because he couldn't swim yet. He was six years old. The rule was the same for all the children. Those who couldn't swim, couldn't ride the inner tubes. The river had a rapid current that was frightening to the parents.

"Most of the afternoon went by, and he was playing games with the younger children. The big kids were down in the river, going up and down in the tubes. You had your back turned. You were helping to clean up from the picnic and talking to people. You had been keeping a pretty close eye on him because you knew he wanted to be with the big boys. But it seemed that he was having fun playing games with the younger children, so you relaxed.

"As soon as he saw that you were busy, he went down to the river and waited at the edge, trying to catch an inner tube. Sure enough, he caught one, he got on it and was out in the current, just like the big boys. But he was a lot smaller than the big boys. He slipped down inside the inner tube because he couldn't hang on, and he didn't know how to swim.

"His body was found the next day. You were heart-broken and blaming yourself because you didn't keep a close enough eye on him. You knew he always wanted to do what the big boys did.

"It was a little more complex because you were trying hard not to say to the bigger boys: 'Why didn't you watch your little brother?' You knew it wasn't their fault or their responsibility. It was painful, and although you never said it, they could feel the blame. Your inner conflict made you shut down with your other boys, and they also felt guilty.

"You had and have this heartache and sorrow. Because it was never healed in that life, it was carried over into your present life. And Ben, on an unconscious level, is still waiting for you to get mad at him because he disobeyed you and went down the river in the inner tube. One day perhaps you can say, 'I forgive you everything and I hope you do the same for me.' You are both feeling guilty. The guilt serves the purpose of reminding you to forgive each other so that this old wound can heal."

Rachel's relief at having her feelings validated was palpable: "This is exactly the feeling I have. It is so heavy."

M: This tragedy is what has come between you. It left you both feeling confused. When you offer him your approval, the unspoken message is: 'I am not blaming you.' When you let him know this, and say out loud that you love and approve of him, then some of that old pain and guilt starts to wash away. When things are feeling a little more open between you and your son, you may want to say: 'If you have any questions for me, I will try to answer them.' Someday it might even feel right to tell him the whole story."

Rachel's Transformation

Two years later, Rachel's relief at the slow crumbling of the wall between them gave her a new perspective:

"This invisible wall between my son and me was connected to my sense of being overly responsible. Through the Reading, I could understand that the wall was my sorrow and guilt from the other life for not checking on him often enough, and my conviction that this was the reason the accident happened.

"I understood from the Reading that there was an energy of guilt and grief that flowed between my son and me. Unconsciously, I felt the guilt of failing him, but there was also his guilt for not following the rules. But I didn't feel angry at him about it. I still have a feeling of powerlessness.

"He may have taken this guilt feeling with him to his early death. Now we have come together again, unaware that there was always this wall between us, from the past.

"I didn't focus on this story for a long time after the Reading. My daily life was very busy and I was afraid of confronting this story with my oldest son.

"It took about a year until the story began to sink in. My son and I went hiking together last summer, and there was a moment when he criticized me, saying, 'You know, the parents of my friends are financially very supportive of them, and help them fulfill their dreams. But neither of you, my parents, have that much to give me, and I don't have that kind of support from you.'

"I answered him in a way that I couldn't have earlier, saying, 'Ben, I have always tried to give you everything I possibly could!'

"Earlier, I would have been embarrassed; I would have reacted with silence and I would have felt like a failure because I hadn't given enough as a mother. I probably would have felt guilty again!

"At that moment this deep, underlying, heavy guilt feeling was released, and I suddenly felt very clear and free to talk with him about this.

"A short time later, when Ben was sick and I was visiting him, we took a walk together in a nearby botanical garden. Our time together was peaceful.

"I thought that he would soon feel better. But he phoned me later and told me that he was short of breath and that he still felt weak and sick, and was worried that he might have pneumonia. He asked me for advice. I advised him to go to the doctor for an evaluation. At that moment, I could feel our closeness. It was a good, personal, and authentic conversation between mother and son.

"I received a message from him later, 'Thanks, Mama, for letting me call you.' I answered, 'I thank YOU for trusting me.' He wrote back, 'You know when I'm not feeling well, you are always my first comfort station!'

"This is how we communicated, and I could feel his loving presence. An entirely new energy is developing between us, a genuine trust. I can let go of my fear and my feeling that I need to be overly responsible.

"Now I can better support him whenever he needs it. I couldn't do this very well earlier because I always took on too much responsibility. Perhaps this change was a result of understanding the old karmic enmeshment.

"I think we are suspended in a cycle of coming and going, coming and going, and the soul knows which old stories need to be worked through. When I view everything from this perspective, I no longer feel sadness between us.

Perhaps his brief life was fulfilled at the moment when he died in his past life, even though it happened under tragic circumstances and affected me so deeply.

"It is very important to me that he understands that I don't blame him.

"I do feel freer now, though I'm still carefully feeling my way around my son. But it's much, much better than before the Reading. The wall of guilt between us is gone; I am very conscious of this transformation. The pathway between my son and me has once again opened. I have a lot of respect for his decisions. I'm not as judgmental and don't take things as personally. Above all, I don't feel guilty!

"I received valuable advice from the Reading on how to become closer to my son. Today I can praise and strengthen him, and most importantly, I can love him unconditionally!"

The world as we have created it is a process of our thinking. It cannot be changed without changing our thinking. The most important insight of my life is that we live in a loving universe.

—Albert Einstein

For Your Toolkit: Giving a Voice to Inner Conflict

We all experience inner conflict at times. A therapist or a counselor can be of great help at such times. Yes, or a psychic. But what to do if such a person isn't available for some reason? Or, perhaps it's that you just don't want to reveal your inner conflict to anyone else. Maybe you are ashamed, or you don't approve of your feelings. As a result, we bury or push down the feelings we "shouldn't be having" and argue with ourselves endlessly.

When you can find the courage, there is another way to sort things out: You can use a mirror.

Try this: Give a voice to both sides of the conflict and listen. (Imagine you are listening to your own best friend—you are!). Using the mirror, look yourself in the eyes, and state out loud your dilemma. Then say out loud the position that you think you should have. Make your case and say what you think you should do about it. Maybe you think you should just act like an adult and forget about it.

Take a five-minute break, maybe walk around a bit, and then, looking into the mirror again, let those unacceptable feelings come out of your mouth. No editing—express them in the most honest way you can. Swear words are OK if that's what comes out. Listen to your "bad" feelings with empathy and respect, again looking into your own eyes in the mirror (See "Yes, that's me too," pp.16-17). Now say clearly what you would like to do about it, for example, 'Smack him in the face' or 'Send her to jail.'

The idea here is to bring the thoughts that are not OK with you out into the open without judgment. Now that you've heard yourself, it may be immediately obvious what you want to do about the problem. Or, it may take a few days.

An alternative way to do this exercise is to use two chairs and sit in one for the first voice, and then in the other for your second position.

When it's clear, and you know what to do, have a Peace Talk with yourself, acknowledging your new insight and the clarity you've achieved. You may want to declare your intentions for the future.

In some instances, you might have this talk with the other person.

Take a hot bath, or drink a celebratory glass of wine to acknowledge the resolution of the conflict.

Chapter 32: Accidental Death of a Brother: A New Possibility

For Your Toolkit: Loss

(Claudia, born 1960; Claudia's younger brother, Zachery, 1964-1981)

When Claudia, and adult education teacher, came to Maitra for a Reading, she wanted to re-examine the loss of Zachery, her younger brother, and get more insight into what happened. He had died in a car accident on the railway. It was an enormous shock to the whole family to lose him; he was only seventeen. Claudia wanted to know if Maitra could tell her about his early death, and if there is a karmic pattern that might help her to understand it better.

Maitra asked for Zachery's name and birthdate; his spirit was immediately present in the room, and he wanted to tell her about what happened when he died.

"He (Zachery) was so shocked. He couldn't believe that he couldn't get back into his body; he tried again and again. The door was closed. His body wasn't working anymore. Then he went around to one or another family member, saying, 'I'm still here.' Everybody was in pain and crying. This puzzled him: 'But I didn't do anything! Why are you acting this way? I didn't do anything.' At first, he didn't realize he was 'dead.' He didn't understand what happened, and for twenty-four hours he was wandering around in familiar places with familiar people trying to make contact. Then he was in your parents' garden, where a man was sitting on a bench. He sat down beside this man and asked, 'What's wrong? Nobody wants to talk to me.'

"The man said, 'It's because you are not in your body anymore. You are what people call 'dead.'' This man was his guide, and he had realized that Zachery wouldn't be able to see or accept him unless he pretended to be another person sitting on the bench. Your brother was surprised that the man talked to him, and said, 'Nobody else would talk to me.' And the Being said, 'Well, that's because I am not in the body either. I'm here to help you make this transition.' And your brother said, 'Do I have to? I don't want to! I'm not ready!' His guide said, 'You don't realize it yet, but you will understand after a while that you did what you were there to do, and now it's time to move on and prepare for something different.'

"Then Zachery was able to leave with his guide. He came back to the family from time to time over five or six more months. It made him so sad that everyone else was sad. He tried to communicate: 'I'm OK, I didn't want to do this either, but I'm OK.'

"His guide took him to a school. He said, 'You can start today or whenever you are ready. You need to understand some things before you reincarnate.' Your brother said, 'Well ... I've had enough of school for a while.' He didn't like the idea of sitting in a classroom. His guide said, 'OK, we can explore some other things.'

"There were places Zachery had wanted to visit on the earth. He was interested in how people live in other places. He had always planned to travel in the future. He went inside the big pyramid, and some smaller pyramids, and he saw some festivals in India. His guide helped him travel to all the places he was curious to see. He did this sightseeing for a while; it didn't last long.

"Then he looked back at the events of his short life and things that happened in the family. And he looked at the past lives, just enough to understand the karmic patterns a bit. Then he got curious about what the school had to offer. For example, they planned to put him in a seat in the back of the classroom so he could observe, and he said 'I can observe better from the front.' So he went and sat right beside the teacher, surprising everyone, looking out at the class.

(Maitra added an aside to Claudia: "I find him amusing; he's got a little twist to the way he sees things, a kind of freshness, and it makes me laugh.")

"The teacher was good; Zachery's interest was awakened. He began to realize that there was so much more to life than he had known. As he went over what he had learned in his short life, he began to understand things on a deeper level. He was particularly interested in exchanges between people, and his parents' motivation when they wanted, or didn't want, him to do something. He began to realize how much he had been loved."

Claudia's Transformation

Claudia listened with great intensity to what was offered and began to make connections regarding the effect of his death on her life:

"I was deeply touched by the description of my brother's experiences after the accident. Although this was long ago and I can say that I have worked through this shock and loss as well as possible, this insight into Zachery's transition cast a new light on his departure. I was twenty-one years old at the time and I didn't think that physical death was the end. The unbelievable anguish, the shock, and the pain that my parents, siblings, and everyone around us felt, closed us off from the dimension of the afterlife for a while. I was sad to hear that my brother tried to contact us and I didn't get the message. I would have been happy to assist him when he was trying to communicate with us.

"The reality of the death of my brother shook me very deeply at the time. I questioned the meaning of death itself after this experience of how physical life could come to an end from one minute to the next. There was suddenly so much pain, sorrow, and helplessness in the family. It made me question my future. Nothing was the same as it was before. Everything had changed in one fell swoop.

"Psychological guidance, or spiritual support, would have been helpful to us at that time. My parents were given medication so that they could get through the funeral and all the other related tasks.

"Each of us tried in our own way to deal with the trauma and go on living with the shock and loss. My parents suffered enormously and, in their grief, often left me alone with mine. I handled the loss in my way, but as I learned later, this experience was stored in my body and wasn't fully resolved.

"I was able to free myself from this trauma several years later through a strong physical experience, a panic attack. Leading up to this, I had had cardiac arrhythmia, weakness, vertigo, and anxieties that were very disturbing.

Due to a minor incident that occurred when I was at home alone—I had a panic attack and needed help. I called a friend for support. He helped me get through the attack. I could feel how all of that stored-up energy was beginning to permeate my body, especially around my heart. All of my cells began to throb and vibrate; I couldn't stop it, even though I was afraid of dying.

"I remembered later that I was often afraid of death after my brother died. The fear, along with the sorrow, brought a feeling that I might also die soon.

"I became aware that I wasn't dying; my body continued to breathe deeply. All of my muscles, especially those in my legs, began to tremble. My entire body vibrated, and then slowly calmed down; the strong emotions eased. I experienced being fully present and the total relaxation of tension in my entire Being. After this extremely deep experience of panic, and then release of tension, I never again had these fears, nor cardiac arrhythmia. My body and circulation were stabilized.

"In addition, this insight into my brother's transition after death strengthened me. Despite the long period of time that lay between, another dimension of the soul and the spiritual world was revealed to me. I am grateful for this Reading because I became more open, and my fear of the unknown diminished. It became another call for me to intensify my contact with spiritual guides, with my guardian angel, and, in general, to look at all of life from a new perspective. Through this experience, I tell people who are suffering a loss, to seek professional guidance in times of mourning and crisis. Psychics and spiritual healers can also be helpful because they can communicate with the deceased person. This brings comfort, and clarifying insights, and can lessen the pain of separation. This can also help the person, who is now separated from them by death, to be able to make their way in the spiritual world. A Reading can bring clarity to both people and this helps them to integrate and accept the incomprehensibility of death."

In a later Reading, Claudia wanted to revisit the previous Reading. She wanted to know again about the death of her brother, Zachery, and whether there was family karma or a karmic pattern that explains why this happened in her family.

"Yes, there is some karma there, a little different with each person. The strongest karmic energy is between your father and Zachery. Zachery, in a previous life, was your father's nephew, the son of your father's brother. Zachery's father was having problems with gambling and he was killed in a knife fight in a gambling casino. His brother (who was your father) was so embarrassed and judgmental about his brother's gambling and being killed and everybody knowing about how it happened, that he refused to take in his nephew, Zachery. It would have been logical for him to take Zachery in because he had a son the same age. He had enough money and everybody thought that he would, but he refused because he was so angry at his brother for being such an embarrassment. The mother was already gone, having died in childbirth with a second child, and that's why the father was gambling. He was trying to deal with it and not doing well.

"In that previous life, your brother had to go to a more distant relative, a second or third cousin, who had a farm. Zachery, in that life, was the same age as he was when he died in this lifetime, sixteen or seventeen. He went to the farm; the relative needed help on the farm and he didn't want to pay for a worker, which is why he took Zachery.

"This boy had a hard time; he worked from sunup to sundown, he didn't get paid, and was told he should be grateful that he had a roof over his head. When he was nineteen, he ran away and got a job on the railroad (that tells us that the lifetime was very recent); he was killed a couple of years later in a train accident. He was working on the roof of the train while it was moving and he fell off.

"Your father, his uncle, felt such terrible remorse; he just knew that if he had taken this boy in, he would have lived, and would have been happy. He was so angry at himself for having turned this boy away that he said to his family in that life, 'If I ever have another chance like that, I won't be so harsh, punishing a boy for something his father did.'"

Maitra then connected this past life information to Claudia's present life:

"In the present, your father had the opportunity to be Zachery's father, to give him another chance in this life. Zachery did have a happy childhood. But he died, and he left again. Your father felt somehow it might be his fault this time too, but it wasn't. It wasn't anything he did or didn't do. It was just your brother's process. It seems your father wanted to make amends, his actions saying: 'Let me do this. Let me help you this time.'

"His death in this lifetime must have hit your father hard. But he did do what he wanted to do for Zachery. He gave him a happy childhood and a good time with the family. That's karma more than anything else; of course, we could look at every member of the family, but that's the one that was the strongest. Father and son. Karma fulfilled."

For Claudia, there were still some questions. She wanted to know where he is now.

Maitra continued to look, and there was surprisingly another life in the present: "Zachery is back in a body now. I see him, a little boy, in the southern part of the United States where there is marshland. His father is a guide who takes people into the Everglades.

"I am seeing your brother, now called Bobby, right now; he's about three or four years old and he is fascinated with his father's boats. One boat looks strange, with a big wheel on the back that skims over the water. When they go into the marsh with it, they just fly over the water; his father, a naturalist, knows all the pathways.

"His father has a degree in Botanical Science and he knows about all the plants and wildlife in the swamp. He is a teacher. He takes students out into the swamps; he also takes out other professionals, such as scientists and government officials, and gives them a tour.

"The little boy has a collection of boats too, and there is a special place along the edge of the swamp where his father lets him put his boats in the water and play. He is very happy. His dad takes a lot of interest in him. He has a baby sister, about two years younger. At first, it was hard to share his parents, but it didn't take him long before he liked her. He likes doing things for her. It took him twenty-eight years, in our terms, to prepare himself to return to a very happy circumstance with lots of potential for him; his parents are educated people. They are dedicated to ecology, to saving the swamplands, the animals and plants."

A few months later, Claudia shared her reflections on loss:

"The experience of loss, as hard as it hit our family, demands of me, again and again, the acceptance of transience. As much as I like the familiar, life always changes; something new is offered and something else is taken away. I realize I can't know the purpose of another person's life path. I am beginning to understand better the experiential journey and to see life in a much larger context. This was revealed to me through the Reading.

"It was a surprise to me that the Reading spoke about Zachery's next incarnation as 'Bobby' in the southern part of the United States. After I was able to see his life's journey in this way, I experienced another inner transformation of what had happened in my life. It opened up in me an unexpected possibility: That Zachery's soul is reincarnated into a child so that he could experience and learn more.

"Somehow, Zachery's sudden departure demystified my fear of death, and I can look at all of our roles as mother, father, siblings, and friends from a new perspective. My consciousness was expanded through all the insights in the Reading. I am left with a fascination for the possibility of encountering this young boy, Bobby, the soul of my deceased brother, again in his new body and a new life.

"The content of this karmic story moves me because it shows me that there are opportunities, again and again, to repair something and to find balance, with new realizations that are meaningful and loving. I am grateful from the bottom of my heart for this insight."

No mud, No lotus.

—Thích Nhất Hạnh

For Your Toolkit: Loss

If you, too, are struggling with feelings of loss and sadness, whether you have a good explanation for these feelings or not, this will help. The first step is to determine what you really want. Do you see your sadness as a sign of how much you loved this person? If you do, perhaps you are not ready to let go of it. Only when the answer inside of you is an unequivocal 'Yes! I want to let go of this sadness and move on with my life,' are you ready to do this little ritual.

Then, instead of trying to deny or control the sad feelings, let yourself feel them fully, even exaggerating them a bit.

Imagine that you have a reservoir of unshed tears, and today you are beginning to empty the reservoir. Look at photos and remember times with the one you have lost. Watch sad movies. Do whatever will evoke even more sad feelings. Notice that it can feel good to cry, really CRY! Embrace the sadness and embrace yourself with the sadness; many painful memories can be shed with your tears. Cry until you can't cry anymore—then stop and notice what you are feeling. Is there a peaceful feeling of emptiness?

There is healing hiding in the sadness. There is joy in the letting go, and an opening into new possibilities. Your letting go says, "I trust that the cycle of life and death is a natural one and that the universe is unfolding in a way that benefits us all."

Reflections: Big and Small by Maitra

Maybe it's a miracle we can communicate with each other at all. We all know how rare and precious it is to be on the same wavelength with another person. George Bernard Shaw said, "The single biggest problem in communication is the illusion that it has taken place." This challenge was exacerbated during my years in Europe by the need to have everything translated since I only have a smattering of German. Consequently, I agree with Ken Liu when he says, "Every act of communication is a miracle of translation." That makes this book a story of many miracles.

The feeling of oneness in communication has been happening to me more and more, lately, as my consciousness continues to expand. Perhaps it happens in the space between the words. I wonder if this is the way consciousness unfolds naturally for all of us. We grow up aware of one level of reality, and then, when we are ready, another level begins to emerge, unbidden.

Opening the heart is crucial to the movement into higher levels of awareness in our communications with others. The heart is where all the accumulated wisdom and experience of all our lifetimes is vibrating, waiting to be set free, to be shared. True soul-to-soul communication can be soul-shaking joy, bliss, and even exhilaration, but it can also take us into very painful experiences if that pain is what is blocking us from realizing our potential. This merging of consciousness is always a cherished experience.

The Readings that I love so much to do for clients are for my benefit too; I continue to discover how each person reflects some part of myself. Reader and Recipient roles are interchangeable. Some time ago, I read for a woman who came to me, wanting to open her heart. She didn't realize that her heart was already open, but obscured by pain from the past—some conscious, some partially conscious, and some unconscious. This is our dilemma when we want to open our hearts. Rumi explains it this way: "Your task is not to seek for love but merely to find all the barriers within yourself that you have built against it."

Mine is an exquisite contradiction: Everything shrinking into the present moment and its uniqueness, and at the same time, I become aware of my unfathomable expansion into the far reaches of this universe. And I'm not even counting the many other universes of which I am (as we all are) a part. Eternity is in the present moment.

I find I can live with all this quite well. Yes!

I am filled with gratitude for Karin and Barbara and all who contributed to the adventure of the creation of this book—what a ride!

May we all come to know we are One.

—Maitra

Gratitude by Karin Stettler

I thank everyone who allowed me to include their personal Readings in this volume and trusted me to witness these deeply moving moments in their lives. It has been a wonderful gift and a valuable learning experience for me to be with Maitra and accompany her as she assists people to come into alignment with the Soul. Learning to trust the guidance of our own Inner Voice, also called the Inner Teacher, awakens us to our potential.

I likewise thank everyone who allowed me, through their trust and openness, to transcribe their Readings, and make their life experiences available to others.

I am deeply grateful to all contributors for their support, and their encouragement to stay with this book project and complete it. The transformational power and the deep spiritual insights in the Readings have moved me again and again, and contributed to my healing, through the many hours of writing this book.

I am moved by the spiritual depth, maturity, wisdom, and love of all the participants. I hope with all my heart that many readers will also experience these Readings in this way.

And I thank Maitra from the bottom of my heart for her great inspiration, her unconditional love, and her guidance in my learning and life process over many years.

Her powerful teachings, her wisdom, and her luminous presence have put me in touch with my Soul. She helped me to awaken my potential, supported my creativity, and strengthened my belief in my healing abilities.

With her help, I have liberated myself from many old limiting patterns and have discovered a loving universe full of wonder.

**A great power
awakens in you
when you know
that nothing
can sway you
from Truth.**

—Mooji

Glossary

- **Akashic Records** are a compilation of all universal events, thoughts, words, emotions, and intent that have ever occurred in the past, present, or future of all life forms. They are stored in a non-physical plane of existence known as the mental plane, which is one of the planes—or levels—available in the human aura.

- **Aura** refers to the field of luminous, multicolored radiant energy that permeates and surrounds the body of a living creature. In it are contained the etheric, emotional, mental, and spiritual planes or levels. The bodies associated with these—by the same name—are sometimes referred to as **'light bodies.'**

- **Astral plane** is the plane of the emotions; it includes polar opposites such as hope and fear, sentimental love and hate, happiness, and suffering. This is the subtle plane closest to the physical plane. The emotional or Astral body is the form we take (a counterpart of the physical body) when we travel in the astral plane while sleeping.

- **Chakras** are energy centers (vortices or wheels) in the etheric body that are related to the spine and the seven most important endocrine glands. They are responsible for the coordination and vitalization of all the bodies (physical, etheric, emotional, mental, spiritual) and their correlation with the soul, the main center of consciousness. There are seven major chakras:

1. The Root Chakra: Muladhara

2. The Sacral Chakra: Svadhisthana

3. The Solar Plexus Chakra: Manipura

4. The Heart Chakra: Anahata

5. The Throat Chakra: Vishuddha

6. The Third Eye Chakra: Ajna

7. The Crown Chakra: Sahasrara

There are many books available on chakras if you want to study this essential part of the human experience, which has a continuing effect on us whether we are conscious of it or not.

- **Etheric Body** is the energetic counterpart of the physical body. It contains the seven major centers (chakras) and forty-nine minor centers. Blockages in the etheric body can result in physical illness or even death. When we die, the etheric body leaves the physical body and there is a measurable difference in our weight.

- **Karma** is also known as the Law of Cause and Effect. It is the basic law that governs our existence in our solar system. Every thought that we have, every action that we carry out, sets into motion a cause. These causes have their effects, which determine our lives, for good or ill.   This is expressed in the biblical quote, "As you sow, so shall you reap," and in scientific terms, in Newton's Third Law of Motion, "For every action, there is an equal and opposite reaction." In popular terms: "what goes around, comes around".

- **Past-Life Regression** is a method that uses hypnosis to recover memories of past lives or incarnations. It can be therapeutic, helping to uncover the roots of trauma and allowing healing to take place. This is different from a reading, in that the subject himself has the memory and its accompanying emotions.

- **Self-Realization** is the process of recognizing and expressing our divine nature. It can bring the experience of our essential Oneness. It is the fulfillment and activation of one's potential.

- **Subtle Body** is a 'quasi-material' aspect/substance of the human body; it is neither solely physical nor solely spiritual, according to esoteric, occult, and mystical teachings. The etheric, emotional, mental, and spiritual levels of subtle bodies (each a unique level of vibration) combine to form an energy field around the physical body, which is known as the aura.

- **Theta waves**: Below is a list of measurable (EEG, biofeedback) brain waves. Theta brain waves (4-7.9 Hz) occur during dreaming sleep (REM), trances, hypnosis, and daydreaming. These waves are the goal of meditation and self-hypnosis.

1. Gamma Waves (31+ Hz)Hyper alert, good for insights and higher learning.

2. Beta Waves (14-30 Hz) The awake state. Engaged in activities and conversation.

3. Alpha Waves (8-13.9 Hz) Relaxed, daydreaming, and light meditation.

4. Theta Waves (4-7 Hz) Dreaming sleep (REM), this is the goal ofn-meditation or self-hypnosis.

5. Delta Waves(0.1-3.9 Hz) When in a deep, dreamless sleep. Newborns sleep innthis stage, adults less so.

- **Third Eye** (see Chakra #6) is located in the forehead. It provides access to perceptions that are beyond ordinary sight. It offers humans a path to inner realms and spaces of higher consciousness. It is often associated with visions, healing, clairvoyance and out-of-body experiences. We all have a third eye; many people use it without knowing what they are doing. It can be trained. Many children today are born with it already active and it can be overwhelming. In classes with children, the first thing I taught them was how to open and close the third eye, which was a great relief to them and their parents. People who have developed their capacity to access their third eye are often known as psychics or seers.

- **Karin Stettler** has her therapeutic practice in Lucerne, Switzerland, where she counsels people through their life's challenges. She trains foot reflexology therapists at the Healing Arts College of Lucerne in Ebikon, Switzerland.
As an artist, she teaches courses in spiritual development and creativity. Among her published writings, is *On the Path to Freedom/Der Weg in die Freiheit*, which includes many examples of her artwork. Karin Stettler has been living in Dierikon/Lucerne, Switzerland since 1995.

- **Maitra** (https://maitra.net) has been teaching *Opening the Lotus Seminars and Workshops*, speaking and giving talks and readings professionally for over forty years in Europe and Asia, as well as in the USA. For many years, she had a radio show—*Psychic Insights*—near her home in Watsonville, CA. Maitra is a proud and grateful mother to three, a grandmother to three, and a great-grandmother to three, which is her best training for the work she loves.

- **Barbara S. Stone** is a Professor Emeritus of German and Humanities at Shimer College. She has translated a variety of academic texts in the humanities and social sciences, as well as memoirs and family histories. She lives in Evanston, IL.

Recommended Reading on Reincarnation

- *Initiation* by Elizabeth Haich

- *Song of the Pearl* by Ruth Nichols

- *You Have Been Here Before* by Dr. Edith Fiore

- *Many Mansions* by Gina Cerminara (Edgar Casey readings)

- *Past Lives, Future Loves* by Dick Sutphen

- *Education of Oversoul Seven (& other Seth Books)* by Jane Roberts

- *Hypersentience* by Marcia Moore

- *Scarlet Feather* (far-memory series) by Joan Grant

- *A Souls Journey (between-life experiences)* by Peter Richelieu

- *Origin and Destiny of Man (Edgar Casey)* by Lyle Robinson.

- *Reliving Past Lives* by Helen Wambach

OTHER RECOMMENDATIONS:

- *Teachings of Don Juan (and others)* by Carlos Casteneda

- *Diamond Heart (and others)* by A.H. Almaas

- *Be Here Now* by Ram Dass

- *Hands Of Light* by Barbara Brennen

- *Wheels of Light (chakras)* by Roselyn Gruyere

- *The Alchemy of the Heart (and others)* by Reshad Field

- *The Adventure of Self-Discovery* by Stanislav Grof

- *Avalanche* by W. Brugh Joy, M.D.

- *The Enneagram* by Helen Palmer

- *The Spiritual Dimensions of the Enneagram* by Maitri

- *The Way of the Peaceful Warrior* by Dan Millman

- *The Handbook to Higher Consciousness* by Ken Keyes.

- *The Impersonal Life* by Joseph Brenner

- *Right Use of Will* – (Emotional body) by Ceanne DeRohan